T0295966

PRAISE FOR *UNDERSTANDING DECENTRALIZED FINANCE*

'Rhian Lewis presents a balanced and informative view that expertly intertwines the evolution of money and markets with this novel, and potentially game changing, set of technologies whilst unravelling and demystifying the lexicon of arcane terminology and acronyms that have followed the hype into the public psyche in recent years.'
Paul Gordon, Founder, Coinscrum

'If you think about the factors stopping DeFi to fulfil its potential, many cite regulation (or lack of regulation) and lack of understanding/knowledge of this space. As it is difficult to control the regulatory part, we can build a deep understanding of what DeFi represents, its components, and the exciting new opportunities it offers – as well as the considerable challenges that occur when the old system collides head-on with the new. I found it exciting that you can boost your knowledge by learning cool concepts such as DeFi mullet, social trading, finfluencer, crypto meme culture and more.'
Mirela Ciobanu, Lead Editor, Banking and Fintech, The Paypers

'Weaving together concepts, definitions and real-world examples, Rhian Lewis covers the basics of decentralized finance, the realities of today, the hopes of tomorrow, and the potential blocks to the realization of truly decentralized finances. A must-read for those interested in moving from online hype posts to broader comprehension of the space.'
Lloyd Evans, Product Manager - Ventures, 11:FS

'*Understanding Decentralized Finance* not only gives you a good input into the world of decentralized finance, but also enables you to deep-dive into topics around this phenomenon.'
Christian Steiner, Head of Regulatory, Bitpanda

'*Understanding Decentralized Finance* is a comprehensive and thought-provoking look at the future of finance, including the intersection of gaming and finance. It offers insights on the challenges of creating a universal system that captures the economic activity of games. A must-read for anyone in the DeFi industry, as well as gamers and enthusiasts.'
Julien Paredes, Head of Partnerships, Tropee

'The world of decentralized finance (DeFi) is one of the most exciting, fast evolving areas of money, operating at the intersection of technology and finance. Many jobs will be created and good opportunities. This book will give you a good way to imagine the future of DeFi. I highly recommend this book.'
Tram Anh Nguyen, Co-founder, Centre for Finance, Technology and Entrepreneurship (CFTE)

'Understanding Decentralized Finance is a comprehensive guide to the world of DeFi. In a space that is fast moving and hard to navigate, Rhian takes the reader by the hand and describes the promise, the evolution and the current state of this emerging technology. A great read for newcomers and degens alike.'
Jonas Seiferth, RetroPGF Lead, Optimism Foundation

'This book is a comprehensive guide for beginners or experienced professionals seeking to expand their knowledge and understanding of decentralized finance (DeFi). The author, Rhian Lewis, possesses extensive knowledge and expertise and has effectively simplified and communicated complex DeFi concepts clearly and captivatingly.'
Enrico Mariotti, CEO, Skytale Finance

Understanding Decentralized Finance

How DeFi is Changing the Future of Money

Rhian Lewis

KoganPage

First published in Great Britain and the United States in 2023 by Kogan Page Limited

2nd Floor, 45 Gee Street	c/o Martin P Hill Consulting	4737/23 Ansari Road
London	122 W 27th St, 10th Floor	Daryaganj
EC1V 3RS	New York, NY 10001	New Delhi 110002
United Kingdom	USA	India

www.koganpage.com

ISBNs

Hardback   978 1 3986 0939 6
Paperback 978 1 3986 0937 2
Ebook   978 1 3986 0938 9

British Library Cataloguing-in-Publication Data

A CIP record for this book is available from the British Library.

Library of Congress Cataloging-in-Publication Data
Names: Lewis, Rhian, 1964- author.
Title: Understanding decentralized finance : how DeFi is changing the
    future of money / Rhian Lewis.
Description: London ; New York, NY : Kogan Page, 2022. | Includes bibliographical references and index. |
    Summary: "Understanding Decentralized Finance demystifies DeFi, locating the integration points between decentralised and centralized finance to help finance professionals unlock valuable opportunities.DeFi - the next evolution of cryptocurrency - has brought a new wave of investors into the world of finance. As fintechs and financial institutions seek to integrate with DeFi, this book explores its history, its present context, and its future. It explains the world of DeFi by comparing it to the traditional finance sector, highlighting points of similarity, difference and integration. Understanding Decentralized Finance explores the technologies underlying the DeFi market and how they differ from those of traditional financial markets. It scrutinizes the difference between centralized and decentralized cryptocurrency exchanges, how NFTs fit into DeFi and how collectibles can be financialized. Readers will also find out how collateralized loans, derivatives, margin trading and liquidity provision work in a world where there is no centralized institution to coordinate these activities - and how regulators in different jurisdictions are ensuring that financial regulations keep up with these innovations. With examples from key actors in the field, including the movement of luxury organizations like Christie's and Sotheby's into the NFT space and the SushiSwap vampire attack, this is an essential read for anyone working in finance, fintech and technology who needs to understand the fast-moving world of DeFi"– Provided by publisher.
Identifiers: LCCN 2022061527 | ISBN 9781398609372 (paperback) | ISBN
    9781398609396 (hardback) | ISBN 9781398609389 (ebook)
Subjects: LCSH: Digital currency. | Cryptocurrencies. |
    Finance–Technological innovations.
Classification: LCC HG1710 .L4983 2022 | DDC 332.4–dc23/eng/20230106
LC record available at https://lccn.loc.gov/2022061527

Typeset by Integra Software Services, Pondicherry
Print production managed by Jellyfish
Printed and bound by CPI Group (UK) Ltd, Croydon CR0 4YY

For my father, Colin David Lewis

CONTENTS

LIST OF FIGURES AND TABLES

PREFACE

Compound interest is the eighth wonder of the world. He who understands it, earns it. He who doesn't, pays it.

ALBERT EINSTEIN

The existing global financial system has grown up piecemeal and is a mass of contradictions and inefficiencies. In my previous book, *The Cryptocurrency Revolution*, I wrote about how blockchain technology offers – in theory, at least – the ability to make low-cost payments across global borders without the inefficiencies and pain points that are involved in existing settlement systems.

Out of the fast-moving and sometimes controversial cryptocurrency ecosystem has now sprung a plethora of new, decentralized financial products and instruments that aim to replicate many of the functions of their traditional equivalents. The networks of protocols and smart contracts that make up this system are known collectively as decentralized finance – DeFi for short.

Permissionless and borderless, these new digital assets promise to bring investment opportunities and financial inclusion to a much wider market. Governments, and in many cases, financial institutions have not yet fully understood the potential and implications of these rapidly evolving technological developments.

Nevertheless, financial companies both large and small are moving ahead with DeFi integrations. As described in Chapters 4 and 9, J.P. Morgan is, via its Onyx project, tokenizing financial assets such as bonds and money market fund shares for use in both traditional markets and DeFi, unlocking potentially trillions of dollars of value. And Huntingdon Valley Bank, a small institution in Pennsylvania, became the first traditional bank to tokenize real-world assets on the MakerDAO protocol.

Conversely, DeFi-native projects are developing new products and services to attract institutional players. Leading lending protocol Aave, about which we discuss more later, has launched Aave Arc, the new permissioned DeFi liquidity pool for financial institutions, and it is not alone in this ambition.

As regulators and TradFi decision-makers alike grapple with the challenges arising from the intersection point of two very different financial systems, I felt it would be useful to lay out in a book exactly where we are at the moment, including what developments have happened so far and how investors – primarily retail – are leveraging these opportunities. In the final chapter, I look ahead at how the landscape is evolving and what the future may hold for institutions wishing to integrate with these revolutionary new technologies.

First, let's ask the question, 'What is DeFi?' In the Introduction, we present some definitions of the decentralized finance sector and a brief history of how it evolved.

ACKNOWLEDGEMENTS

The DeFi and crypto landscape has been transformed in the last decade, but one thing that has not changed is the generosity of those in the ecosystem who have willingly given up their time to share their knowledge and otherwise encourage me in my writing. Profound thanks go to my interviewees: Justin Banon, Rachel Black, Max Coniglio, Arthur Doohan, Ian Grigg, Ala Haddad, Gilbert Hill, Angie Jones, Izabella Kaminska, Mauricio Magaldi, Hanan Nor, Igor Pejic, Ioana Surpateanu and Simon Taylor. Further thanks to Professor Dr Philipp Sandner, who allowed material from his *Medium* to be reproduced.

Thank you, too, to those people who have been supportive of my writing endeavours and with whom I have had interesting conversations that have given me ideas and influenced me in various ways: all at Outlier Ventures; all at Boson Protocol; Enrico, Massi and all at Skytale Finance; the B9Lab team; Martin Jee, Mattina Hiwaizi, Victoria May Gimigliano, Patryk Baranowski, Neha M, Nind and Paul Gordon.

Thanks to my family and friends outside the crypto space, especially my mother Diana Lewis; Andrew Todd; and Amelia and Clare. Thank you to Mark White for help and support when I needed it the most. And, of course, to Isabelle Cheng for commissioning this book, and Nick Hoar, Catherine Wood and Roanne Charles for their work on it.

Introduction

CHAPTER OBJECTIVES

- What is decentralized finance?
- The building blocks of DeFi
- Understand how Bitcoin works
- Smart contracts
- What are the megatrends influencing adoption?
- What financial institutions are considering DeFi integration?
- Where do NFTs fit into DeFi?
- What are some of the challenges and risks?

The world of decentralized finance (DeFi) is one of the most exciting, fast-evolving areas of money, operating at the intersection of technology and finance. The Ethereum Foundation (see https://ethereum.org/en/defi/) describes DeFi as 'an open and global financial system built for the internet age.' Yet few people – including many who work within traditional finance markets – understand this fast-moving, jargon-heavy sector in which fortunes can be made or, more frequently, lost in seconds and where the decision-makers are not located in a stereotypical corporate setting but are just as likely to be developers or entrepreneurs loosely organized into distributed communities who may have only met online.

Imagine brokerages and asset exchanges that operate silently 24/7, every day of the year in every country in the world, requiring a fraction of the staff numbers to operate and without expensive bricks-and-mortar headquarters to maintain. Imagine settlements that happen more or less instantaneously, with no manual processes or back offices required. Imagine transactions that can be picked up immediately and analysed programmatically by compliance teams instead of requiring painstaking data collation in individual banks.

Too good to be true?

That is indeed an overly positive view of DeFi, which should be tempered with caution. As we will discover throughout this book, while the technologies themselves offer huge potential to reimagine a natively digital and global system for transferring value, exchanging assets and generating yield, the headlines have – justifiably – focused on lost savings and unethical behaviour by high-profile figures within the space.

Detractors of decentralized finance argue that it is an unregulated minefield of scams, the permissionless nature of which means that its networks and protocols can be run by shadowy, anonymous operators. They point to the bear market of 2022 and the high-profile failure of several entities within, and adjacent to, DeFi that left thousands of investors around the world desperate and angry after their life savings were wiped out, with no government guarantees or possibilities for restitution. The collapse of FTX was indeed only the visible tip of an iceberg of fraud, negligence and criminal behaviour in the cryptocurrency sector, rightly prompting demands for change and clarity.

However, as traditional financial institutions take their first steps towards experimenting with the DeFi system and, as regulators in different countries seek to improve consumer protections without stifling the innovation and creativity that has been the hallmark of this sector so far, it is no longer an option for people working in traditional finance simply to ignore the DeFi phenomenon and hope it goes away.

Ratings agency S&P has already taken the first steps towards expanding its services to encompass DeFi, for example, with Elizabeth Mann, CFO at S&P Global Ratings, stating that decentralized finance has the potential to redefine the financial markets (McQuaid, 2022).

To understand DeFi means digging deep below the layers of jargon and hype to discover a new wave of products and services that are, nonetheless, completely alien to anyone steeped in the established way of doing things. While many of the promised returns on investment are undoubtedly too good to be true, the cost savings and efficiencies that are offered by these technological advances are something of a Pandora's box: once the technology has been unleashed on the world, it is very difficult to ignore or put back.

Ioana Surpateanu, Web3/DeFi investor, advisor and entrepreneur and board member of the Multichain Asset Managers Association, paints a compelling vision for the future of DeFi:

> We're moving to something that I'm extremely excited about, which is a composability between various different protocols, coupled with programmability. We're moving towards an era of DeFi protocols that have no analogy in the TradFi world. So far, we have imported processes and products and instruments from TradFi into DeFi and redesigned them to cut out intermediaries or replace them with code. But now because the ecosystem is evolving, we're going to see combinations and permutations that will lead to something really alternative, something that will have no analogy in the traditional world.

This phenomenon is growing too quickly to ignore, and, while this book has been written with traditional finance professionals in mind, it has also been written with the hope that other more general readers may also find it useful.

It is not a book that will help you get rich by investing in DeFi (although I would argue that it might inject some realism into the debate and prevent readers from committing funds to projects that are fraudulent or dangerous). Instead, it is aimed at anyone in the world of finance who wants to understand the exciting new opportunities offered by DeFi – as well as the considerable risks of committing funds to technology that is currently in its infancy and the challenges that occur when the old system collides head-on with the new.

What is decentralized finance?

Decentralized finance means different things to different people. Izabella Kaminska, financial journalist and founder editor of *The Blind Spot*, points out that decentralized markets existed long before crypto:

> Commodity markets were always decentralized, they were always bilateral, they were always OTC – and that was seen as a problem after the global financial crisis. So now we've ended up creating central counterparts, and some might argue that we've got a concentration of risk that has ended up in the clearing houses instead. That's why I don't think it's so fantastically novel that there's decentralized finance, because commodity markets even up until the Noughties, were decentralized.

Banker and activist Arthur Doohan concurs with this view:

> If markets were still decentralized in the way they were 150 years ago, where banks could fail and companies could go bust and had to be aware then that's my idea of decentralized finance. However, the central banks have come to dominate in a way that was not envisaged. They were meant to be the lenders of last resort and now they are the prime movers of policy.
>
> So, the markets were initially characterized by innovation and competition. But we're in a situation now where central banks set interest rates almost in lockstep across the globe. And so we've come to a point where with zero interest rate policies and everybody's using the same tools such as quantitative easing at the same time in the same direction that we've ended up at quite a centralized place.

These comments add an interesting counterpoint to something that we often take for granted: that decentralized finance is purely an innovation related to cryptocurrency. Kaminska and Doohan both make the point that, in fact, certain parts of the financial sector have been decentralized in the past, and it is only in recent years that the tendency towards centralization on a global scale has won out. However, the expression 'decentralized finance' (or DeFi) is usually presumed to refer to the idea of permissionless financial instruments transacted via blockchains – and that specific idea is the topic of this book.

The Ethereum Foundation's definition of DeFi in the opening paragraph is true enough: DeFi is indeed 'an open and global financial system built for the internet age'. But what does this actually mean in practice? Instead of thinking about what DeFi *is*, let's think instead about what a typical person might *do* with it.

Let's think about a typical small investor, in a post-industrial country such as the United Kingdom, the United States, France or Germany. We will see later that DeFi has the power to open up the world of financial products and services to people who may not have previously been able to participate in this world, but, for now, let's imagine someone who is not excluded in this way, who has a pension, a tax-optimized savings account and who might dabble in retail investment using a variety of different digital platforms or mobile apps.

A retail investor generally has one aim: to make their money work for them and earn some kind of return that will, at the very least, keep up with inflation, and, in the best case, outperform inflation, so that they end up with a pot of value that will purchase more real-world goods and services than if they had left it sitting in their checking account.

Higher returns normally reflect a higher degree of risk, so, depending on the investor's personality type and life stage (people often become more cautious as they get older and their time-window to recoup losses gets shorter), their choice of investment vehicles may include stocks and shares, bonds (both private and government issued), commodities or government treasuries. Sophisticated investors may indulge in trading foreign currencies or other high-risk activities, such as spread betting – where the trader does not own the underlying asset but places a bet on its price movement – or margin trading, which is essentially trading with borrowed funds. Additionally, a retail investor will usually consume other financial services, such as loans of various types, insurance plans or aggregated funds where a professional investor makes purchases on their behalf.

These financial products are usually offered and regulated on a national basis, so investors are unable to use geographical arbitrage to shop around for the products offering the highest return. Someone in Ghana might find that their local banks offer a low return on their savings, but unless they are high-net-worth individuals with accountants, lawyers and addresses in multiple countries, they cannot shop around for the best rates in Germany, Japan or Turkey.

Digital currencies, however, allow investors to participate in a truly global system. Twitter founder Jack Dorsey believes that the new, decentralized exchange tbDEX, which is being developed within his payments giant Block, has the capacity to expand financial opportunities for everyone with its ambition to create non-custodial and permissionless services. Technologies such as tbDEX are designed to pull together internet-native currency and decentralized identity into an open, permissionless network that can build trust relationships between individuals and institutions.

In order to understand why these problems need to be solved, let's look first at how the current system came into being, and understand how digital currencies can help.

How the financial system evolved

While money developed around the world in different forms, with the earliest types coming into existence many thousands of years ago, people have spent the last few centuries accustomed to the idea that currencies are issued by the governments of nation states. The strength of a country's currency is often seen as a proxy for the strength of the country itself, and some national currencies are more desirable than others. In many countries, especially those whose national currency is perceived as weak, merchants are often prepared to accept US dollars as payment for goods or services. Payments in dollars, pounds, euros or any of the other government-issued currencies in the world are routed via the banking system, which can be a slow and cumbersome process, especially when these payments are made across international borders.

This system also requires a high degree of public trust, both in the government's central bank, and in the private banks and other financial institutions in which people and businesses deposit their money. Any individual must believe that their government intends to – and is able to – maintain policies to ensure that a fixed amount of money will not catastrophically lose its purchasing power, and also that the bank that runs their accounts does not suddenly go out of business and announce that their money has been lost.

In many countries, the fear of national currency collapse or bank failures has receded into the past. Within living memory, however, there have been many instances of hyperinflation and bank failures, from the Weimar Republic in Germany in the 1930s to post-Soviet Russia in 1992, when prices increased by more than 2500 per cent.

The UK 'mini-budget' in September 2022, in which the then Chancellor of the Exchequer Kwasi Kwarteng announced sweeping tax cuts and implied increased government borrowing, which was followed by a steep fall in the exchange rate of the pound, is a salient reminder that inflation, with all its attendant dangers, is still a threat.

In fact, although no one is expecting Weimar-style hyperinflation, the UK has been immune to neither inflation nor bank failures. The global financial crisis of 2007–2008 triggered a potentially catastrophic near-collapse of Northern Rock, a building society that had become a bank. The vision of thousands of savers queuing to remove their cash and the anticipated knock-on effects for other banks was sufficient to induce the UK government to nationalize the bank.

The saga of the near-collapse of a minor British bank may have faded into obscurity – but for cryptocurrency historians all over the world, the story of Northern Rock is important for one reason: the message that

Satoshi Nakamoto, the mysterious inventor of Bitcoin, encoded into the very first block of the Bitcoin blockchain.

Cryptocurrency: the foundational building block of DeFi

DeFi offers an alternative to an approach based on traditional companies and national borders by relying on blockchain technology and cryptocurrencies, using a stack of technologies commonly referred to as Web3. This is not a book about cryptocurrency itself (*The Cryptocurrency Revolution* goes into more detail about how cryptocurrencies were invented and evolved), but it is necessary to offer a potted history of cryptocurrency and its underlying technology before we can start understanding how DeFi works.

How Bitcoin works

Here we spend a few moments looking at Bitcoin and how it works because, without Bitcoin and all the other cryptocurrencies that have come after it, there would be no decentralized finance ecosystem.

It is important to note that the system of central-bank-issued currencies described earlier – whose payment rails are administered by banks and centralized financial institutions – is one that has been adapted to the digital age from an existing system that once depended on physical notes and coins.

This idea of physical cash, handed from one individual to another and then either passed around in another transaction or deposited at a bank, is thousands of years old. The cash itself may not be intrinsically valuable in the way that early silver or gold coins were, but, as long as you trust that the coins or notes that you receive have not been forged, you can have a reasonable degree of certainty that you will be able to keep them or hand them over to someone else in payment for goods or services that you require.

The introduction of the internet brought a new kind of challenge: creating payment systems that could be used in a situation where the purchaser was geographically distant from the seller and was not known to them. For this example, the use of an intermediary organisation such as a bank or credit card issuer was crucial. The buyer could 'sign' a transaction by clicking a payment button on a shopping website or similar and entering their credit card details. The merchant or other supplier of the product or service would know that when they received this notification, it meant that the buyer's bank would settle up with their own bank and that their account would be credited with the right amount of money. A complex balance of ledgers and settlement processes that are regulated and overseen by government authorities in each country guarantees that digital payments can be made reliably in this way.

This adaptation of an analogue model to the digital world is not without problems. Simon Taylor, head of strategy and content at leading compliance platform Sardine, whose 'Brainfood' newsletter is an essential resource for anyone wanting to understand the fintech landscape, says:

> The existing system isn't global. It was globalized. What you actually saw was a series of national systems that have evolved over decades and were built by the best technology we had at the time, for the context of the time. And there were major upgrades when they were implemented. The nature of Swift in the Seventies, for example, was a massive upgrade from sending cheques around the world and dealing with different central banks and trying to make phone calls to people. We digitized something that wasn't digital before. It was cutting edge when it was built. However, we did it with limited hardware, limited memory, limited bandwidth, and a lot of the standards that we use to this very day still harken back to what we built in the Seventies.

Solving the double-spend problem

To create a natively digital payment system based on digital cash, some fundamental problems needed to be solved. Bitcoin, remarkably, solved the one problem that had previously halted all attempts to create a fully digital equivalent of cash: the 'double spend' problem. If someone pays someone else in cash, there does not need to be a bank involved because the recipient can see and feel that they have physically received the payment. But if you try to send someone $10 digitally without involving a bank, you could send the same $10 to multiple other people without having to back up the promise that you had these funds.

Because Bitcoin transactions are recorded in a special type of ledger that is very difficult indeed to rewrite, and whose history is present in multiple locations, it means that the shared history of financial transactions has to be agreed on by the thousands of different computers in the network – a process known as consensus. The computer code that underpins this consensus mechanism is open source, which means that anyone in the world can inspect or download the code, unlike the proprietary software that is found within the private banking system, where the inner workings are hidden away from public view.

Permissionless payments

The entire history of all the transactions on the Bitcoin network is in the public domain and any computer can be added to or removed from its network without a single person or organisation giving permission. The network is governed by a set of rules and incentives that have been encoded into its inner workings, and anyone in the world can submit proposals for changes to the code. To people who are used to currencies and payments being governed by other people, who are involved in a constant process of decision-making about how things should work, it may seem impossible that a network that is run by consensus and computer code can even exist, let alone grow more resilient in the nearly 15 years since its inception, but this has indeed been the case.

Of course, nothing in life is free, and just as banks charge fees for transactions, so do the owners of the computers that make up the Bitcoin network. Because Bitcoin is totally subject to the rules of market forces, this can mean that, when the network is under heavy load, fees can rise to a level that makes small payments uneconomic. This is often used as an argument against Bitcoin, whereas it has instead provided the incentive for investment in innovative solutions including the development of Layer 2 networks such as Lightning.

It is important to point out that, as the first truly digitally native payment system, Bitcoin is without parallel, allowing near-instantaneous payments of any size to anyone in the world. International payments via the traditional banking system can be cumbersome and expensive – and in countries where there are infrastructure problems, such as those caused by war or conflict, it can take days or even weeks before a payment reaches its intended recipient. The parties in a blockchain payment do not need to know each other's names, account details, nationality or any other personal identifying information (PII). It is easy for anyone to set up a Bitcoin wallet, which simply consists of two long alphanumeric strings, of which one can be given to anyone to allow them to pay you, and the other the private key that allows you to unlock your funds and which should be kept secret at all times. In reality, many people choose to use the Bitcoin and other cryptocurrency networks via an interface where they have set up an account with their real name and address, but the preferable scenario is to create your own wallet and retain its recovery details yourself, which means that you never have to trust a third party to keep your funds and your private information safe.

FAST CROSS-BORDER PAYMENTS

We have seen the true power of Bitcoin and other cryptocurrencies during the conflict in Ukraine, where the Ukrainian government's crypto wallets received an inflow of more than $60 million within the first three weeks of its appeal.

Bitcoin proved that it was possible to run a universal payments network without human intermediaries and without the permission of national or state governments. Anyone, anywhere in the world, can set up a Bitcoin wallet as long as they have an internet connection. Initial panic by governments about the ability of criminals to launder funds using the Bitcoin network have been mitigated by the open nature of Bitcoin's ledger. The proliferation of crypto forensics specialists such as Chainalysis and Elliptic has shown that Bitcoin is, in fact, a far-from-opaque solution for anyone wanting to cover their tracks.

Payments, of course, are simply one component of the global financial system. While it is possible to use the Bitcoin network as an underlying proof system for other types of transaction than simple payments, by 2013 a young developer named Vitalik Buterin had started to explore the idea of using a similarly decentralized network to allow anyone, anywhere in the world, to execute complicated agreements and transactions without involving third parties.

Ethereum and smart contracts

There are more blockchain networks than just Bitcoin, of course, and the blockchain that is most widely used in DeFi is Ethereum, which has a fascinating history of its own.

We don't have room here to document all the twists and turns in the story of Ethereum, and those readers who want to know more about its development, along with the involvement of the various larger-than-life characters involved in its gestation and birth, can read either or both of two excellent books on the subject: *The Cryptopians* by Laura Shin and *The Infinite Machine* by Camila Russo. In later chapters, however, we take a deep dive into specific DeFi projects that have been created on top of Ethereum, including how Ethereum's architecture has enabled or hindered the evolution of different use cases.

Like Bitcoin, Ethereum is publicly available, open-source code that anyone can use or fork (make a copy and subsequently change the code of the copy) for their own purposes. Also, like Bitcoin, its code runs on thousands of computers all over the world, whose users have joined the network of their own volition, incentivized by financial reward to maintain the validation of transactions and record the history of the ledger. It is possible to use the network to make simple payments from one party to another, using the native currency of the blockchain, Ether. In another similarity with Bitcoin, transactions are ordered into blocks before these are agreed on by the validators.

The above processes work in roughly the same way as Bitcoin, but there are some differences, most notably that Ethereum uses a consensus mechanism known as proof of stake. This difference is discussed later in the book. Other differences involve block-creation speed and the way fees are calculated. A new Bitcoin block is created every 10 minutes, while the block time for Ethereum is 12–14 seconds. Another difference is that, while Bitcoin transaction fees are calculated and deducted in the same currency as the payment itself, Ethereum's transaction fees are payable in a different currency, known as gas. The gas price fluctuates according to how many transactions are being processed on the network at any given time, rising at times of high demand and falling at times of low demand.

What can you do with Ethereum that you can't do with Bitcoin?

With these differences in mind, it is probably easier to understand the capabilities of Ethereum and the Ethereum Virtual Machine (EVM) by giving a specific example of how Ethereum tends to be used for applications other than payments. Let's take the simplest scenario possible. Imagine two people want to make a bet with each other about what the gas price will be at some point in the future. It is possible to use the block height (the sequential number of the blocks that make up the blockchain) as a rough predictor of date and time. Alice bets that the gas price will be higher than a nominated value at x block height, and Bob bets that it will be lower.

If Alice and Bob wanted to make a bet like this without using a public blockchain, they would either have to trust each other completely that the loser of the bet would hand over the money, or else use a betting platform run by an intermediary, who would be the arbitrator of who had won the bet. This third party would also be responsible for holding the funds of both Alice and Bob until the bet was settled, and also for sending the payment to the winning party. All these processes add friction and expense.

While – as we shall see later in the book – Ethereum and similar blockchains have their shortcomings, a case like this is where they excel. Someone – whether this is Alice, Bob, or another person – writes some instructions to the Ethereum blockchain in a specific programming language. This set of instructions is called a smart contract, and contains a set of conditions and then an instruction about what should be done if this condition is met. When these instructions are written to the blockchain, an address is generated that is simply a long alphanumeric string that denotes the contract's timestamped location on the network.

Committing to the bet is as simple as sending the chosen quantity of Ethereum to this address. The contract acts as a container for the funds and, when the specified time has elapsed, it will read the gas price from the blockchain and automatically pay the winner. There are no extra records to be updated, no checks that need to be done and no possibility that someone will forget to send the funds or that the funds will go astray. The process is fully automated – and the results can be viewed by anyone, anywhere in the world.

This is a minimal example of a smart contract, which I chose because it does not require any input of information from outside the blockchain itself. In the real world, someone is unlikely to get excited about the possibility of making a bet about gas prices and is more likely to want to bet on the price of, say, Tesla shares or the US dollar exchange rate for Ethereum. In this case, the data that triggers the action of paying out the reward for the winning bet would have to be provided via a mechanism known as an oracle.

WHAT IS AN ORACLE?

In a permissionless system where smart contracts execute transactions that depend on information outside the blockchain, it is important that this information can be trusted. Imagine a smart contract that pays out when the price of a particular stock reaches a certain level.

Oracles are decentralized information sources that form a bridge between the blockchain and the real world, and whose source can be independently verified as reliable.

The DeFi ecosystem is, of course, about far more than simple bets between two parties. This trivial example, however, demonstrates how it is possible for a smart contract to hold funds in escrow and then pay out automatically to a particular wallet address dependent on certain data being correct at a specified time. These principles lay the foundation for many different types of contracts and financial instruments that together make up the complex and sometimes bewildering infrastructure of the current DeFi landscape.

Challenges facing Ethereum

Bitcoin and Ethereum are not the only blockchains any more, and barely a month seems to go by without someone launching a new chain that is billed as the new 'Ethereum killer'. Recent years have seen the launch of EOS, Cardano, Avalanche, Solana, Fantom, NEAR and many more. No doubt, by the time this book is published, there will be others.

However, the network effects of Ethereum mean that, even when it is under heavy load and suffering from long confirmation times and high gas fees, it remains the default platform for smart contract execution, and hence retains its place in the foundational layer of DeFi infrastructure. Having said this, competitors have sprung up in response to the shortcomings that have raised challenges for Ethereum's ecosystem participants since its inception.

While it is not entirely fair to compare the transaction throughput of Ethereum with that of a payment network such as Visa, the disparity is remarkable – and not in Ethereum's favour. Ethereum can handle only 13 transactions per second, whereas the figure for Visa is somewhere in the region of 1700 per second. In addition, as Ethereum has seen greater and greater adoption, gas fees have risen alarmingly. It is true that this is a feature rather than a bug. If the price of executing smart contracts were to be set at an artificially low rate, this would enable bad actors to spam the network with meaningless transactions and slow down the processing rate for genuine ones. So, a price that increases along with scarcity is a good thing.

High gas fees are, however, a significant pain point for all but the very wealthiest participants, and limit the network's usefulness for small-to-medium-value DeFi transactions. For example, if you want to send $1000 worth of Ether to a smart contract in order to generate yield (more on this in later chapters), the fees need to be substantially less than the potential yield in order to make the transaction worthwhile – especially as you will need to pay the same again in fees to withdraw the Ether to your wallet. With fees that are often in excess of $100 per transaction, it is not hard to see how Ethereum has been criticized for simply being a plaything of the crypto rich, rather than as a tool for improving and democratizing financial access.

Some of Ethereum's more immediate issues with scaling look likely to be solved with its eventual, multi-stage migration to an entirely different architecture. The first stage of this was concluded in September 2022 by a software change known as 'the Merge', which moved Ethereum from a proof-of-work consensus model to proof of stake. The former means that the validating computers have to compete to solve a puzzle in order to show they have used sufficient computing power to validate the blocks they are adding to the blockchain, which has led to criticism in some quarters for adding to the problem of anthropogenic climate change. Proof-of-stake consensus relies on incentivizing honest behaviour by requiring validators to commit a certain number of tokens and lock it up so that it can't be withdrawn.

While environmental campaigners applauded Ethereum's move to proof of stake as being more energy efficient, the Merge itself does not yet solve Ethereum's scaling issues and comparatively high fees. Block space on the main Ethereum network is a desirable commodity and will likely continue to be expensive. Future changes to Ethereum's architecture are, however, expected to bring improvements.

Ethereum's move to proof of stake also raises questions for validators about how they respond to censorship and the imposition of sanctions by different governments. This issue is explored in more depth in Chapter 8, which looks at regulatory issues raised by the sanctioning of Tornado Cash.

What are Layer 2 networks – and how can they help?

Whether or not the ongoing software development effort towards Ethereum 2.0 helps solve scalability challenges in the way developers expect, there are other useful initiatives, which involve the creation of Layer 2 networks. This book is not a technical manual, so I would recommend that you follow the links at the end of the chapter if you are interested in reading more about Ethereum 2.0 scaling solutions or exactly how Layer 2s work, but here is a brief explanation.

The idea of a Layer 2 network is that, while only a network that has thousands of validators can be trusted as an ultimate source of truth, it is possible to run some of the processing on a different, more lightweight network, which reports back to the primary blockchain periodically to bundle and record the outcome of the transactions.

The mechanisms that these Layer 2s use varies: some have their own proof-of-stake consensus mechanism, whereas others pass messages backwards and forwards between smart contracts on the Layer 2 and Ethereum's main chain. Polygon and Arbitrum are probably the best known Ethereum Layer 2 networks. In a similar way, the Lightning network is a lightweight – and so-far successful – solution for carrying out multiple cheap payments on the Bitcoin network without every single transaction having to be written separately to the main Bitcoin blockchain.

The success of Layer 2 blockchains has led to a substantial uptick in their use within DeFi. A useful measure of DeFi activity is TVL (total value locked). This indicates the collective balance (usually denominated in dollars) of funds that are held in smart contracts within a particular DeFi protocol – or within the ecosystem itself. The value locked in Layer 2 solutions was around $3.5 billion in the second half of 2022.

Why is decentralization important – and is it achievable?

It is worth taking time to consider why decentralization is seen as worthwhile. The cypherpunk movement from which Bitcoin emerged was filled with idealists who believed that the freedom to transact without the intervention of governments and the punitive fees charged by many financial institutions is a right that should be available to people everywhere.

Chapter 8 takes a closer look at how regulators in different countries are dealing with the challenges of drawing up frameworks that offer consumer protection for those using these protocols, but it is also true to say that many developers and entrepreneurs working in the DeFi ecosystem now have a more pragmatic and conciliatory view of working with governments than the early generation of crypto enthusiasts had.

There is a need for pragmatism on both sides – yet with the advent of central bank digital currencies (CBDCs) we see the potential for unprecedented surveillance of our financial habits by governments and large corporations. So, it remains important for law-abiding citizens to retain the expectation of privacy in their financial transactions. Later chapters explore how DeFi transactions can be pseudonymous and private, yet remain compliant with requirements such as tax reporting and money laundering regulations.

Decentralization, however, is very much in the eye of the beholder. The truth is that, for many applications and platforms, true decentralization is an aspiration rather than a reality, primarily because of the technical challenges inherent in implementing truly decentralized solutions. Due to the aforementioned scalability challenges facing Ethereum, the trade-off between decentralization and efficiency means that many services and integration points are as centralized as anything in the legacy financial system. For example, the sheer size and unwieldiness of the existing Ethereum chain data – in excess of 660GB at the time of writing – means that many services choose to write to and read from the network via a centralized API such as Infura or Alchemy. If there is a temporary problem with either of these services, the much-vaunted high availability of a decentralized blockchain is of no use at all.

Similarly, bringing new users on board can be challenging. Creating and backing up a self-hosted wallet, with the attendant risk of losing funds, has meant that the majority of new entrants to DeFi and to cryptocurrency ownership in general have been introduced through centralized services such as Coinbase.

Some investors may take the next steps of working through the complexities of setting up an unhosted wallet and interacting with DeFi protocols, but many will stay with the simpler option of storing cryptocurrencies or NFTs (non-fungible tokens) in a wallet on a centralized exchange. This opens the door for new financial products at the intersection of fintech and DeFi that can smooth the onboarding process – but also raises the risk that investors will place too much trust in centralized services masquerading as decentralized.

DEMOGRAPHIC DRIVERS

When it comes to handling the complexities of self-hosted wallets and complicated user interfaces, it is probably fair to say that digitally native younger generations have an advantage. However, there are also cultural reasons why the landscape is dominated by younger investors. In many ways, the popularity of DeFi investments, particularly among younger millennials and Generation Z, mirrors the meme stock phenomenon, particularly around the subculture in channels such as the WallStreetBets subreddit.

The accredited investor legislation in the United States, and corresponding frameworks in other countries, had in the past acted as a limitation on the number of people directly involved with the most profitable investments, and the world of finance was seen as rather dull, usually intermediated by financial advisers who abstracted away most of the mechanics of how the system worked.

Social trading

The twin phenomena of stock trading apps, such as Robinhood or eToro, and cryptocurrency trading brought in a fast-moving, exciting and gamified experience where the social element of trading experiences was almost as important as gains or losses. This built on a feeling that younger generations had been largely excluded from the huge gains in value of more traditional assets held by their parents or grandparents, who had benefited from burgeoning property prices and generous pension schemes.

Rachel Black, founder of DeFi savings app HaloFi, sees first-hand the attraction of such investments for younger generations:

> I'm an elder millennial, and the amount that people speak about finance and investing now compared to when I was a teenager or in my early twenties is so much bigger. I think it's now become part of pop culture in a way that it wasn't then, so I think it's definitely made things a lot more accessible.

This is even more the case for Generation Z, she thinks:

> They definitely had a bit of pre-warning compared to older millennials, who were basically screwed over because we were given no financial education and then plunged right into the worst recession of our lifetime and tried to figure that out with no information or warning. So that was painful for millennials – but Generation Z followed and saw what had happened to us and their experience is very different.

At the same time, crypto trading was exploding in popularity, apps such as Robinhood were prompting a surge in trading more traditional assets among the crypto generation. The famous short squeeze on GameStop in late 2020 caught those in institutional finance by surprise, as the sheer numbers of people involved in the meme stock enthusiasm had largely gone under the radar. Almost 900,000 separate accounts traded GameStop shares in a single day at the height of the frenzy, accompanied by entertaining commentary and an endless supply of memes on Reddit and Twitter.

We can, therefore, see the entrance of younger investors into both the meme stocks and cryptocurrency arenas as part of a wider, disruptive trend.

In the three years since I wrote *The Cryptocurrency Revolution*, the cultural and regulatory landscape around cryptocurrencies has changed beyond recognition. A survey in March 2022, for example, showed that more than one in five Americans had bought cryptocurrency at least once (Franck, 2022). And in April 2021, Coinbase launched its IPO to much fanfare. Its stock, along with those of Bitcoin miners such as Riot, Marathon and Hut, allows investors to gain indirect exposure to the price movement of cryptocurrencies without having to deal with the complexities of self-custody that are involved in directly holding digital assets.

How mainstream are cryptocurrencies and DeFi?

There is no clearer sign of DeFi hitting the mainstream than the new offering from Bitcoin Suisse, a regulated Swiss finance company with more than 300 employees offering cryptocurrency services to private clients and businesses, with guarantees from the state-backed Swiss Cantonal Bank (Horsfall, 2022). In addition to the cryptocurrency trading services that had been the core of its business, in April 2022, it announced that customers would be able to deposit ETH (Ethereum's native token ether) to mint a stablecoin called LUSD using the Liquity protocol. If this sounds like gobbledygook, the next chapter looks into exactly what this means.

The launch of the Bitcoin Suisse DeFi offering should not come as a surprise to anyone who has been tracking the trajectory of cryptocurrencies over the last 10 years – and DeFi in particular.

Legacy banks and institutions move into the space

One might expect a modern fintech company such as Block to be a first mover in this area, but when it comes to crypto, even some of the world's oldest and most venerable institutions are eyeing the sector.

Germany's Commerzbank, founded in 1870 and headquartered in Frankfurt, that most staid and traditional of European banking centres, applied for a crypto licence in April 2022 that would allow it to offer custodial services for crypto-assets in tandem with offering digital asset exchange services. While its initial products are to be aimed at institutional customers rather than the retail market, the direction of travel is clear (Singh, 2022). Nasdaq and BlackRock have also offered cryptocurrency custody solutions aimed at institutions.

Meanwhile, across the Atlantic, Fidelity is set to roll out an option for employees to save up to 20 per cent of their 401(k) pension plan in Bitcoin, on condition that their employer approves this (Roth, 2022). Microstrategy, which had repeatedly hit the headlines for the bullish Bitcoin pronouncements of its CEO Michael Saylor, is reportedly set to become the first company in the USA to take advantage of the product.

Technological innovations such as Bitcoin's Lightning network are smoothing the path for the mainstream adoption of Bitcoin as a payment method, as acknowledged by Morgan Stanley. The company pointed to the integration of Strike into the NCR point-of-sale network as an example, a move which will allow the widespread use of cryptocurrency as a payment method in bricks-and-mortar premises (Quiroz-Gutierrez, 2022).

These are all examples of cryptocurrency integrations rather than specifically DeFi, but we are beginning to see the green shoots of institutions working out how they can interact with these new product offerings. For example, Huntington Valley Bank became the first bank to raise a loan with MakerDAO. Its $ 100 million loan in the US dollar-pegged stablecoin Dai was collateralized with its own stock. This news should be qualified with the observation that it came at a time when the MakerDAO community was rethinking its use of real-world assets as collateral, but it is interesting to see a very traditional bank interacting directly with a DeFi protocol in this way.

Payments giant Visa has already taken its first steps in the world of stablecoins by allowing settlements using another stablecoin, USDC. Arguably this is rather less decentralized than the Huntington Valley integration as USDC is issued by a consortium rather than a DAO (decentralized autonomous organization) and payments go via Visa's Ethereum address at crypto bank Anchorage, but given the prevalence of USDC within DeFi, it is still an interesting move. Visa additionally announced in December 2022 that it was working with StarkWare to develop auto-recurring payments for self-custodial wallets.

DEFI MEETS GAMING

More recently, the growth in popularity of NFTs representing collectable artwork, music or membership services shows no signs of slowing, and has brought in yet another wave of people for whom the idea of investing in anything even vaguely related to finance would have been unthinkable a few years ago. In addition, metaverse-based games whose economies are based on blockchains and tokens have also hit the headlines within the last two years. This integration of gaming and DeFi – GameFi or MetaFi – is a significant enough development to warrant an entire chapter in this book.

There is an argument that the initial growth of cryptocurrency as a cultural phenomenon was limited by the number of people interested enough in either finance or technology to invest significant amounts of their personal time investigating it. However, the heady mix of art, music and gaming, along with the opportunity for a lucky few to make life-changing sums of money, has attracted an entirely new market into crypto, aided by celebrity endorsements.

No one should underestimate the power of exclusivity in driving demand, and the phenomenon of Bored Ape Yacht Club, a collection of images of fed-up simians, each one unique and registered on the Ethereum blockchain, is a case in point. Their creators, Yuga Labs, must be delighted that Ape holders include Eminem, Jimmy Fallon, Post Malone, Marshmello, Shaquille O'Neal, Neymar and Madonna.

Meanwhile Reese Witherspoon has partnered with NFT collective World of Women with a view to creating TV shows or films based on the creative concept, and fashion houses such as Louis Vuitton, Hermes, Dolce & Gabbana and Tommy Hilfiger have dropped their own fashion NFTs so that your digital presence can be as well dressed as your real-world self. With savvy investors snapping up the tokens that they predict will be the fashion collectables of the future, this intersection of finance and culture is driving an unprecedented interest in blockchain technology and cryptocurrencies.

As discussed later on in the book, the ability to financialize almost anything and to plug it into DeFi infrastructure opens up funding opportunities and wealth-building potential to a whole new market of investors to whom this world was previously alien.

The cryptocurrency bear market

From the highs and optimism of 2020's 'DeFi summer', a backdrop of falling cryptocurrency prices and some high-profile collapses of centralized projects within the sector have tempered the enthusiasm of would-be investors and reduced the market capitalization of the DeFi ecosystem. The total value locked in DeFi protocols fell precipitously from more than $180 billion in December 2021 to a little over $54 billion nine months later.

At the height of the DeFi boom, tempted by returns that were simply too good to be true, retail investors piled into schemes that had not been stress-tested in a market where background prices were falling. Later chapters examine the various reasons for the collapse of Terra's ill-fated stablecoin and the subsequent failure of Three Arrows Capital, along with some high-profile hacks. All these were eclipsed by the scale of the FTX implosion, and all have tainted the reputation of the entire sector as far as casual observers are concerned.

However, it would be a mistake to dismiss an entire wave of innovation simply because of the incompetence and/or dishonesty of certain individuals and organizations. It is important to recognize that, despite dramatic price volatility, the main DeFi exchange and lending protocols have continued to operate exactly as designed. The failure of overly centralized applications and projects built on top of these foundational layers has been traumatic and has rightly drawn the attention of regulators, yet we should draw a distinction between the underlying technology and its misuse.

Managing risk within the DeFi system

The chance for scammers and fraudsters to prey on those who are naive about both the technology and the principles of financial investment is a story as old as time. While many would argue that the accredited investor rules in the USA are too heavy-handed, it is clear that an ongoing process of education is needed to protect those who might otherwise leap into risky or outright fraudulent investment opportunities and lose life-changing sums of money. This poses an unenviable challenge for regulators, who must choose between protecting consumers and allowing new technological ideas and investment products to flourish so that their jurisdiction does not fall behind in the competitive fintech sector.

Fintech and crypto companies are among the most mobile in the world, able to move easily to territories that have the most helpful approach to regulation, which – as discussed in Chapter 8 – does not necessarily mean the most lax approach. Clarity, rather than an 'anything goes' approach is what companies need.

In summary, while consumers and regulators are now much more comfortable with the idea of cryptocurrencies as a mainstream investment, the world of DeFi poses huge challenges. However, it also offers huge opportunities, and it is possible to see a future where decentralized and centralized finance blend together so seamlessly that consumers are barely aware of the difference.

The following chapters look in detail at the current landscape and how it may evolve, in technological, financial and political terms, beginning with a deep dive into how these technologies evolved – and what it means for someone who wants to get hands-on with some of these exciting new products.

References

Franck, T (2022) 'One in five adults has invested in, traded or used cryptocurrency, NBC News poll shows', CNBC: https://www.cnbc.com/2022/03/31/cryptocurrency-news-21percent-of-adults-have-traded-or-used-crypto-nbc-poll-shows.html (archived at https://perma.cc/D8ZJ-8JMM)

Horsfall, F (2022) 'Bitcoin Suisse launches decentralised finance offering', CityWire Switzerland: https://citywire.com/ch/news/bitcoin-suisse-launches-decentralised-finance-offering/a2385646 (archived at https://perma.cc/RH8A-GU6L)

McQuaid, D (2022) 'S&P Global Ratings announces DeFi strategy group', Currency.com: https://currency.com/s-p-global-ratings-announces-defi-strategy-group (archived at https://perma.cc/XDY6-952G)

Quiroz-Gutierrez, M (2022) 'Partnerships with brick-and-mortar stores critical to the future of Bitcoin, Morgan Stanley contends', Fortune: https://fortune.com/2022/04/21/morgan-stanley-brick-and-mortar-stores-critical-bitcoin-future/ (archived at https://perma.cc/XVR3-RJDC)

Roth, E (2022) 'Fidelity is rolling out Bitcoin investing for 401(k) plans', The Verge: https://www.theverge.com/2022/4/26/23043424/fidelity-rolling-out-bitcoin-investing-401-k-plans-cryptocurrency-microstrategy (archived at https://perma.cc/C5KD-7WEW)

Singh, A (2022) 'Germany's Commerzbank applies for local crypto license', Coindesk: https://www.coindesk.com/business/2022/04/21/germanys-commerzbank-applies-for-local-crypto-licence-report (archived at https://perma.cc/463N-HNKS)

Further reading

Jack Dorsey, 'Square is creating a new business…', Twitter, 15 July 2021: https://twitter.com/jack/status/1415765941904941061 (archived at https://perma.cc/9MXR-N3UN)

Ethereum Foundation, 'Decentralized finance (DeFi): https://ethereum.org/en/defi/ (archived at https://perma.cc/JBR4-2PRT)

01

Why DeFi developed and how it works

In order for a whole new industry sector to be created and reach a critical mass of adoption, two main elements need to be in place: the technical and business innovations that allow the sector to develop; and a demand from potential users based on a problem that is waiting to be solved. In other words, sometimes technical innovations dreamt up by entrepreneurs might result in a product or service that looks impressive but which no one actually needs.

This chapter looks at the development of the technologies surrounding blockchains and cryptocurrencies that make up the fundamental building blocks of decentralized finance. The different types of token standard within the Ethereum ecosystem are defined and explained. The chapter also examines the timeline from the emergence of the first stablecoins in 2014 to the birth of the sprawling spiders' webs of decentralized finance we see today.

But first we look at the specific market needs and changing social attitudes that are driving the adoption of cryptocurrencies and DeFi. There is no denying that this is an extremely high-risk sector, in which the partial or even total loss of capital is always a possibility. So, if you live in a modern economy with ready access to bank savings accounts or consumer-focused trading apps and platforms, what is the big demand-side draw of DeFi?

Cultural movements and low returns on investment

Much of the activity in the cryptocurrency sector, from speculation on the price of tokens to the multi-million-dollar sale of NFTs that are sometimes little more than crude pixelated images, is little more than gambling of the riskiest kind. Many first-time buyers are lured by the amazing – and true – stories of the early adopters who, through a combination of awareness and luck, made millions or even billions of dollars by being in the right place at the right time. Some of these influencers are prominent on social media, flaunting their wealth in endless photographs of luxury holidays and that favoured crypto status symbol: Lambos (Lamborghinis).

Naturally, this does not represent the experience of most people who have invested – or gambled – with these protocols and tokens. Even before the 2022 crypto bear market, there have been seemingly countless stories of traders who fell victim to scams, invested in worthless projects or who followed influencers, got the timing wrong and lost everything. With nothing in the way of consumer protection, large numbers of people have suffered rug pulls (where those running a project 'pull the rug out' from underneath investors by taking profits and abandoning it), hacks and thefts – and the sector has thus gained an appalling reputation that is, in many cases, entirely justified.

Yet there is still an irrepressible enthusiasm around the whole crypto scene – and much of it is for reasons that are cultural as well as financial. We see no better illustration of this than the popularity of meme coins.

Meme coins and the NFT craze

Meme coins are tokens that are created or transferred on a blockchain in the same way as Bitcoin, but they do not usually have special, innovative properties. Instead, they become desirable for their cult status and because of their similarity to other tokens that have previously risen in price.

Shiba Inu is an example of this. Shiba Inu is the breed of Japanese dog that was popularized via the Doge meme, which in turn inspired Dogecoin. Dogecoin has not only survived more than eight years since its launch in 2014, but has had its cult status enhanced massively by Elon Musk's cheerleading.

Crypto traders who felt that they had missed out on big profits from holding Dogecoin then turned instead to lookalike dog-themed and even cat-themed currencies – of which there are hundreds. Many of them made short-term gains from this strategy, even though prices quickly fell after their initial launch. However, Shiba Inu was the one coin that went stratospheric, with a 700,000 per cent price rise during 2021. This meant that traders who had spent just a few thousand dollars at the right time suddenly found themselves multi-millionaires (Kraterou, 2021).

Similarly, the price of NFTs also hit the mainstream press during 2021, with a work by the artist Beeple reaching $69 million at a Christies auction, and desirable cartoon-like NFTs from the CryptoPunks and Bored Ape Yacht Club collections on sale for millions.

These extreme examples may have captured the imagination of the mainstream world outside crypto – but while such rags-to-riches tales paint a colourful background to the story of DeFi, there were more prosaic reasons luring traders and savers to crypto in general and DeFi in particular.

The low-yield environment

Most rational investors – or even speculators – do not expect to make thousands of times their initial investment, let alone in the first few months or the first year. Instead, most people are simply seeking a return – any kind of return, however modest – on their capital.

Before 1990, it was possible for even the most cautious investors to raise an income from their savings. Retired people were able to buy government bonds or even leave their money in cash and gain a return that could allow them to eke out a modest existence from their life savings, even if they were not very rich. The Bank of England base rate, as shown in Figure 1.1, was well into double figures for the majority of the years between 1975 and 1990, and even at its lowest did not fall below 5 per cent for many years. Compare this with the 0.1 per cent record low rate in the last quarter of 2021. Its rise to 2.25 per cent by the third quarter of 2022 was received with shock, yet compared with its pre-financial crisis rates, it was still very low.

FIGURE 1.1 Bank of England base interest rate, 1975–2022

While savings accounts and bonds normally return a little over the base rate, it still means that it is impossible to derive a meaningful income from savings, and savers are suffering capital loss in terms of purchasing power. This becomes even more important in an environment where there are inflationary pressures, as evidenced by the rising prices of staples such as food and energy that began to set in during the Covid pandemic and accelerated during 2022. If your savings are earning 1 per cent but the price of food, fuel and other essentials is rising at 10 per cent or more, it does not take long before the real value of your savings is rapidly eroded.

With prudence apparently being penalized in such a way, some of society's most vulnerable people are sometimes tempted to risk their capital in schemes that are high risk or even outright fraudulent. Many valid criticisms have been levelled at cryptocurrencies for encouraging naive investors to risk losing everything, but, at the same time, investors have lost millions of pounds of savings to schemes that sounded – and were – too good to be true, such as overseas property developments that never materialized or non-existent truffle farms.

Many outside the fast-moving, hype-driven world of crypto write disapprovingly about risk-taking millennials and Generation Z traders who poured their savings uncritically into the notoriously unstable DeFi and NFT ecosystem. However, skewed incentives created by low yields have precipitated risky behaviour across all generations.

The new freedoms accorded to holders of private pensions in the UK, who were allowed to transfer their funds from defined benefit schemes into other, more risky pension products, have resulted in many sad stories of life savings lost to fraudulent or badly managed get-rich-quick projects, particularly in the real estate sector.

Developments that enabled the growth of DeFi

Given the pre-existing and growing appetite for a new type of investment, what were the innovations that allowed DeFi to exist? Bitcoin developed as a decentralized payment mechanism, but other things also needed to happen before decentralized finance in its current form could evolve.

Stablecoins

Cryptocurrency prices have been notoriously volatile since the birth of Bitcoin in 2009, but what if investors and savers could benefit from holding their cash in something that tracks the value of state-backed money such as US dollars, euros or pounds, yet can be transmitted via a low-friction, low-cost public, decentralized financial infrastructure?

This compelling question led to the invention of stablecoins. These in turn became the flywheel that accelerated the growth of decentralized finance. It is also important to understand that these assets, while theoretically pegged to the value of government-backed currencies, are not themselves guaranteed to maintain this peg, or to be low risk.

Before we start digging deep into the mechanics, it is first important to understand that stablecoins are simply a type of token issued on a blockchain. Let's quickly recap the different types of tokens that are created using the Ethereum blockchain. While other types of Layer 1 and Layer 2 blockchains are discussed throughout the book, the Ethereum token standards are the fundamental building blocks that we first need to understand.

The ERC20 token specification

In the days after Bitcoin but before Ethereum, if someone wanted to launch their own crypto token, they had to first create their own blockchain. In many cases, these were virtually copy-paste imitations of Bitcoin that could be set up by almost anyone, but, in other cases, they introduced technical innovations that brought in significant differences between networks and involved much complicated work by computer scientists.

In these early days, even coins that had been created on a blockchain that was a copy (fork) of an original blockchain were not interoperable with coins on the original network. You could not connect a Bitcoin wallet to the Bitcoin blockchain and send Dogecoin over the same network. And you could not send Monero to an address on the Cardano or EOS network.

This lack of interoperability slowed down innovation because it meant that, every time someone wanted to create a new project, they were effectively reinventing the wheel. It also meant that the required mass of developers experienced in the programming languages and new frameworks was slow to accumulate. In order to list new cryptocurrencies, crypto exchanges had to go through the technical process of integrating with a new blockchain before the coin could be traded.

Of course, it is equally valid to argue the opposite case: that the genuine time and investment that had to be spent on new projects meant that only the most worthy and technically valid were able to survive in any meaningful sense.

For better or for worse, Ethereum changed all this by introducing standard specifications that, at one stroke, removed much of the technical work that was necessary to develop and to integrate new tokens. As explained in the Introduction, the primary difference between Bitcoin and Ethereum is that, while Bitcoin is used primarily for payment transactions, Ethereum has been specially designed to allow more complex conditional transactions – 'smart contracts' – to be executed.

Who makes decisions about Ethereum's code?

Ethereum and Bitcoin are both open-source software in which changes to the way the code works are governed by consensus. Unlike proprietary software released by a private company, which is designed and authorized by a small team of people who do not have to make their decisions public, Ethereum Improvement Proposals (EIPs) are discussed and debated in calls between the developers working on Ethereum, which are open for the general public to listen to.

If the EIP is deemed worthy of adoption, it goes through a lengthy process of development and testing before being incorporated into the main Ethereum code base. Even once this release has happened, further consensus is required in that the thousands of validators running Ethereum's software have to decide voluntarily to upgrade their software to the newest version. This approach to development may seem unfamiliar to anyone who works within a large financial organization where a small number of people are responsible for making decisions about which software enhancements are developed and deployed and when this should happen.

The now-familiar ERC20 token defines a deliberately minimal level of information that nevertheless provides everything needed to be a transfer mechanism for exchanging such tokens on the Ethereum network. The original specification was proposed by developer Fabian Vogelsteller in 2015 (see GitHub, 2015) and adopted in 2017. Even non-coders should be able to recognize the essential principles laid down in the specification:

- TotalSupply – the total number of tokens that will ever be issued.
- BalanceOf – the account balance of a token owner's account.

- Transfer – automatically executes transfers of a specified number of tokens to a specified address for transactions using the token.
- TransferFrom – automatically executes transfers of a specified number of tokens from a specified address using the token.
- Approve – allows a spender to withdraw a set number of tokens from a specified account, up to a specific amount.
- Allowance – returns a set number of tokens from a spender to the owner.
- Transfer – an event triggered when a transfer is successful (an event).
- Approval – a log of an approved event.

The beauty of these rules lies in their simplicity. An ERC20 token, which can be transferred easily from wallet to wallet and which acts in a similar way to cash, does not have to be able to do very many things or perform any complicated functions. It needs to have a name and a symbol, to distinguish it from other ERC20 tokens. It needs to have a total supply and to have its level of divisibility specified. And it needs to be able to be transferred to any given address, where the balance is incremented, from a given address, where the balance is decremented.

These uniform properties suddenly meant that cryptocurrency exchanges, wallets and decentralized applications that supported Ethereum could now support any tokens that someone else issued on Ethereum with no extra technical work, as long as they conformed to the ERC20 standard.

This had advantages and disadvantages. It brought interoperability and reduced friction, but it also meant that the barrier to entry for creating new tokens and creating fund-raisers for new projects was now open to anyone with a computer and an internet connection, however competent, whether they were well-intentioned or otherwise. All someone needs to do to create a new ERC20 cryptocurrency token is to deploy a smart contract to the Ethereum blockchain. At Etherscan.io, you can go to the contract address of, for example, $SHIB, the Shiba Inu token discussed earlier in this chapter, and see that all transactions can be viewed by anyone in the world and linked to wallet addresses, providing a pseudonymous audit trail and a useful source of data.

This ability to issue one's own token supply without having to assemble a specialist team of cryptocurrency developers prompted a boom in Initial Coin Offerings in 2017, when thousands of crypto and blockchain projects of varying degrees of provenance and honesty raised many millions of dollars in ERC20 tokens from a credulous public.

Very few of these exist today, either because they were run by people with the best of intentions but without the business experience or other expertise to run a successful start-up, or because they were outright scams. The public nature of blockchain transactions was able to provide ample evidence of these activities, and some of the higher-profile projects were retrospectively investigated by the SEC (Securities and Exchange Commission) in the USA for illegally issuing securities.

Nevertheless, this period can be seen as one where there was an overall feeling of innovation and excitement, which opened the eyes of many developers and entrepreneurs to a very different kind of future. The ERC20 standard went on to be adopted outside the Ethereum ecosystem, inspiring the BEP20 standard, which is used on BNB Chain, and the NEP21 standard, which is the equivalent fungible token specification on NEAR Protocol. (BNB Chain is a Layer 1 blockchain originally funded by the Binance exchange). Other Layer 1s include NEAR Protocol, Solana, Flow, Avalanche and Fantom and these all have their own token standards, all with different names.

Rather than reeling off a long list of numbers and letters that denote these standards, it is important to understand the distinction between fungible and non-fungible tokens (NFTs), as both of these principles form important building blocks within DeFi.

FUNGIBLE AND NON-FUNGIBLE TOKENS

In accounting terms, fungibility means that one unit of a commodity is exactly equivalent to and interchangeable for another unit of the same commodity. This is particularly relevant when it comes to settling debts, as it means that, if you owe someone 100 units of a commodity, any random 100 units of that same commodity will have the equivalent value. Hence a barrel of Brent crude oil is considered exactly the same as another barrel of Brent crude, and a gold bar of a set purity is the same as another of the same grade.

This sounds simple, but in fact fungibility is not a completely binary property. Consider the pound or dollar in your pocket. If you walk into a shop and see something that is priced at £5, you can hand over any five £1 coins or a £5 note in exchange for the item and, unless the money has been forged, the shopkeeper will accept the sale. This suggests that one £5 note or one £1 coin is exactly like another £5 note or £1 coin, but in fact there may be subtle differences that make a particular instance of a note or a coin more or less valuable, or at least more or less desirable.

For example, some of the rarer 50p coins in the UK are in such great demand among collectors that people will pay several hundred pounds for them. Some shops and businesses in England refuse to take Scottish bank notes, despite the fact that they are legal tender. Anyone demanding cash for a ransom or in a bank heist knows to ask for new, unmarked notes that could not be used to identify them. So, while currencies are regarded as fungible, this is more of a sliding scale than an absolute truth. At the other end of the sliding scale are extremely non-fungible assets such as Stradivarius violins, antiques, houses and signed memorabilia.

ERC20 tokens are designed to be fungible. Nothing exists in the code of a standard ERC20 smart contract that gives a particular token or subset of tokens within the token supply special properties that make them more valuable than others with the same name and symbol. It is theoretically possible that some tokens may have been passed through the wallet of a fraudster or may have been stolen in a hack, in which case they may be slightly less fungible, but, broadly speaking, ERC20 tokens are designed to be completely fungible.

Now let's consider non-fungibles such as a Stradivarius violin or a house. Houses are built on different plots of land in different places, and have been decorated to the taste of the current owner. The garden may have different plants, and one road may be less busy than another. Even on a newly built development, there is a pecking order. A house may be superficially identical to another, yet one has more sunshine in the morning or may be at an end of the street that has fewer passing vehicles during rush hour. Houses are not fungible at all, and neither are artworks, antiques, pets or a whole host of other items and beings.

The non-fungible equivalent of the ERC20 token is the ERC721 standard for smart contracts, which was later succeeded by the ERC1155 specification, which added more properties. Non-fungible tokens have seized the public imagination, not to mention that of celebrities, sports teams and art collectors. Everyone seems to have an opinion about NFTs, good or bad, but many people miss the point that these tokens are about far more than collecting digital images of apes or superheroes.

The NFT boom

So, if NFTs are more than just JPEGs, what makes an NFT different from an ERC20 token, and what can you do with it?

The ERC721 standard for NFTs was proposed in 2018. In its code, it specifies a *tokenId* property. This identity reference may be used as an input to generate a particular type of output when referenced by an application. The ERC721 contract also has the ability to receive metadata, which can include properties such as an external URI that references an image, for example.

Highly publicized NFT collections such as CryptoPunks, CryptoKitties, Bored Apes and World of Women have resulted in a misconception among some observers that the only point of NFTs is to identify and transfer the latest trendy digital art collectables. NFTs, however, have a variety of different uses, including their use in subscription, membership or loyalty schemes – and also as a utility within DeFi.

Chapter 3 looks closely at the mechanics of how decentralized exchanges (DEXs) work. Some people are surprised that this can involve NFTs. For example, when someone deposits tokens into a liquidity pool on Uniswap, an NFT token denoting their position is automatically sent to their wallet. Its individual properties include the amount they have deposited, and when they remove the liquidity from the contract, the token is sent back and destroyed. Hence, while celebrity-endorsed cartoon images may seem a world away from the world of finance, the underlying technology that is common to both provides a core component of the infrastructure needed for the modern DeFi system.

At this point, it is also worth mentioning the ERC1155 standard, which allows developers to issue a mix of fungible and non-fungible tokens in a single contract. See Chapter 7 for a deep dive into NFTs and how they integrate with DeFi.

DeFi: finance without a central authority

While it is possible to argue that the birth of Bitcoin is in itself a form of decentralized finance, as payment systems are indeed part of the financial system, most people trace the evolution of DeFi in its truest sense to the release of MakerDAO in late 2017. This was not, of course, a planned milestone in the evolution of cryptocurrency and DeFi, but a completely separate project established to leverage Ethereum's capabilities for the purpose of creating a cryptocurrency that would remain at a stable rate against fiat (government-issued) currencies.

If the entire industry had been conceptualized by a single corporation, it is unlikely that progress would have been so rapid: decentralization leads to the involvement of many different people, with many different ideas and points of view. However, as is inevitable in a system that is not controlled by one company, entity or interest group but which emerges organically, the creation of this infrastructure was rapid but not smooth or coordinated in any way.

The chaotic way in which DeFi is organized and governed may come as a shock for professionals who come from a background in traditional finance (TradFi). A protocol that holds many millions of dollars in value may be deployed by a well-funded start-up or alternatively by a totally anonymous developer – the 'shadowy super-coder' of Senator Elizabeth Warren's nightmares (Gotsegen, 2021).

Dabblers in DeFi regularly transact hundreds of thousands of dollars' worth of trade via a browser extension secured only by a passphrase which, if lost, would remove their access to their funds permanently. There is no support telephone line or help desk to consult if the worst happens and a back-up is lost or a wallet is hacked. Even worse, if a hapless user loses funds or faces technical problems and then tweets about it, hordes of malicious bots patrol Twitter for mention of popular wallet brand names and reply with links containing malware that will drain even more of their funds.

MAKERDAO

The aim of the MakerDAO project was to enable anyone to use the Ethereum ecosystem in a way that would not necessarily expose them to the volatile price movements of the underlying cryptocurrency. It enabled investors to borrow a dollar-denominated digital currency by depositing collateral into a contract, without any third-party intermediation or control.

This is a revolutionary idea because, in normal circumstances, if someone wants to borrow dollars, they have to make an application to a centralized lender that checks their credit rating and may approve or reject them based on their identity. MakerDAO and other similar protocols obviate the need for identification and credit checks by forcing lenders to over-collateralize their loans, which are liquidated if they fall below a certain level.

What does this mean in real terms? Imagine you have Ether, which you do not want to sell because you believe the value is going to rise over a set period. However, you also want to take advantage of a trading opportunity in another asset that is denominated in dollars, or even borrow US dollars to fund the purchase of a real-world asset such as a car. To provide a concrete example, the investor sends $3000 worth of Ether to the MakerDAO smart contract using the Oasis app. This allows them to create $2000 worth of Dai (in other words, 2000 Dai, as the value of one Dai token is always pegged to the dollar).

If the investor is successful in their predictions, they have guessed accurately that Ether will remain at more or less the same rate or even gain in value against the US dollar. When they want to reclaim their Ether, they repay the Dai they have borrowed and get their collateral back, minus a small amount of interest. During the period they have owned the Dai, they have had the chance to make money or gain some other advantage from it, and if they are lucky, their Ether will also have appreciated in value. Best of all, the processes are entirely automated, so there is no waiting around for loans to be approved or funds to hit your bank account. It is also a way to take out a long position against the US dollar in whatever collateral you want to deposit: although MakerDAO started out accepting only Ether as collateral, the protocol now accepts a range of different tokens that have been voted as acceptable deposits.

In case this makes the process sound too easy, potential borrowers should also be mindful of the risks. If someone borrows Dai and their collateral falls below the agreed ratio of 150 per cent, then they run the risk of liquidation and having to pay a 13 per cent liquidation penalty. To complicate matters, this liquidation can be performed by anyone at all, with the result that bots are continuously monitoring all open positions, their owners eager to extract the liquidation reward and make a profit.

The example of MakerDAO is relatively simple, yet it shows how a financial product such as a collateralized loan can be opened, administered and closed without any company or institution having involvement or oversight. The entire process is written into encoded instructions that run automatically on the Ethereum blockchain on computers that can be owned and administered by anyone anywhere in the world.

What can you do with stablecoins within the DeFi ecosystem? To give one simple example, if you have minted Dai and wish to earn a return on it while keeping your funds in a dollar-denominated asset, you can lock it in Maker's DSR (Dai Savings Rate) contract and earn interest; or you may deposit it elsewhere in a dizzying array of protocols where you might be able to get a better rate. There are descriptions of some of these protocols and their underlying principles in the following chapters.

Collateralized vs algorithmic stablecoins

While Dai is the best-known example on Ethereum, it was not in fact the world's first stablecoin. Because stablecoins are pegged against government-issued fiat currencies such as dollars or euros, they are useful for performing bridging functions between the cryptocurrency world and the traditional financial domain. They are also a powerful tool for anyone who wants to make transactions that are fast, borderless and frictionless, but who do not want to expose themselves to the fluctuating exchange rate of cryptocurrencies such as Ether.

Tether, for example, predates Ethereum: it was launched in 2014 on a blockchain named Omni (formerly MasterCoin). Unlike Dai, Tether is not decentralized at all, being issued by a private company. But it is similar in that it requires a certain proportion of other assets to be locked up in order to mint the stablecoin. In other words, it is collateralized. Over the years, rumours have surrounded the extent to which Tether is backed, and it briefly lost its peg and fell to $0.88 at one point, returning to its peg when the backing company produced what was deemed sufficient evidence of collateral. Critics of the opacity around Tether's reserves point to the stablecoin as a source of systemic risk to the entire crypto ecosystem. In May 2022, following the de-pegging of the Terra stablecoin UST, Tether also briefly lost its peg.

Another collateralized stablecoin is US Dollar Coin (USDC), which was launched in 2018 by a consortium backed by Coinbase and Circle. Like Dai, USDC was first issued on Ethereum, but is now issued on a range of Layer 1 networks including Avalanche and Solana. As mentioned in the Introduction, USDC has even been used by Visa for settlements.

Providing collateral for a stablecoin may seem like the obvious – and only – way to maintain a constant exchange rate. In recent years, stablecoins that maintain their peg via an algorithm have become more common – although following the high-profile collapse of UST, Terra's algorithmic stablecoin, support for these has become more muted.

ALGORITHMIC STABLECOINS

An algorithmic stablecoin adjusts its supply according to the price of the underlying asset: as the price of the US dollar or other fiat currency rises, so does the supply of the stablecoin. Smart contracts responsible for algorithmic stablecoins use oracles – decentralized, trusted data sources – in order to keep track of real-world exchange rates.

Algorithmic stablecoins were first heavily stress-tested by market conditions in late spring and early summer 2021, when crypto markets fell dramatically and quickly, and their supply struggled to stabilize. Ampleforth (AMP) dropped to $0.48 at one point. This pales into insignificance, however, against the events of May 2022, when the de-pegging of UST caused its sister currency Luna to drop precipitously in value. Indeed, UST lost its dollar parity so dramatically that it fell from 91 cents to 16 cents in a matter of hours. The algorithmic mechanism for maintaining UST's peg meant that, for every 1 UST minted, the equivalent of $1 in Luna is burned. Conversely, as each UST is redeemed for Luna, the supply expands and the Luna price falls. Within just a week, the price of Luna tanked from more than $90 to a fraction of a cent, causing huge instability in the cryptocurrency markets.

The interlinked nature of DeFi meant that contagion quickly spread. Three Arrows Capital, a crypto hedge fund that was staking large sums of Luna, was ordered to liquidate in July 2022, while broker Voyager Digital, which had lent heavily to Three Arrows, declared bankruptcy the same month. All of these events, however, paled into insignificance when compared with the dramatic collapse of the FTX crypto exchange. While FTX was not a DeFi product, its failure led to a loss of confidence in the entire crypto sector.

Key moments in the evolution of DeFi

Stablecoins were the first components of the infrastructure we now recognize as DeFi, but gradually, during 2017 and 2018, other ideas and products began to emerge. While cryptocurrency traders had until then been content simply to trade their tokens for other tokens, the dream of building an entirely new type of financial infrastructure on these new public networks was now becoming real.

Exchange trading was the way most people became involved in crypto, so it is hardly surprising that some of the first platforms to make an appearance were decentralized exchanges (DEXs). We take a detailed look at the development of DEXs in Chapter 3, but a brief overview here can put the rest of the timeline in Figure 1.2 into context.

FIGURE 1.2 Timeline of DeFi developments and events

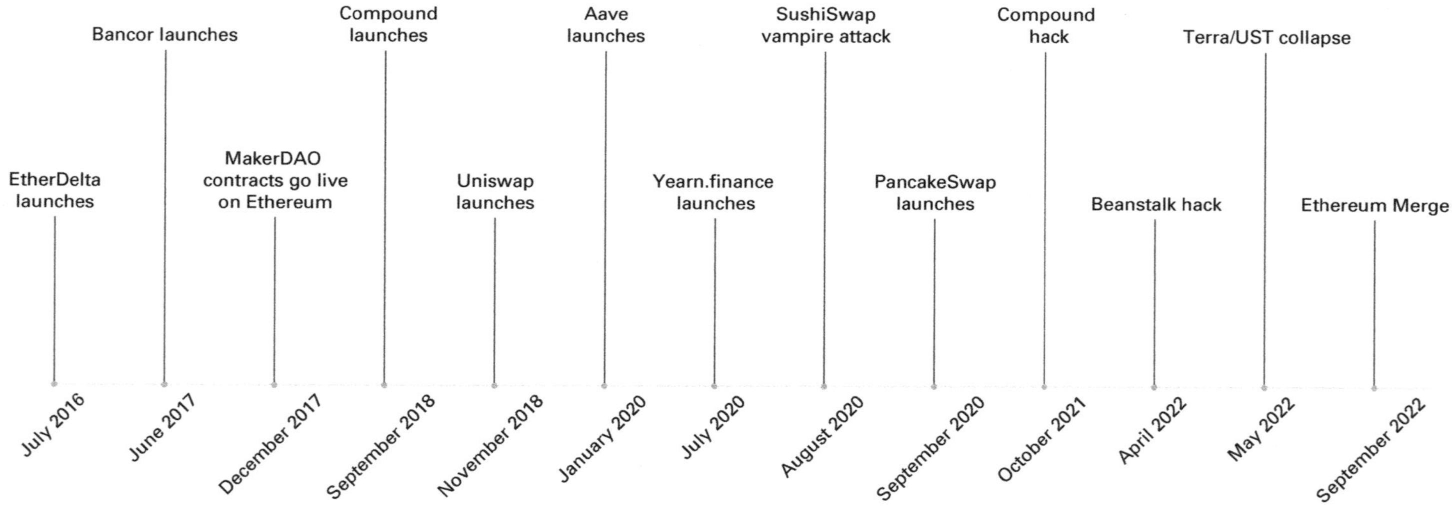

EtherDelta launches — July 2016

Bancor launches — June 2017

MakerDAO contracts go live on Ethereum — December 2017

Compound launches — September 2018

Uniswap launches — November 2018

Aave launches — January 2020

Yearn.finance launches — July 2020

SushiSwap vampire attack — August 2020

PancakeSwap launches — September 2020

Compound hack — October 2021

Beanstalk hack — April 2022

Terra/UST collapse — May 2022

Ethereum Merge — September 2022

The first crypto exchanges began to emerge as early as 2010 when the original Bitcoin hobby miners began to cash in, and less tech-savvy types who had heard about Bitcoin but did not have the inclination or means to run a mining operation bought these novel new currency tokens.

Early exchanges were plagued with amateurish technology and it was often difficult to distinguish losses caused by external hacks from those that were perpetrated by the people who ran the exchanges. Names such as MtGox, MintPal, Cryptsy and Quadriga have now faded into crypto history, but for those who lost thousands of dollars' worth of crypto (which would be multi-millions today), the trauma is still real.

While the newer generation of centralized exchanges lent an air of professionalism and slickness to proceedings, the idea of keeping large amounts of cryptocurrency in wallets that were under the control of unknown parties was anathema to those who had been through the growing pains of losing funds on first- and second-generation exchanges.

Hence the idea of exchanges that consisted purely of verifiable smart contracts – where you kept custody of your assets yourself – became an increasingly appealing option. The earliest DEXs, such as EtherDelta and Kyber Network, had limited success. While hardcore enthusiasts appreciated the opportunity to retain control over their own funds, low liquidity and high transaction fees meant that these exchanges struggled to compete against the slicker interfaces and low trading fees of the new centralized exchange. As platforms such as Coinbase increased the range of tokens they sold, a new breed of trader was drawn in, who was more used to interacting with traditional fintech applications and thus had higher expectations of user interfaces and customer service support.

Chapter 3 looks at how DEXs such as Uniswap began to make inroads into the market share of the centralized exchanges. In the meantime, other financial applications were springing up in the DeFi sector and opening people's eyes to a wide range of new possibilities.

The phenomenon of initial coin offerings (ICOs) sparked something of a crypto gold rush in 2017 and 2018. While many of the associated projects quietly died in the following year or so, some of those that received ICO funding at around this time have gone on to create the backbone of the decentralized finance infrastructure we see today. Between December 2017 and February 2018, two noteworthy projects that launched ICOs were Aave and Synthetix.

Aave

Aave is a lending and borrowing protocol that allows users to deposit digital assets which can be borrowed by other users, and thus earn passive income. The rate earned is based on current demand, and can fluctuate. As we saw earlier with MakerDAO, the big difference between lending on a centralized platform and a DeFi platform is the fact that no one needs to approve you or check your credit rating.

Synthetix

DeFi offers decentralized alternatives to traditional financial products. By 2018 other elements were coming into play, such as Synthetix, which allows investors to trade derivatives. We will examine later in the book exactly how this happens, but the point of highlighting Aave and Synthetix is that innovators were gradually starting to find solutions to the previously intractable problem of how to recreate elements of traditional finance within DeFi.

TVL

Anyone who spends time investigating DeFi will soon find a swathe of acronyms and unfamiliar terms. Many of these are covered in the Glossary. An expression that is often heared is Total Value Locked, or TVL. Because DeFi protocols – whether they are lending, borrowing, trading, or anything else – require funds to be sent to a smart contract address, where they remain until the particular investment or transaction has ended, these funds, either Ether or other types of collateral, are said to be 'locked'.

Tens of billions of dollars' worth of value are locked in different protocols at any given time. There are various websites that show the total TVL, as well as the individual TVLs, for any particular project. Figure 1.3 gives an indication of the very rapid growth of the sector over the last five years.

It is worth bearing in mind that, while transactions on open blockchains are publicly visible and it should be possible therefore to validate TVL claims, there is still a certain amount of wriggle room that means some figures may be inflated. An example of this is the action taken by US developer Ian Macalinao that resulted in Solana's TVL being dramatically overvalued. Every dollar's worth of crypto that is added to the ecosystem can be counted multiple times if it is lent out more than once. Hence Macalinao built protocols that were layered on

FIGURE 1.3 DeFi total value locked, 2019–2022

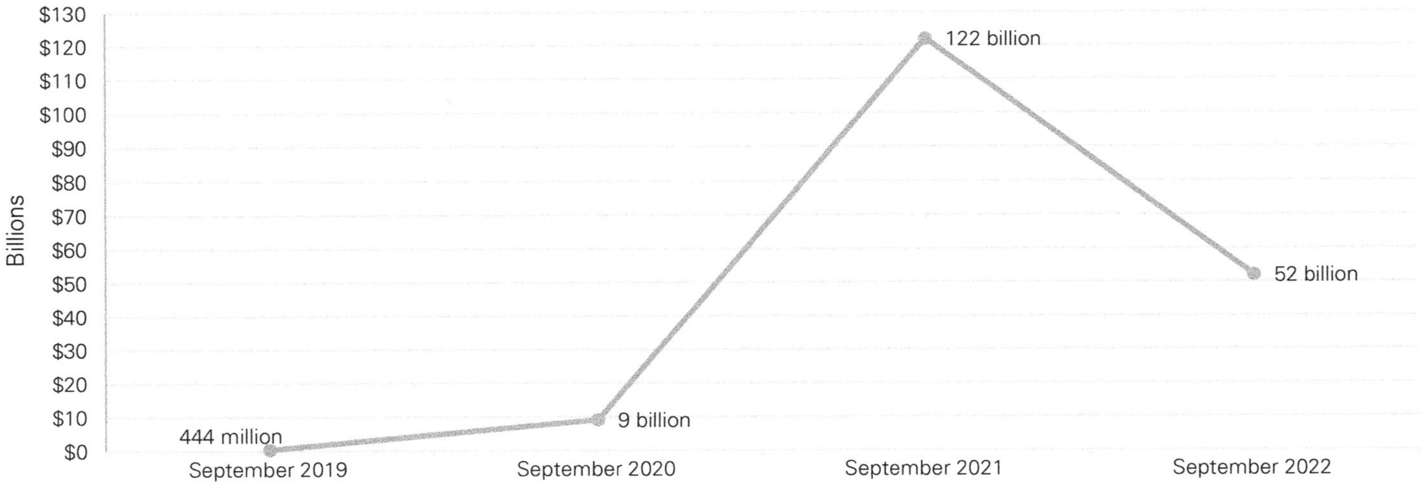

FIGURES from DefiLlama

top of other protocols, so that tokens lent on one platform could be lent again on another. This is not in any way illegal as the transparent nature of public blockchains enables traders to see that this is the case – although one could argue that Macalinao's assumption of different pseudonyms to do this added some opacity to this move. (Nelson and Wang, 2022).

Before moving on, let's take time to consider the implications of this growth in TVL. Tens of billions of dollars of investor funds are deposited in smart contracts consisting of code that could have been written by anyone in the world, running on computers all over the world on a network that anyone can join. There is no corporation guaranteeing the safety of funds, and no customer support if anything goes wrong. Yet – somehow – enough people trust the integrity of this system to commit their capital to it.

The DeFi summer of 2020

Other protocols that launched during 2018–2019 were Uniswap and Compound, both hugely important pillars of the growing ecosystem. Chapter 3 looks at the major differences between Uniswap and the DEXs that had preceded it, while Chapter 4 includes a deeper dive into Compound.

Compound allows investors to deposit a variety of different tokens, which can then be borrowed by other users. APY varies according to the token and also varies over time. Compound had launched in 2018, but the real gamechanger, both for Compound itself and for DeFi as a whole, was its decision to launch the Comp token in April 2020. Comp could be earned as a reward, on top of the lending fees that investors made on their deposits. The chance to earn what was effectively double interest on deposits sparked even greater interest from those dabbling in DeFi, and the concept of DeFi liquidity mining (see Glossary) was born.

The advantages were double-edged: not only was it a great incentive for depositors to earn Comp tokens, which could be traded for other cryptocurrencies or fiat currencies on exchanges, but it was also beneficial for the protocol to be able to distribute its tokens in this way. The tokens did not simply act as an incentive, but also provided a mechanism through which the users of the protocol could vote on decisions affecting it. The topic of DeFi governance is so important that a whole chapter (Chapter 6) is dedicated to the topic of DAOs.

Liquidity mining sparked something of a gold rush into DeFi protocols, and depositors began frantically moving funds from token to token to take advantage of those offering the highest returns – an activity known as 'yield farming'.

A developer named Andre Cronje launched a new protocol, Yearn Finance, in early 2020. Like Compound, Yearn had its own token, YFI. Yearn is an automated lending aggregator where depositors can lock their funds that are lent out on other platforms including Aave and Compound, and is periodically rebalanced by an algorithm to ensure yield is always maximized.

To traditional finance experts, this idea that users should be paid simply for using a particular platform was – and remains – perplexing. Yet, particularly in a bull market, the rising price of the reward tokens, driven by the high underlying price of Ether and other cryptocurrencies, provided a powerful incentive to try out the latest exciting platform.

The food token craze

In the meme-driven countercultural world of crypto, the concept of yield farming and its parallels with real-life farming became a social media phenomenon. It was not long before it prompted a wave of platforms and tokens with ridiculous names that referenced crops or food, and soon the cryptocurrency price rankings were awash with tokens with names like Sushi, Yam, Burger, Pizza and Kimchi.

However, one of the most interesting aspects of this period is the growth of composability between protocols, or as some DeFi enthusiasts would have it, 'DeFi Lego'. What does this mean? In its simplest terms, it means that different projects and protocols could be used in conjunction with each other in order to maximize yield. To use some projects already mentioned as examples, a savvy investor could deposit a particular token on Compound, earn fees from this and also Comp tokens. These Comp tokens could then be staked on another platform such as Yam, to gain an even higher return.

Of course, something that some people see as exciting and innovative composability and interoperability looks to other people remarkably like a dangerously teetering edifice driven by greed and unrealistic expectations. The truth, as ever, is somewhere between the two extremes, but optimism and confidence stayed high for some time. While the summer of 2020 is generally acknowledged as the 'DeFi summer', 2021 was also a wildly successful year for new protocols and for decentralized finance as a whole. In May 2021, the price of Comp was riding high at more than $800, and YFI at $42.

By the summer of 2022, after a long crypto bear market, prices were hovering around a sixth of their peaks. Having said this, the fact that many of the underlying protocols have been thoroughly battle-tested and are still attracting investor funds and doing what they are supposed to do is a marker that the system as a whole appears, at least at the moment, able to withstand the excesses of inflated price expectations and settle down to a more realistic equilibrium.

Izabella Kaminska sees the DeFi bear market as an inevitable consequence of the cyclical nature of markets and frames it in terms of anacyclosis theory:

> I think what's interesting about the whole DeFi collapse in the last year is how resilient people in the market are. The market hasn't failed – it's just had that cyclical readjustment... As long as you do those controlled shakeouts in this way, you don't let them spill over. If the system stays in stasis just too long, then the collateral damage from the next tip of the cycle is going to be way more excessive.

Beyond Ethereum: other Layer 1 networks

The volatility of APYs between different protocols and different token pools – some of which were temporarily in excess of 1000 per cent – and the chance to make many times one's original return through a combination of rising crypto prices, high APYs and compounded token rewards led to a great deal of excitement on social media during 2020 and 2021 as investors shared tips and hyped the latest platforms, some of which were released with a minimum of development and testing time. (See Chapter 5 for the consequences of some of these rushed and inadequately audited software releases.)

Yet, even when excitement was running high, there was something that everyone cited as a downside of DeFi: high transaction fees on the Ethereum network. While the opportunity to make astonishingly high returns on capital was open to anyone in the world, whoever and wherever you were, these opportunities had become increasingly limited to those who were already crypto-wealthy. Small investors who would otherwise have been quite happy to lock away a few hundred dollars' worth of tokens here or there were not able to take advantage of these stratospheric returns, as transaction fees of well over $50 would have wiped out the short-term profit. For those who were able and willing to commit tens or hundreds of thousands of dollars, the higher transaction fees were nothing more than an annoyance. However, for the developers and entrepreneurs creating new Layer 1 blockchains, the potential to create new and cheaper-to-use DeFi protocols on top of them provided a new impetus.

Ethereum is still the most popular blockchain for DeFi, but it is followed by BNB Chain and Avalanche, which are rapidly gaining ground and which have significantly lower transaction fees. Ethereum's supporters argue that the scalability improvements due in the later stages of the migration to Ethereum 2.0 should lower fees, but if the other chains have a chance to establish themselves as low-fee competitors before this happens, it is likely to bring about a permanent change in the competitive landscape.

BNB Chain is worth a mention because it evolved as a decentralized spin-off project from the popular global cryptocurrency exchange Binance, run by the charismatic Changpeng Zhao (CZ). Originally named Binance Smart Chain (BSC) and since rebranded as BNB Chain to reinforce its association with its BNB native token, it was launched in 2020, in time to take full advantage of the DeFi summer boom. Its most popular dApp, PancakeSwap, looks like a parody site with its cartoonish graphics and bright colours, but has proved itself an integral component of the wider DeFi system, with around $5 billion TVL at any given time, and its Cake token hovering in the top 50 cryptocurrency rankings. With fees that are often only cents, and a popular lottery game, it quickly proved to be an easy entry point into the arcane world of DeFi for people who had never before been involved in the financial world.

The fast-moving world of memes, colourful interfaces and dramas that play out daily on social media could not be further away from the perception of finance as a rather staid field. Yet to characterize DeFi as purely a plaything for crypto enthusiasts would be inaccurate. There has been a steady flow of employees from traditional finance incumbents into DeFi, attracted by the lure of building a technology-first, frictionless, democratic investment ecosystem that includes rather than excludes.

It is also true to say that the ideas and concept behind decentralized finance, while executed completely differently from traditional finance, are all borrowed from the same principles. Opinions differ about how well or badly these are implemented within DeFi, but many people concede that both sectors have plenty to learn from each other.

The next chapter looks at how retail investors participate and invest in existing financial products and examines why they might be tempted to enter the world of decentralized finance.

References

GitHub (2015) 'ERC: Token standard #20': https://github.com/ethereum/eips/issues/20 (archived at https://perma.cc/APH3-8EKH)

Gotsegen, W (2021) 'Senator Warren: Crypto puts financial system in the hands of "shadowy super-coders"', Decrypt: https://decrypt.co/76997/elizabeth-warren-crypto-big-banks-shadowy-super-coders (archived at https://perma.cc/QFN8-XDN2)

Kraterou, A (2021) 'Shiba Inu millionaire retires at the age of 35 after $8,000 bet', *New York Post*: https://nypost.com/2021/11/09/shiba-inu-millionaire-retires-at-the-age-of-35-after-8000-bet/ (archived at https://perma.cc/M4Y4-8GX4)

Nelson, D and Wang, T (2022) 'Master of anons: how a crypto developer faked a defi ecosystem': www.coindesk.com/layer2/2022/08/04/master-of-anons-how-a-crypto-developer-faked-a-defi-ecosystem/ (archived at https://perma.cc/ZGA5-FFB7)

02

The current face of retail finance

CHAPTER OBJECTIVES

- How retail customers invest
- The difference between retail and institutional
- How changing demographics change attitudes to risk
- The rise of the influencer
- Understanding why fintech developed
- Fintech × DeFi
- The DeFi mullet
- WallStreetBets and the growth of meme stocks

For many people in countries such as the UK, financial services are something to which they may not give much thought. Advice in the personal finance sections of many newspapers and websites tends to centre around comparing mortgage deals or energy provider contracts, or on tips for economizing on daily expenses rather than how to make your capital work harder for you or on getting the best returns from your investments. In general, the UK is not really a nation of shareholders, once managed products such as pensions are excluded.

The reality is that, even where individuals seek investment vehicles that will give them a good return, much of the underlying detail is abstracted away. Very few people invest directly in stocks and shares, for example, although their pensions, overseen by third-party fund managers, contain them. Until something goes wrong and hits the headlines – as the Northern Rock crisis did in 2007 – the majority of the public remains unaware of the sheer interconnectedness of the global economy.

This chapter looks specifically at how customers interact with the traditional financial sector and how this picture is slowly changing as banks transform themselves into technology companies, and fintech apps make inroads into the territory previously occupied by banks. It also studies the demographic and cultural shifts that are leading to a greater interest in stocks, shares and cryptocurrencies among younger people, and takes a speculative view of how banks, or more likely, fintech companies, may integrate their products into the DeFi ecosystem in future.

Retail customers and their attitude to risk

As few people will have been left in doubt after the crisis of 2007–2008, the world's financial markets are inextricably linked in webs of complicated transactions and dependencies that criss-cross the entire globe. Others may prefer to see it as a precarious house of cards rather than an interconnected web, with debts and obligations stacked in layers on top of each other, ready to collapse at a moment's notice.

Regardless of this interconnectedness, because the regulatory structures in most countries provide specified consumer protections, individuals who entrust their savings to banks, fintech companies or pension providers can generally do so with a degree of confidence that they will be protected from fraud or negligence. This being the case, most people go about their business without paying much attention to what happens to their money once it is safely locked away.

Fifteen years on from the Northern Rock crisis that shook Britain, and which was recorded for posterity in Bitcoin's genesis block, the shockwaves have receded. At the time, however, many Northern Rock savers were surprised by the extent of their bank's dependency on events happening on another continent. The subprime mortgage crisis, documented so compellingly in Adam McKay's 2015 film *The Big Short*, might have had its roots in the United States, but the knock-on effects on global credit markets meant that overexposed banks all over the world started suffering liquidity issues.

One of the luxuries of living in a country with effective financial regulation is that one does not generally have to worry about what happens to one's money once deposited in the bank. So, it came as a shock for many people to realize in 2008 that their funds were not just sitting there, ready for them to access at any time. It is usually only the threat of crisis that makes people examine what is actually happening behind the reassuring bricks and mortar frontage of their high street bank.

As we will see in this chapter, the global financial crisis, the coming of age of Generation Z and the increasing importance of fintech – defined as any technology that delivers financial services through software – have led to seismic changes in the way people think about money, financial products and investing. Before we can start truly understanding the ways in which consumers may take advantage of decentralized finance in future, we need first to understand public perceptions of the financial sector as a whole and find out how retail investors currently consume financial products in the existing landscape.

We also need to take into account how those responsible for decision-making within banks and financial institutions view the possibility of offering integrations with DeFi systems. Given that most institutions are wary even about the possibility of involvement with cryptocurrencies at even the most basic level, it is unlikely that we will see this happening any time soon. However, the first seeds are beginning to take root, as Igor Pejic, banker and author of the award-winning *Blockchain Babel*, explains:

> Banks are starting to warm up to cryptocurrencies, but as investment assets. It's currently very limited... So you have big banks such as Morgan Stanley and Goldman Sachs, allowing institutional investors or private wealth management clients a limited exposure to cryptocurrencies in their investment portfolios. But I wouldn't say that they have plans to offer things such as yield aggregators or decentralized exchanges in the short term. It is too early. But they have started looking into it. ING, for example, has done some first analyses on DeFi.
>
> In the end, I believe you have to differentiate not so much between retail and institutional banking, but between three broad categories of banks. The first category is made up of the regional, smaller banks. They are generally not really looking into blockchain topics. Some of them are, but then as part of consortia or some bigger collaborative projects. Then you have the big banks like JP Morgan Chase who are doing quite a lot. They came up with their own stablecoin very early on, developed Quorum and so on.
>
> And then you have those I would call the first pioneers, which are digital-first banks, but significantly smaller in size. You have banks such as Revolut or N26 that offered cryptocurrencies earlier than their mainstream counterparts. But even within this group, you have a more specialized segment, which is catering specifically to a crypto-affluent market. They are also starting to implement DeFi applications. Silver Bank would be such an example. So, broadly banks are starting to warm up to the whole decentralized finance idea, albeit cautiously.

Why this book focuses on DeFi for retail customers

So far, we have discussed the current market as it pertains to retail customers. In fact, retail is a comparatively small proportion of the financial markets, with the lion's share taken up by institutional activities. When lay people talk about financial products and services, however, they often mean the kind of products that are available to individual investors, in other words, the retail sector. These may include pensions, life insurance policies, stockbroker services, personal loans or savings bonds. This book focuses on retail markets, as that is where virtually all DeFi activity is currently concentrated. Just as cryptocurrency – primarily Bitcoin – is gradually and cautiously being integrated by institutions after initial adoption by the retail market, many people assume that, over time, once regulation is clearer, there will be opportunities within DeFi for institutional clients.

Developers and organizations within the sector are already gearing up for the demand to grow, with Metamask, for example, offering a specific institutional version of its wallet. Nasdaq and BlackRock are among those offering custody services for institutions to hold their digital assets without the perceived complexity and risk of self-managed and self-hosted wallets.

While crypto-native institutional customers will undoubtedly continue to provide the first demand for institutional DeFi – such as Web3 hedge funds – once confidence builds in the sector, other organizations will follow. However, as this is as yet in its very early stages, it makes sense to focus on detailing the current state of play with retail.

Comparing institutional and retail activities

Let's start by making a clear distinction between retail and institutional investment activity. Institutional investors are responsible for investing other people's money, whether that is directly, as with fund managers who take deposits from retail investors, or indirectly, as in those who manage company treasuries or otherwise invest on behalf of companies and their shareholders. Institutional activities make up the vast majority of all financial market transactions.

In previous decades, retail investors would normally access financial services through their bank or through a broker, whom they would telephone to place trades. Over time, the traditional image of a broker has been updated and is now much more likely to be a company offering brokerage services through a website or mobile app, supported by a call centre.

Institutional investors are distinguished by the tools, equipment and data they have at their disposal. Teams of analysts, drawn from the world's most promising graduates, use artificial intelligence, giant data warehouses and high-speed connections to make vast sums by way of transactions that may take place in tiny fractions of a second. Retail investors, in contrast, have to rely on their own research and knowledge and the limited tools available to them on consumer-facing trading platforms.

While changing demographics and global cultural shifts have encouraged more and more people to dip their toe into investing in shares, for example, lack of knowledge is still holding many people back. A report by the Financial Conduct Authority in the UK in 2021 showed that there is a wide gap between the total pool of 15.6 million adults who have investable assets (judged to be £10,000 or more) and the 2.2 million who have a stocks and shares ISA, which is one of the most tax-efficient ways to gain exposure to the markets. Of the 15.6 million, 37 per cent hold their assets entirely in cash and a further 18 per cent hold more than 75 per cent in cash (FCA, 2021).

In an environment where inflation remains persistently high and where the real cost of goods and services is increasing rapidly, this preference for cash means that savers are not only missing out on substantial potential gains, but also risk losing significant sums to inflation over the longer term, as the returns on savings fail to keep up with the rising cost of living. However, as the same report points out, it is no use encouraging people to enter the investment market if they do not have sufficient knowledge to participate. Rather worryingly, it also stated that nearly half (45 per cent) of new self-directed investors were unaware that they were at risk of losing some of their money if their chosen investments fell in value. Perhaps this perception has been reinforced by an environment where share prices have appeared to defy gravity and gone on rising for years at a time. Falling markets in the time since the survey was conducted have no doubt gone some way towards challenging this assumption.

Education is also key in ensuring that potential investors are aware that they may lose money to temporary market movements – and that some investments are much riskier than others – and in protecting people from fraudsters and scammers.

Changing rules around withdrawing funds from pensions and transferring pensions from one provider to another brought welcome flexibility for older people in the UK, but also sparked a wave of fraudulent activity as criminals proved themselves ready to profit from the naivety of those who had not dealt with their own investments before. Huge sums of money were lost, especially in overseas property opportunities offering returns that were too good to be true. The figures are alarming: a 2021 Parliamentary report suggested that, in the years since 2015, an estimated 40,000 people had been defrauded out of a collective £10 billion of pension savings (House of Commons, 2021).

While pensioners are often targeted by scammers because of their perceived vulnerability and because some have had time to build up extensive savings pots, investment fraud is by no means limited to pension transfer schemes. In fact, the FCA 2021 report contained the astonishing statistic that, in the year April 2020 to March 2021 alone, 23,378 consumers reported losing an estimated £59 million to investment fraud. On average, consumers lost over £24,000 each.

Potential investor naivety and the importance of protecting consumers are often cited as arguments against the legal existence of cryptocurrencies and DeFi, yet we can see from these statistics that improving retail investor education and awareness is important across the whole sector, and that fraudsters and criminals are already adept at parting people from their money through a variety of avenues that do not involve crypto.

Demographics and retail investment

The age and gender profile of people who access financial services varies hugely by country, and changes rapidly over time. Much of this depends on the demographics of a particular country, as well as the type of service being analysed. This even applies to something as elementary as retail banking services: in China, 53 per cent of retail banking revenues come from the millennial generation, while, in the US, 50 cent of retail banking revenues come from baby boomers.

Demarcation by gender is also something that can vary dramatically from region to region. A McKinsey survey showed that women made up only 7.6 per cent of active retail investors in India, while the UK and US varied between 23 to 30 per cent, rising to near gender parity in younger age groups such as Generation Z (Dietz et al, 2020).

One of the most striking changes over time – and particularly over the last 10 years – has been a rising enthusiasm for investors in much younger age groups, driven by the development of the fintech sector and the growth of financial social media and the influencers found on these platforms. An influential report by BNY Mellon (2021) found that 22 per cent of new investors were under 30, against only 6 per cent before 2020. The report also found interesting statistics within these segments, for example that, among the 17 per of new investors who were African American, 53 per cent were women.

Hanan Nor, a programme manager at Outlier Ventures, explains why younger generations have been so quick to adapt to the investment opportunities offered by DeFi:

> If you look at my generation, in between millennials and Generation Z, the reason why we're able to quickly adapt to blockchain or cryptocurrency is because we've been exposed so early to the utility of crypto tokens and NFTs, so it's easy to figure out how to use them in DeFi.
>
> For example, we can understand very, very simply that we can use our own NFT as collateral for things that we want to trade, or we can use an NFT as a way to support members of our community. It has a unique value in its utility. And then in general, stablecoins are an easy concept to understand. Digital currency is quite synonymous to the way we grow up as a generation because we don't really see the value of cash. We didn't grow up with cash. So digital currency like a stablecoin is just another type of currency that we keep in our wallet, in the same way as USD or GBP.

COPY TRADING

Applications such as eToro or Iris that allow copy trading – in which investors who do not feel sufficiently confident to pick their own trades simply mirror the portfolios of more successful or celebrity investors – have fuelled the growth of this intersection between finance and social media. The term 'copy trading', or 'coattail investing', as it is sometimes known, has been around for at least 10 years.

Imitating the tactics of successful investors might sound like a sensible strategy, but it carries its own risks, of course. The investor whose strategies you are following might simply have hit a lucky streak, or may have different long-term goals from you. It also, when taken to extremes, carries some systemic risk. If a much-followed investor decides to dump shares and all their followers do the same, it may cause dramatic price swings that would otherwise not have occurred.

The rise of the finfluencer

Whatever the downside, it seems that 'finfluencers', social trading and the new-found enthusiasm of Generation Z for retail investment are here to stay. The rise of social trading and the finfluencer movement on social media platforms such as Instagram are also a significant factor in drawing younger investors into the formerly staid world of financial services. We look more closely at this trend later in the chapter.

It is difficult to understate the effect of this demographic change in the investment customer base. Younger markets are usually more technology-literate and less risk-averse, making them key players in the evolution of new products and new sectors. Financial inclusion – whether this is opening up access to investment opportunities for younger people or those in developing countries or the less wealthy, or all three – is not simply something that can be seen as a moral imperative, but makes great business sense for any company wishing to pursue innovation and growth. While there is clearly an education gap that needs filling in relation to the investor market as a whole, the new breed of younger, tech-savvy entrants seems remarkably clued up.

The most-used financial services

As one might predict, the most popular financial services are those relating to payments. A recent survey in the UK by Statista showed that a current (checking) account is the most popular product, used by 79 per cent of respondents (Kunst, 2022). Credit cards and loans were the next most popular, followed by passive investments such as pension plans and different types of life insurance. Of people who owned any type of equity or bonds, the majority invested passively: saving into a scheme where a professional money manager handled their capital on their behalf. Meanwhile, only 14 per cent of respondents replied that they had any kind of account where they invested directly.

If the average consumer decides that they are going to bite the bullet and start directly buying their own investments, what do they buy? Stocks and shares, as well as government bonds, are the most common investments, with only a tiny fraction of the population in any country dipping their toe into more complex financial products such as options or contracts for difference (CFD).

Riskier investments

The growing availability of financial products, however, such as options on digital trading platforms, has prompted a rapid growth in people willing to engage in riskier activities. In the USA, for example, it is reported that 11 per cent of Robinhood users have traded options at least once in 2021, despite the fact that, for most, it is a losing bet.

Similarly, contracts for difference, from which retail investors are banned in the USA, result in 70 to 80 per cent of retail participants losing money. A CFD allows traders to speculate on the future market movements of an underlying asset, without actually owning or taking physical delivery of the underlying asset. CFDs are allowed in the UK and in various other countries, but subject to restrictions that stipulate the maximum permissible margin.

The availability of trading apps and websites, driven by the fintech sector, and by existing financial services companies such as AJ Bell and Hargreaves Lansdown, has increased the choice and availability of investment opportunities in the retail market, but fees can be a deterrent, especially for those wishing to make small, incremental investments, as can extra costs such as currency conversion expenses.

Some platforms charge a flat fee per deal, which can eat into any potential gains, particularly when the investment is small. Others may charge more for currency conversion fees for trading shares on global markets. Traders should be mindful that, where some platforms offer commission-free trades, this may be offset by other fees such as higher withdrawal charges. Table 2.1 shows the most-used trading apps and websites in the UK.

Banks or technology companies?

One of the most striking trends of the last 10 years has been the steady encroachment of tech companies into banking and a commensurate shift in the number of banks that are effectively becoming technology companies. Such is the huge shift in culture that not all banks are truly well placed to

TABLE 2.1 Most popular trading apps and websites in the UK

	Number of active monthly users
eToro	151868
IG Trading	101469
Plus500	67657
WeBull	18370
AvaTrade	12162

Data from Statista (www.statista.com/statistics/1259954/etrading-app-monthly-active-users-uk/)

take advantage of it. The challenge is universal across retail banking and investment banking, but investment banks have been swifter to transform themselves than retail institutions.

Goldman Sachs is well known for its innovative approach to technology. In 2017, then-CEO Lloyd Blankfein stated categorically that it was a technology company. It is a theme that has been running through investment banking for more than 20 years now. Even the most cursory look at the insights section of Goldman Sachs's website reveals pages and pages of blog posts about Web3 and the potential of blockchain technology – and this theme is repeated by its competitors.

For retail banks, it is a different story. Heavily dependent on cumbersome systems built on legacy software that are increasingly expensive to maintain and difficult to integrate with other applications, they are rapidly being left behind in a world where fintech companies are driving the majority of the innovation.

The growth of fintechs at the expense of banks is a global phenomenon, particularly in countries that have introduced formal open banking legislation. A good example of how banks have been outcompeted by fintechs is in share brokerage platforms. While many retail banks offer share dealing services to their customers, these platforms lack the usability and high profile of standalone products such as Robinhood or eToro.

The growth of fintech

A decade ago, a search for finance apps would have revealed a top 10 dominated by banking apps. Today, the plethora of fintechs aimed at helping people make the most of their money and investments means that the banks are pushed way down the list. This means that integration points that allow retail investors to access DeFi infrastructure through existing applications and interfaces are, in the short term, far more likely to come from fintech than from existing banking products and services.

And if you were left in any doubt as to how pervasive the growth of fintech has been, you only need to look at Ernst and Young's Global FinTech Adoption Index, which, in 2019, cited the adoption rate of fintech as more than 64 per cent globally, up from 16 per cent in 2015.

The reasons for this transition are varied, but a key factor is the difference in culture between software development and product design across organizations and companies. Both are fast-evolving fields, and there is a constant tension between the 'move fast and break things' culture of Web3 and DeFi, and the need to protect brand values and support integrations with existing systems, which prevents large retail banks from doing the same. Company culture takes a long time to change – and while the wilder edges of DeFi are prepared to take the risk of innovating without complying with existing regulations, this is not a choice for banks.

Banks and cryptocurrency: the slow burn

Web3/DeFi entrepreneur, chief innovation officer at Swash, and Multichain Asset Managers Association executive board member Ioana Surpateanu is almost uniquely positioned to see both sides of the equation, having previously been co-head of European government affairs – innovation strategy lead at Citi. Speaking about the prevailing attitudes within banking and the chasm between their products and the DeFi ecosystem, she points out:

> Obviously, one of the most cited friction factors is regulation, or lack of regulation when it comes to DeFi and over-regulation when it comes to traditional finance. Even if this regulatory risk is exaggerated and at times almost used as an excuse to justify inaction, the gap between how the world is perceived in a traditional finance setting versus a DeFi one is a genuine one.
>
> There is an additional gap related to product development speed. It takes ages to develop something in traditional finance. Even if you have the best idea and there actually are sophisticated and groundbreaking ideas in TradFi – by the time it gets filtered through compliance, legal and gets all of the cross-entity approval stamps it almost loses relevance.
>
> As a result, it is impossible to compare and compete with the pace of development in DeFi, where from one week to the other, you can plan an upgrade or an alteration to a protocol and deploy it, sometimes even via a DAO governance vote which presupposes a swift synchronization of the community sentiment. So as a result of both the regulatory and agility constraints, I would say that irrespective of the will to implement innovation, the overall TradFi ecosystem operates at an implementation disadvantage. Some would argue that it is not that relevant anyway because they have the capital to offset that disadvantage.

Surpateanu also cites lack of knowledge as an issue:

> I don't think there is sufficient understanding of DeFi within TradFi, at scale. There are various teams within very relevant traditional financial services entities that do understand crypto, but in a more generic fashion. And

some teams are equipped with DeFi experts, but it's small teams of people compared to the overall magnitude of that specific institution. So that's another constraint – a lack of deep understanding of what DeFi represents, what it will evolve into, and where various DeFi TradFi symbioses can materialize.

Major banks such as my alma mater, Citigroup, are equipped with crypto-knowledgeable people and they have recently ramped up hiring for more. Some other banks of the same caliber (J.P. Morgan, Goldman Sachs, etc) emulate this model. So, there is a visible improvement in that strategic sense. But when applying the filter of the mind-blowing possibilities of what can be created at the intersection of DeFi and TradFi, I don't think enough is happening. Like I said, sometimes the potential regulatory issues are almost used as an excuse for inaction.

Fintech × DeFi

There are two main areas where DeFi and fintech are likely to cross over:

- fintech apps giving customers the opportunity to interact with decentralized finance protocols using familiar interfaces and branding, for example buying, lending or borrowing digital assets via the same tools they use to trade traditional equities
- integrations with DeFi services such as stablecoins that happen on the back end, so that the customer does not realize they are using them.

In the meme-driven world of DeFi, this latter scenario is known as the 'DeFi mullet'. If you are wondering what a 1970s-inspired hairstyle has to do with either finance or technology, you are probably not alone. The context is a photograph of a smooth, moustached man with a flamboyant mullet haircut, which had previously done the rounds as a meme with the caption, 'Business at the front, party at the back.' This was repurposed as 'Fintech at the front, DeFi at the back' to denote an app or a platform where the front end is a familiar, professional-looking interface but where the back is plugged into decentralized finance in order to return higher yields and the greater range of innovative products enabled by DeFi. 'Bank at the front, DeFi at the back' simply would not work as a concept because of the considerable technology and culture barriers that would have to be overcome in order for a mainstream bank to make such an offering, but it is entirely feasible that teams within a fintech would have both the technical knowledge and the will to make such products a reality.

There may also be less of a gap in regulatory terms than there first appears. As we will see in Chapter 8, many founders of DeFi projects are actively seeking regulatory clarity, and there is an increasing acceptance among governments that decentralized technologies can genuinely offer something useful. With the World Economic Forum predicting that as much as 10 per cent of global GDP could be stored on blockchains by 2025, their adoption may be upon us sooner than we realize.

The 'DeFi mullet' in practice

Examples of the DeFi mullet in the real world include remittance apps that use stablecoins behind the scenes to facilitate low-fee international payments, or pre-pay debit cards that offer rewards on balances held on the card that are generated by staking tokens on DeFi protocols.

As anyone who has ever tried to fund or withdraw from a cryptocurrency wallet with fiat currency can attest, the biggest friction points are the on-ramps and off-ramps where users move in and out of the crypto ecosystem. In addition to providing a speedy pipeline for converting in and out of crypto, the DeFi mullet model also provides user interfaces that are familiar to anyone who uses conventional financial services, and authentication processes that depend on traditional mechanisms involving usernames and passwords.

However, this principle has received a certain amount of pushback among some members of the Web3 community, on the basis that a halfway house between decentralization and fintech is unlikely to meet the needs of either party. There is a real danger that presenting consumers with interfaces that look and feel like those they already know and understand can result in a situation where they assume that the same guarantees and processes are being followed. In other words, the user interface of DeFi products should be as easy to use as possible while still transparently showing the decentralized principles that underlie it.

Wallstreetbets, meme stocks and crypto meme culture

We have already discussed the intersection of fintech and DeFi in terms of the DeFi mullet meme, so this is a good moment to turn our attention to meme culture in general, and the rise of its importance in the retail investment landscape.

The growth of the internet since the 1990s has led to a shared culture and consciousness in which, in many cases, generational or internet-tribal similarities have become more important than those found within national borders. Different countries do have their own memes, of course, especially those that play on a word or phrase in a particular language. However, many are universal, and some of the best-known memes, such as the Distracted Boyfriend or the Coffin Dancers, crop up time and time again in multiple platforms, languages and contexts. (As a side note, when the Coffin Dancers meme was minted as an NFT, its sale price exceeded $1 million. We discuss the role of NFTs in DeFi in Chapter 7.)

Financial services might seem an odd place to go looking for memes. However, just as the macho, bravado-laden 1980s culture depicted in the films *Wolf of Wall Street* and *American Psycho* displaced the rather dull and staid world of bowler-hatted brokers that preceded it, 2020s financial meme culture is ushering in yet another wave of social and technological change.

The 'memification' of finance has been gathering pace on social media for several years, largely flying under the radar of the mainstream finance media. In 2012, Reddit user Jaime Rogozinski created the r/wallstreetbets subreddit (forum). Six years later, it had more subscribers than there were users of the Bloomberg terminal. By the time Wallstreetbets shot to the top of the world's financial headlines in January 2021, its subscribers had reached a critical mass that had the power to move markets, catching established financial commentators entirely by surprise. The subreddit's subscribers are known for their irreverent, high-octane and high-risk approach to investing in which huge losses are shared and celebrated in the same way as huge gains.

The liberal use of memes such as the Stonks guy (based on an intentional misspelling of 'stocks'), symbols of excessive wealth and an apparent obsession with Elon Musk – often seen as the patron saint of meme finance – meant that readers and posters were entertained as much as they were informed, and spawned – or at least popularized – a new vocabulary of trading-related jargon and slang.

The same slang and memes permeated the subreddits devoted to cryptocurrency trading and other channels such as Crypto Twitter, which was a key driver of the altcoin trading frenzy of 2014–2018. Many traders dabble in both areas, although there are plenty of diehard crypto traders who prefer not to touch centralized assets, as well as stock market investors who steer clear of cryptocurrency.

THE GAMESTOP SHORT SQUEEZE

If financial markets had been a serious place before, forums such as Wallstreetbets turned them into a source of entertainment. Robinhood was the preferred trading platform for those who sat up all night, trading and posting and sharing tips. In an investment world where institutional money was king, the Wallstreetbets community saw themselves as underdogs, and it could even be said that there was an element of folk-hero mythology in some of the narrative. Just as *The Big Short* had woven a seemingly dull tale of obscure financial products into a gripping suspense story, so there emerged a new drama that briefly dominated the news at the start of 2021.

The story centred around a global chain of stores selling games and collectables called GameStop. In common with many other bricks-and-mortar retailers, by 2020, the business was closing stores and its perceived value was falling. Institutional money had made the judgement that the value of the stock would decrease – and hence the stock was being shorted. Taking out a short position is effectively betting that the value of whatever is being shorted will fall. Given GameStop's position as a real-world business fighting a tide of digital competitors, the decision to short the stock did not seem controversial.

However, the Wallstreetbets community had other ideas. Making money was seemingly only part of the motivation: a desire to troll the professional traders of Wall Street was undoubtedly a big part of the thrill. For whatever reason, they had decided that GameStop was worth saving, and, primarily using Robinhood, they started buying GameStop options, pushing the price up 1500 per cent over a two-week period in January 2021. The surge was given impetus by Elon Musk tweeting 'GameStonk' with a link to the community, bringing in even more buyers.

The rising price caused what is known as a short squeeze: professional investors had to borrow increasingly large amounts to cover their positions. It caused huge losses to several hedge funds, including Melvin Capital, who were forced to close their short and accept a $3 billion injection. Eventually Robinhood restricted traders from opening new positions in GameStop and the stock slid back. However, a Rubicon had been crossed in that the saga demonstrated that memes could move markets and that the smallest of retail investors, affiliated only by their involvement in a social media phenomenon, could take on hugely capitalized hedge funds and win – at least for a while.

The GameStop affair was judged newsworthy enough to merit its own report by the SEC, amid suspicions that market opinion may have been swayed on either side by large players, but nothing suggesting organized misinformation was found.

The GameStop story highlights how regulatory bodies such as the SEC are having to respond to a rapidly changing environment where swirling rumours on social media are more influential than the headlines in the business pages.

Turning from stocks to cryptocurrency, we find a world that is strongly driven – one might almost say primarily driven – by sentiment, social media and memes, and where true innovation and financial judgement can be over-ridden in a matter of seconds by a tweet or a rumour.

The surge in value of meme coins inspired by Dogecoin is a case in point, with many traders grumbling in 2021 that their carefully derived trading strategies based on studying the fundamentals of serious blockchain projects had been far outstripped in terms of profit by new entrants who had simply lucked out by gambling a few thousand dollars on tokens such as Shiba Inu.

FinTwit, StockTok and traditional influencers

We will look more closely in Chapter 8 at how regulators are handling the challenges of establishing solid regulatory frameworks for cryptocurrency and DeFi. Meanwhile, no discussion of the current investing landscape would be complete without mentioning the new breed of Gen Z finfluencers producing short-form content and videos on Twitter, YouTube and TikTok.

It is a fine line between sitting in a café with friends and recommending the latest shares you have bought, and telling your hundreds of thousands of followers the same thing. TikTok is awash with content from traders seeking to enhance their reputations and their profits by recommending the shares they hold to new would-be day-traders with short attention spans. With the world of DeFi even more prone to social media hype than traditional financial markets, it is hard not to see this trend becoming amplified in the years ahead.

It is also important to remember that while today's YouTubers and TikTokkers may be grabbing the headlines, retail investors have always sought the opinions of well-known and successful investors. Billionaire hedge fund managers Ray Dalio, founder of Bridgewater Associates, and Paul Tudor

Jones, of Tudor Investment Corporation, are two examples of this, whose pronouncements are eagerly awaited and regularly make the front pages of the financial press.

Dalio, a former cryptocurrency sceptic, stated in 2021 that he holds Bitcoin as part of a diversified portfolio, and praised the digital asset for its resilience (Locke, 2022). Tudor Jones has been even more positive about cryptocurrencies, stating a preference for Bitcoin over gold as an inflation hedge (McShane, 2021).

While Tudor Jones has for several years expressed positive sentiment towards crypto, there are still voices within traditional investing who remain extremely negative towards digital assets and, by extension, decentralized finance. Berkshire Hathaway CEO Warren Buffett – 'the sage of Omaha', renowned for being one of the most successful investors of all time – said in May 2022 that he would not buy all the Bitcoin in the world for $25 (Vega, 2022). His voice is becoming drowned out, however, by the numbers of traditional investors and analysts expressing positive sentiment for digital assets – including the International Monetary Fund (IMF). Its 2022 Global Financial Stability Report (IMF, 2022) singled out DeFi in a chapter on fintech, highlighting the associated risks but noting that DeFi has the potential to bring even greater efficiency to financial services.

Opportunities and challenges

The challenge for traditional financial service companies is how to draw in a new generation of traders with a slick user experience, possibly extending to gamification, while at the same time including checks and balances to protect their customers. It is also worth noting the headwinds that some may face from activists who see any investment activities related to cryptocurrency as a contributory factor to climate change. Chapter 4 looks more closely at some of the arguments surrounding the proof of work and proof of stake consensus mechanisms and their impact on energy consumption. Investors who apply ESG (environmental, social and governance) principles to their investments may, therefore, push back against financial service providers who embrace cryptocurrency and DeFi. The reality is more complicated than it appears, and anyone wishing to integrate with the DeFi ecosystem should understand the implications, both positive and negative, of these systems.

Managing risk is also important, as is communicating this risk to clients. For many inexperienced investors, the danger is not so much that they will be scammed, but merely that, even if they are buying shares in legitimate companies using legitimate platforms, they simply may not understand the percentages they could lose. Tesla – the ultimate meme stock, exceptionally popular among the finfluencer crowd – has followed such a steep trajectory upwards that it has possibly skewed expectations of how normal growth shares behave.

Some would argue that the steeper learning curve required to interact with DeFi protocols is in itself a check and balance and requires a higher level of knowledge and understanding of risk than expected by the common trading apps. However, if the true nature and complexity of DeFi is abstracted away by slick, gamified applications, this removes these natural checkpoints and frictions, and service providers need to work even harder to communicate exactly what is happening under the hood of the app or platform. And, if a potential investor is interacting with platforms that are essentially beta products, then these risks should be clearly signposted, not hidden away in the fine print of terms and conditions.

One insider I spoke to points out that there is much work still to do in order to encourage people to try DeFi applications:

> When it comes to problems with adoption with retail, the question really is how the product should be presented to them. Because a lot of people don't understand the current financial system. They don't really understand how the bank works or where the money are being stored.
>
> And also at the same time, a lot of people just don't care about these things. They don't want the hassle of managing their own money end to end because managing a portfolio can be a full-time job, especially for those with larger portfolios. So one of the hurdles to that adoption is essentially producing products that are easy enough to use and also feed into generalized use-cases.

The following two chapters look at some of these use cases as part of a deeper dive into two of the most common categories of DeFi products and services: decentralized exchanges and borrowing and earning protocols.

References

BNY Mellon (2021) 'The evolving landscape of U.S. retail investing': www.bnymellon.com/content/dam/bnymellon/documents/pdf/insights/the-evolving-landscape-of-us-retail-investing.pdf.coredownload.pdf (archived at https://perma.cc/SJS9-57XS)

Dietz, M et al (2020) 'Charting retail banking revenues by generation', McKinsey & Company: www.mckinsey.com/industries/financial-services/our-insights/charting-retail-banking-revenues-by-generation (archived at https://perma.cc/V7G8-VJXB)

FCA (2021) 'Consumer investments: strategy and feedback statement': www.fca.org.uk/publications/corporate-documents/consumer-investments-strategy (archived at https://perma.cc/DP6A-X467)

House of Commons (2021) 'Protecting pension savers – five years on from the pension freedoms': https://committees.parliament.uk/publications/5322/documents/53036/default/ (archived at https://perma.cc/PL7J-GX65)

IMF (2022) 'Global financial stability report': www.imf.org/en/Publications/GFSR/Issues/2022/04/19/global-financial-stability-report-april-2022 (archived at https://perma.cc/J7MW-LCZT)

Kunst, A (2022) 'Financial product usage in the UK in 2022': www.statista.com/forecasts/997877/financial-product-usage-in-the-uk (archived at https://perma.cc/VSP9-9VQ3)

Locke, T (2022) 'Ray Dalio's Bridgewater reportedly backing a crypto fund means the world's largest hedge fund and one of Bitcoin's former skeptics is taking it seriously', *Fortune*: https://fortune.com/2022/03/22/ray-dalio-bridgewater-crypto-fund/ (archived at https://perma.cc/YXP3-DJUK)

McShane, A (2021) 'Billionaire Paul Tudor Jones now prefers Bitcoin over gold', *Nasdaq*: www.nasdaq.com/articles/billionaire-paul-tudor-jones-now-prefers-bitcoin-over-gold-2021-10-20 (archived at https://perma.cc/Y9FS-XTLK)

Vega, N (2022) 'Warren Buffett wouldn't buy "all of the bitcoin in the world" for $25', CNBC *Make It*: www.cnbc.com/2022/05/02/warren-buffett-wouldnt-spend-25-on-all-of-the-bitcoin-in-the-world.html (archived at https://perma.cc/GD8T-4YBP)

03

Decentralized exchanges: the start of DeFi

CHAPTER OBJECTIVES

- Read about the history of centralized crypto exchanges
- Evaluate the risk of hacks and fraud
- Understand why decentralized exchanges exist
- Recognize automated market makers and liquidity pools
- Learn how to add and remove liquidity
- Learn about non-Ethereum DEXs
- Understand how NFT DEXs work

For almost as long as Bitcoin has existed, people have wanted to buy and sell it in exchange for currencies such as dollars, euros, pounds, yen, Swiss francs or Brazilian *real*. As soon as other cryptocurrencies arrived on the scene, traders wanted to buy and sell them in exchange for Bitcoin in addition to their local currencies.

There are various reasons for this. Investors may, for example, wish to exchange cryptocurrencies they have mined or earned for dollars in their bank account that they can spend on food or other products. But by far the biggest reason investors trade cryptocurrencies is for speculation: either to hold their cash in Bitcoin, Ethereum or another digital asset, or to make a profit from betting on the constantly moving prices.

In this respect, crypto exchanges are very similar to stock, foreign exchange and commodity exchanges. Many traders discovered cryptocurrency trading as a diversification from these types of trading, and the interfaces and processes will be familiar to anyone who has used one of these traditional platforms.

Centralized crypto exchanges

Cryptocurrency exchanges have existed in some form for more than 10 years. In the extremely early days of Bitcoin, exchanging this new type of digital money for familiar state-backed currencies required a certain amount of ingenuity. Most people who owned Bitcoin in 2009 and 2010 had acquired it from running mining software, in the days when it was still possible to make a profit from mining on home computers.

If you were a less tech-savvy member of the public who had read or heard about this new 'magic' internet money but lacked the know-how to mine it for yourself, the only option was to find someone on an internet forum or in real life who would sell it to you. By October 2009, nine months after Bitcoin's genesis block was mined, the first 'official' price was quoted: 1309.3 Bitcoin to 1 US dollar.

This price was not quoted on an exchange: Bitcoin's first buying and selling service was as far from a traditional financial market as it was possible to get. The self-styled New Liberty Standard Exchange was a service that connected buyers and sellers, enabling them to pay for Bitcoins using PayPal. The rate was not set through anything like price discovery, instead being derived from the price of electricity used to produce the Bitcoin.

The first Bitcoin exchanges

When a Bitcoin enthusiast known as dwdollar set up Bitcoin Market in early 2010, he stated his intention that his new exchange, as elementary as it was, should match buyers and sellers and allow the price to operate as a genuine free market. Bitcoin Market is regarded as the first exchange in the true sense of the word – although, like all the other exchanges that followed in the next year or so, it was very much a one-man operation.

By July 2010, the infamous MtGox exchange was launched with an announcement on the BitcoinTalk forum – the world's primary source for cryptocurrency information at that time (Figure 3.1). Its original founder,

FIGURE 3.1 Announcement of the MtGox exchange launch

Jed McCaleb (who went on to become well known as the founder of Ripple), sold the exchange to Mark Karpeles in early 2011.

Other exchanges followed in the years 2011–2013, most notably Kraken in 2011, which has navigated the choppy waters of competition and regulation to emerge as one of the world's best known crypto trading platforms. Coinbase and Bitfinex followed in 2012.

By late 2013, more and more people were trading Bitcoin, and there was an immediate need for exchanges that allowed the trading of one digital currency against another. From 2013 onwards, there was an explosion in the number of alternative cryptocurrencies as other people forked the Bitcoin blockchain, either to work out new and exciting uses for it or simply to launch a meme coin and make a buck or two. (A decade later, more than 10,000 different cryptocurrencies are listed on the main crypto ranking sites, and that doesn't include the thousands that have fallen by the wayside.)

The rise of altcoin exchanges

For a while, it seemed that as many crypto exchanges were opening as there were new currencies being launched. Many were amateurish affairs run by hobby developers, but others were serious operations. Cryptsy, MintPal, Cryptopia and Poloniex were all familiar names during this period, and crypto enthusiasts on Twitter and Reddit speculated frantically that the tokens they held would be the next to be listed. Like other sites, Poloniex had a 'trollbox' feature where traders could chat while trading – and trollboxes and Crypto Twitter between them spawned many memes. 'When Polo?' was a familiar question from traders to coin creators demanding to know when their coin would be listed on Poloniex.

It is easy to get misty-eyed about these enthusiastic, amateurish days, but the truth is that plenty of people had their life savings wiped out by criminality or incompetence, and it is something of a relief that many of the early enterprises have now either disappeared or developed into more professional outfits. The sorry sagas of Quadriga CX and MtGox are detailed below, and it is also worth remembering that, of the exchanges mentioned above, Cryptsy, MintPal and Cryptopia all failed with the loss of customer funds to some extent or other.

By the time Binance – now the world's largest crypto exchange by volume – launched in 2017, the crypto exchange landscape had been transformed beyond recognition. With its slick user interface and easy on- and off-ramps, Binance was a world away from the rickety operations that had been prevalent five years earlier. So was FTX – or at least this is the impression it gave until it spectacularly imploded at the end of 2022.

It is worth a reminder at this point that all the exchanges mentioned are centralized and not part of the DeFi system at all, but it is important to be aware of the history of cryptocurrency trading to set in context the growth of decentralized exchanges.

Hacks and fraud

To understand the momentum that led to decentralized exchanges, we need to be aware of the considerable risks of using centralized exchanges. Plenty of people who cut their trading teeth in the early days of crypto remember the sinking feeling of hearing rumours of yet another hack, realizing it was an exchange where they held funds and of scrambling to withdraw their crypto before the rumour became reality – which was usually impossible.

Erica Stanford covers many of these events in her excellent book *Crypto Wars*, so there is no need to describe all of them in detail, but there are many salutary tales that demonstrate why many people prefer to use decentralized exchanges rather than commit their hard-earned cash to someone else's safe-keeping.

Issues with centralized exchanges

It is important to understand that, when you trade on a centralized exchange, it is similar to using a bank, except, without the checks, balances and guarantees. You use your wallet to deposit cryptocurrency into a central wallet controlled by the people who run the exchange, and they keep an internal, off-chain ledger that shows the balances in everyone's accounts. When you set up an account with a centralized exchange, therefore, you sign up with a username and login, usually with two-factor authentication, and are provided with the means to retrieve your funds if you accidentally lock yourself out of your account. The user-friendly interface and the available support offer a level of convenience and reassurance that is often welcomed by newcomers to crypto, but that must be balanced against the risk of entrusting your funds to someone else. We are used to doing this with banks or with traditional trading platforms – but these are all covered by legislation, insurance and, in some cases, an assurance by governments that funds will be underwritten if lost.

Having said this, it is also important to note that the processes in place within most modern crypto exchanges are usually more professional than they used to be, when often the only person holding the private key containing everyone's crypto would be the owner/operator of the exchange.

CASE STUDY
MtGox and Quadriga CX

It might seem unthinkable to someone from a traditional financial background that there should ever be a situation where one person was entrusted with something as important as the key to millions of dollars' worth of other people's assets, but that has indeed been the case with centralized cryptocurrency exchanges.

There have been so many hacks and abuses over the years that it is pointless to list them all, but a few stand out. The scenario of the single holder of the private key turned out to be an expensive nightmare for anyone with funds on Canada's Quadriga CX exchange, when owner Gerald Cotten apparently died at the age of 30 while on holiday in India in 2018, taking to his grave the knowledge of the all-important private keys to the exchange's $190 million deposits. The story has since taken a mysterious turn as investigators probe whether Cotten faked his death and absconded with the money, but whichever is true, both scenarios highlight the dangers of trusting one's funds to someone else's wallet.

While the Quadriga CX saga is the subject of a Netflix documentary, *Trust No One: The Hunt for the Crypto King*, even Quadriga is not the best-known exchange synonymous with Bitcoin hacks. For that, we must go back to 2014, to MtGox, which was responsible for a huge 70 per cent of all the world's Bitcoin exchange trade volume.

In February 2014, following multiple complaints about long withdrawal times, the exchange was abruptly closed and declared insolvent. It emerged that a series of hacks dating from 2011 had drained the exchange's reserves and that Mark Karpeles, completely out of his depth, had manipulated data to give the impression that nothing was wrong. For years, rumours circulated that Karpeles himself had embezzled the Bitcoin. In March 2019, a Japanese court acquitted him of theft but found him guilty of data manipulation.

The fallout from MtGox continues to this day, and has been a powerful driver in the sentiment against centralized exchanges and any protocol that required individuals to relinquish power over their own cryptocurrency.

The decentralization dream

Within the crypto community, the mantra 'Not your keys, not your Bitcoin' has resonated across the years – and has, of course, been applied to many other assets than Bitcoin. Holding one's own assets, without interference from the state, or from private corporations who might use your data to discover and disseminate facts about you that you would rather keep to yourself, is one of the political ideals that has shaped the direction of the cryptocurrency community since its inception. It is true that a certain degree of pragmatism, and a recognition of the need to work with governments rather than against them, has been adopted by the community at large, but the overriding philosophy still tends towards self-reliance.

The threat of hacks and theft may have been instrumental as a warning against degrees of centralization, but many people had loftier ideals than merely not wanting to lose their money. Deriving ideas of self-sovereignty from works of economics and philosophy by Austrian economists such as Ludwig von Mises and Murray Rothbard, the idea that individuals should be able to hold and spend their wealth as they wish, independent from the interference of central banks and nation states, was seductive to many Bitcoiners.

While many early Bitcoiners rejected the idea of state control outright, a growing realism in the crypto community has led many to seek constructive dialogue with regulators to ensure that they comply with existing legislation and help to shape the frameworks of the future. There has, in fact, been a boom in funding and developing technologies that allow individuals and institutions to remain in control of their own money while also remaining compliant with local and global regulations, and enabling easy reporting of this compliance. Chapter 8 looks in more detail at these regulatory challenges and opportunities.

Turning cryptocurrency exchanges from centralized to decentralized entities, though, is a much more challenging process than simply enabling peer-to-peer payments. Various evolutionary stages had to be navigated before the current situation with exchanges could be developed so that internal processes and architecture could run purely on smart contracts.

The first decentralized exchanges: ShapeShift and EtherDelta

The earliest exchange with a claim to being decentralized was ShapeShift, founded in 2014 by Eric Vorhees, who saw the need for an antidote to centralized exchanges. He launched ShapeShift within months of the MtGox collapse. He was determined to build an exchange that did not hold traders' funds in custodial wallets from where they could be stolen.

In reality, while revolutionary for its time and about as decentralized as it was then possible to be, ShapeShift operated in many ways like a centralized exchange, complying with KYC (know your customer) regulations from 2018 onwards and blocking access to users in New York State in 2015 following the state's BitLicense regulation that would have forced ShapeShift to collect extra data about its users. Additionally, ShapeShift at this point still relied heavily on the traditional model of liquidity provision and order books. In recent years, it has moved forward, launching a new web application to take advantage of integrating with DeFi protocols such as Uniswap and also reinventing itself as a DAO (decentralized autonomous organization).

It is easy to forget, however, that ShapeShift was still a huge step forward in empowering individuals to retain custody of their own funds and not entrust them to the best efforts of someone else's security team, however well-intentioned and honest these people might be.

There are also parallels between ShapeShift and EtherDelta. While EtherDelta, launched in 2016, also operated on a fully self-custodial basis, trades were matched in an off-chain order book before being settled directly on Ethereum. While this distinction may seem like a purely technical one, it has significant implications for the regulatory status of such exchanges. Despite EtherDelta's settlement and custody being fully decentralized, the ambiguous and hybrid nature of the enterprise meant that EtherDelta's founder Zachary Coburn was retrospectively (in 2018) charged by the SEC for running an unregistered securities exchange (SEC, 2018).

By this time, however, the concept of what constituted a decentralized exchange was changing. Key to this is a particular sort of smart contract known as an automated market maker.

Automated market makers and liquidity pools

When Bancor was launched in 2017, followed by Uniswap in November 2018, they were like no other exchanges that had been seen before, centralized or decentralized. While neither ShapeShift nor EtherDelta took a custodial approach to investor deposits, meaning that they were to some extent decentralized, their mechanism for matching buyers to sellers relied on a traditional order-book approach.

Automated market makers

In contrast, decentralized exchanges (DEX) like Bancor and Uniswap use a mechanism called automated market makers (AMMs). At an initial glance, a DEX may look similar to a traditional exchange in that assets are listed in pairs, such as ETH-Dai (Ether traded against the Dai collateralized stablecoin issued by MakerDAO, which is pegged to the US dollar). The big difference from the trader's point of view is that they do not have to wait for a counterparty. In other words, if they want to buy a particular amount of a token, they do not have to wait for their 'buy' order to be matched in the order book. Instead, they simply purchase the token at whatever price is set by the AMM algorithm in the liquidity pool, which contains tokens on both sides of the trade. As the proportion of tokens in the pool changes, the algorithm adjusts the price to reflect current demand and the purchase can be made immediately.

On the other side of the equation, AMMs opened up a new income-generation opportunity for token-holders wishing to make a return from their capital. Under the traditional model, liquidity is supplied by specialist market makers. In contrast, AMMs allow anyone at all to provide liquidity and be rewarded for it. (See Table 3.1.)

Uniswap has now gone through three different iterations, each bringing innovation and improvements in areas such as efficiency and liquidity. Uniswap v3 is by far the most popular DEX, so we will use this as an example throughout of how a typical decentralized exchange works.

Let's take a closer look at how AMMs and liquidity pools work in the context of DEXs. The mechanism underlying DEXs is an important principle for understanding how the rest of the DeFi ecosystem works, so it is worth spending some time to understand it.

TABLE 3.1 Comparison of order books and automated market makers

Order book	AMM
Uses a matching engine	Uses an algorithm that calculates price according to ratio of tokens in pool
Generally used by centralized exchanges with a custodial wallet	No custodial wallet required – users interact directly
Trades can happen off-chain	Trades happen on-chain
Slippage is generally low	Slippage can be high
Better for tokens with high liquidity	Works for all liquidity levels
Permissioned	Permissionless

Liquidity pools

One of the benefits of a truly decentralized exchange is that anyone at all can create a liquidity pool. This has implications for both transparency and the potential of a much wider cross-section of token-holders to earn yield, as, previously, market-making was the domain of big players.

Previously, any project launching a token was entirely dependent on the centralized exchanges to list its token. In the past, many centralized exchanges gained a somewhat shady reputation for the wheeling and dealing that happens around token listings. The publicity gained from being listed on a big exchange can send the price of a token shooting up, even if the lift is only temporary, and there have been rumours of insider trading on various exchanges as employees tip off friends and family about upcoming listings. Even the highest-profile exchanges are not immune to this, with former Coinbase product manager Ishan Wahi's brother pleading guilty to profiting from the knowledge of upcoming listings (SEC, 2022). It can also be an expensive process, with some exchanges charging extortionate sums of money for a listing.

In contrast, anyone can create a liquidity pool on Uniswap for a token pair that is not currently listed simply by depositing a pair of ERC20 tokens at a ratio that denotes a price that they believe is at the correct level. The incentives encoded in the smart contract come into play here, as it is highly unlikely that the pool creator would be able to game the system by setting an incorrect price. Even if they were tempted to do this, it is highly likely that someone else, or more likely a bot, would take advantage of the arbitrage opportunity. This is a nice example of game theory playing out in DeFi real life.

FIGURE 3.2 Adding liquidity to a pool on Uniswap

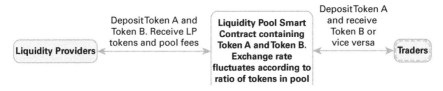

Uniswap v3

When someone decides to create a liquidity pool, this happens immediately and the transaction that creates the pool is immediately visible on the block-chain, meaning that there is equal opportunity for everyone to make trades or to contribute liquidity to the pool.

ADDING AND REMOVING LIQUIDITY

As more liquidity providers join the pool, they must deposit tokens that represent both sides of the trade, at a value set by the current price. Figure 3.2 shows how liquidity is added to a pool on Uniswap.

Once you have added liquidity, you will see an unusual type of token appear in your wallet. It is an ERC721 NFT, which represents your liquidity position. This is normally known as an LP token or an LP NFT. Because of the decentralized, anonymous nature of exchanges such as Uniswap, it is perfectly permissible to trade, sell or give away this token, just as you would any other fungible or non-fungible token.

When you want to remove liquidity – in other words, restore the token balances to your wallet, along with any trading fees that may have accrued – you simply connect your wallet and the smart contract that governs the pool detects your LP token and allows you to withdraw your funds. If you have sold or otherwise passed on your LP token, you will not, of course, be able to withdraw your funds and that privilege will have transferred to whoever now owns the LP token.

IMPERMANENT LOSS

If this sounds like an excellent arrangement and you are poised ready to add liquidity to your first pool, you should also be aware that, as with many other things in life, there is a catch. In the case of liquidity pools, this catch is something called impermanent loss. Depositing liquidity in a pool is not a decision that should be taken lightly, as there is always a trade-off around whether it would have been more profitable simply to hold your funds your-self and benefited from price volatility if the market is rising market.

What is impermanent loss, exactly? To provide a simple example, consider a pool where you have contributed ETH and the equivalent value of Dai – say, $3000 worth of each. If the price of ETH suddenly rises, this will not be reflected in your pool until the ratio of tokens alters. This means that traders will spot the arbitrage opportunity and buy ETH at the lower price in your pool until the price reflects prices elsewhere. This will ultimately leave you with an imbalance of fewer ETH and more Dai as your share of the pool. If you had simply held the ETH, you would have been in profit from the rising price. In this situation, even your trading fees and any other exchange tokens you earned may not be enough to offset the loss.

However, it is called 'impermanent' for a reason: it does not actually become a loss until you withdraw your liquidity. Unless you are unlucky, or provide your liquidity at an unfortunate moment, it is possible that price movements will rebalance your holdings, the loss may cancel itself out and your proportion of the pool's trading fees will more than offset your loss, possibly augmented by your share of any reward tokens issued by the platform.

OTHER RISKS OF LIQUIDITY POOLS

The other big risk with liquidity pools is that there may be a bug – intentional or otherwise – in the code that governs the smart contract, and all your funds may disappear. Unlike a bank that suffers a liquidity crisis and closes its doors, decentralized exchanges, like every other component of the DeFi system, are not governed by similar consumer protection laws that give depositors recourse to refunds in case of loss.

In reality, someone who provided a deliberately fraudulent smart contract and sat there skimming off the deposits of those who trusted it would, in most countries, be subject to existing criminal laws. The wheels of justice may grind slowly, but the transparent nature of blockchain technology means that sooner or later – even if it is years later – the long arm of the law is likely to catch up with deliberate perpetrators of outright fraud.

Incompetence, however, is frequently not a criminal matter, and countless millions of dollars have been lost to faulty smart contracts that have been deployed hastily or without adequate testing. Because smart contracts are essentially a giant testing site for human behaviour in the form of game theory, even something that is not necessarily a bug in the code but merely someone using the contract in a way that had not been foreseen can cause major problems.

FRONT-RUNNING

One of the challenges facing decentralized exchanges, examined in deeper technical detail in Chapter 5, is that of front-running. Front-running is not unique to DEXs, of course, or to financial applications that run on blockchains. It refers to the practice of using insider knowledge of a forthcoming transaction that will affect an asset's price to inform one's own investing decisions. Traditionally, it referred to individual brokers or brokerage firms using knowledge of a client's instructions to carry out a market-moving transaction in order to make their own trades.

Because trades on Ethereum are not made using brokerages, the front-running process is slightly different – and much harder to prohibit, as it is based around the incentive design of the underlying technology. In the Introduction, we looked at how Ethereum's gas fees provide the reward to the miners for ordering transactions into blocks and adding them to the blockchain. Higher gas fees allow transactions to be processed as priority traffic – in other words, they are written to the blockchain before those with a lower fee.

Before the transactions are added to a block, they are broadcast to the network, where they sit in what is called the mempool. This is the point at which the transactions can be front-run. Bots continuously scan the mempool for interesting transactions, identifying profitable opportunities, and then quickly submit their own transactions, with a higher gas fee so that they are processed before the original transaction.

When the original transaction is processed, the submitter will find that the profit they calculated in creating the transaction has been eroded by the price change of the asset that has resulted from the front-runner's transaction.

Miner extractable value

Front-running in Ethereum is a vast and complex topic, normally discussed in conjunction with a concept called MEV (miner extractable value). Projects such as FlashBots have been set up to investigate the extent of the problem and to research mitigations.

It is important to realize that this remains an issue of which anyone interacting with DeFi needs to be aware. (There is more on this in Chapter 5.) It is also set to persist after the migration to the Ethereum 2.0 proof of stake system. To give an idea of the scale of the front-running problem, a study by Christof Ferreira Torres (2021) at the University of Luxembourg identified a total of 199,725 attacks and 1580 attacker accounts over a period of five years.

'Pump and dump' tokens

Regulation is a topic in its own right (see Chapter 8 for an in-depth evaluation of the current state of play). Decentralized exchanges are a high-risk environment, suitable only for traders who understand that, for all the unprecedentedly high returns on offer, the risks are considerable and the process is far more akin to gambling than investing as things stand at the moment.

One important point to remember is that a decentralized exchange is exactly what it says on the tin. A smart contract running on the Ethereum blockchain does not demand to see the credentials of someone who interacts with it, or make policy decisions about who should be allowed to use the contract to create new liquidity pools. As we have seen, the sole requirement for anyone wishing to create a new liquidity pool is that they have tokens for both sides of the new pair in their wallet, along with enough Ether to cover the gas fees. This means that someone can create a new ERC20 token on Ethereum and set up a trading pair against another token, such as Dai or Ether, with a few mouse clicks. There is no quality control or approval process to ensure that the tokens are reputable or issued by an entity that has been vetted in some way.

Seasoned crypto watchers – and, in fact, most people who have read the basics about decentralized systems – are aware that, of the many thousands of tokens listed on coin ranking sites, most are completely worthless – their value influenced only by how loudly their cheerleaders are promoting them on social media. Meme coins come and go, while any genuinely successful and innovative project is immediately copied by opportunists trying to jump on the bandwagon.

It is fair to say that the liquidity pools on Uniswap and similar exchanges leave a very long trail indeed, with each DEX having hundreds of pools. On Uniswap, the most popular pools contain hundreds of millions of dollars in TVL, while the least popular lie abandoned, with just a few cents left in them.

> The class action launched on 4 April 2022 by trader Nessa Risley centred on these little-known, low-capitalization altcoins. She alleged that her substantial losses in such tokens as EthereumMax, Matrix Samurai, Rocket Bunny, Alphawolf Finance, Bezoge Earth and BoomBaby were caused by Uniswap's failure to restrict access to its platform and implement sufficient checks against Ponzi schemes and 'pump and dump' operations (Haig, 2022).

The lawsuit also alleged that Uniswap's entire incentives and fees infrastructure encouraged such fraud by paying liquidity miners guaranteed fees for every trade, regardless of the reputation or origin of the tokens. It is an interesting case because it calls into question exactly how decentralized a DEX is in practice.

The Uniswap protocol, running entirely independently on the Ethereum blockchain, is governed in a way that is popular among many decentralized projects: holders of the project's native token, Uni, vote on changes to the code, which are then carried out by developers. We look in more depth at token-based governance models and DAOs in Chapter 6.

Thus, while it can be argued that the protocol itself is not directly under the control of one entity, the front end of the application – the Uniswap website – is created and administered by Uniswap Labs (which is named in the Risley lawsuit, along with some of the venture capital firms that funded Uniswap Labs). Previously, Uniswap had removed from its website certain types of synthetic assets – those that track the price of listed stocks, as well as precious metals and stock market indices – in order to comply with securities legislation (Regan, 2021).

It is worth emphasizing, however, that anyone who wishes to interact directly with the protocol without accessing it via Uniswap's website, is able to create whatever pools they like by interacting directly with the computer code in the smart contracts. We will return to this distinction between parts of an application that are decentralized and parts that are less so in Chapter 8.

Forked codebases and vampire attacks

So far, this chapter has focused on Uniswap, as it is by far the biggest and most well-known of Ethereum DEXs, or, in fact, all DEXs. For anyone who is interested in monitoring the relative popularity of different DEXs and other DeFi protocols, ranking sites such as DeFi Pulse, DappRadar and DefiLlama provide plenty of fascinating insights into TVL and other statistics.

There are hundreds of DEXs, although, as with Uniswap pools and their tokens, we see a distinct long-tail effect. The top exchanges count their volume in hundreds of millions of dollars, while those in the lower ranks languish with a volume of close to zero.

Perhaps it should not be surprising that DEXs have proliferated over the last three or four years. Unlike the considerable expense and legal complexities involved in setting up a traditional exchange, creating a DEX in its simplest form requires only writing and deploying a series of smart contracts on a public blockchain. Because participants hold their own funds, other than when they are locked in a smart contract, there is no need to construct layers of security around users' funds, and no requirement to employ support staff to assist investors who may be having problems with their accounts.

We mentioned earlier some of the highest-profile hacks and thefts from centralized exchanges. Using a DEX rather than a centralized exchange does not, of course, guarantee that you are immune from such risks. It merely shifts the responsibility onto individual users – which is seen in some quarters as sophistry, given that the majority of traders are unlikely ever to read the code in a smart contract. And it is also true to say that DEXs and other DeFi protocols have proved to be a honeypot for hackers (something we dig into further in Chapter 5). Perhaps, given the speed with which this ecosystem is developing, and the high-octane pace with which new protocols are sometimes deployed, such exploits are unavoidable.

The SushiSwap vampire attack

In an example that perfectly illustrates the gulf in process and philosophy between the worlds of centralized and decentralized finance, let's look at the cautionary tale of SushiSwap.

Traditional financial institutions generally develop their software in a controlled and private environment, locked away from the eyes of hackers and competitors. The code undergoes cycles and cycles of careful testing, initially in an isolated environment and then at integration points with other areas of software, such as APIs and customer-facing applications.

DeFi protocols are often developed publicly – and even if the code repository is private, the contracts are usually published on sites such as EtherScan. This allows other developers to piggyback on existing work and rapidly develop and evolve new ideas that incorporate the best of what went before. Making a copy of a code repository and adding your own changes to it is known as 'forking'.

In 2020, after Uniswap was launched but before the governance token Uni was released, an anonymous developer known only as Chef Nomi forked the Uniswap code base and used it as the foundation for a new DEX, which he named SushiSwap in a nod to the trend for DeFi food-themed tokens that we mentioned in Chapter 1.

Not content with creating what he saw as an improved competitor to Uniswap, his next move was to drain liquidity from Uniswap into SushiSwap by first allowing Uniswap liquidity providers to stake their liquidity tokens for SushiSwap's own Sushi tokens and then proposing to redeem the liquidity tokens for assets that would be transferred from Uniswap. This action took place over a two-week period and was played out largely on social media, primarily Twitter. This liquidity draining was referred to as a vampire attack – and the twists and turns in the saga, combined with Chef Nomi's anonymity, created a compelling drama that, once again, underlined the significant differences between traditional finance and DeFi.

A further twist in the tale, in which Chef Nomi cashed out the Sushi development fund for 38,000 ETH, causing the price of Sushi to plummet 70 per cent, seized the attention of DeFi news watchers. The situation was soon resolved by Chef Nomi returning the tokens and voluntarily agreeing to hand over the private key controlling the development fund to none other than Sam Bankman-Fried, the billionaire founder of the FTX exchange.

In typical fairy-tale 'all's well that ends well' fashion, Uniswap's liquidity soon recovered, even exceeding its pre-SushiSwap volume, and the price of Sushi also recovered. Despite the dramas, SushiSwap remains a top 20 DEX, and the whole saga, while a cautionary tale regarding the swashbuckling, 'anything goes' ethos of DeFi, does underline how open-source development and conversations conducted publicly on social media can ultimately strengthen public confidence in the underlying technology.

Non-Ethereum DEXs

With hundreds of decentralized exchanges in existence, it is hard to underestimate the effect that the invention of AMM technology has had on the sector. For those without the time to research and calculate where their funds will make the best return, there are aggregation services such as 1inch, Orion and Matcha, which can be used to deposit your funds in a single place while they use algorithms to assign the funds to liquidity pools.

Before deciding which DEX or even which aggregator to use, however, investors must first decide which blockchain to use. Cross-chain interoperability of assets is, at the moment, complex, and nascent technologies mean that, while a multichain future is likely, trading and liquidity mining today takes place on one chain at a time.

For all the hype around competing Layer 1 networks such as Avalanche, NEAR and Solana, the most popular non-Ethereum DEX is not deployed on any of those chains. A glance at the DEX rankings shows that in second place to Uniswap v3 is the BNB chain-based PancakeSwap, with a 24-hour volume in excess of $0.5 billion. With its cartoony aesthetic, easy-to-use interface, fun lotteries and competitive pool-liquidity rewards, PancakeSwap shows that, however innovative and technically impressive your product is, user loyalty and a good user experience can still outweigh many other factors.

It is also worth mentioning that non-Ethereum DEXs have the huge advantage of much, much lower transaction fees – though lower liquidity on these exchanges may counteract a lot of this advantage.

NFT exchanges

The year 2022 was undoubtedly the year of the NFT. In Chapter 1, we described the ERC721 token standard on Ethereum, and how this techno-logical innovation has led to an explosion in the demand for digital collectables, often in the form of a JPG. In Chapter 7, we focus on non-fungible tokens and how they interface with DeFi, but it is worth briefly considering here how the ability to trade these tokens influenced the huge NFT boom.

OpenSea is by far the largest NFT marketplace in the world, with a trad-ing volume that regularly exceeds $100 million per day (according to DappRadar). Users are able to buy and sell either at a fixed price or via an auction process, and all sales are peer-to-peer. With a user base that grew from 4000 to 600,000 in just over two years, OpenSea was a product of the well-known Y Combinator accelerator and is notable for its slick and intui-tive interface.

However, while transactions take place peer-to-peer and users access the site from their crypto wallet rather than via a traditional login, OpenSea is a private company rather than a decentralized entity and cannot be described in any sense as a decentralized exchange. In contrast, OpenSea's main competitors – LooksRare and Rarible – despite having much smaller customer bases, are DEXs that are community-owned, with governance linked to their native tokens, Looks and Rari respectively.

What is a wallet?

These chapters have made frequent mention of wallets, and of connecting them to various applications. It would be useful to look at this in greater detail, as the ability to hold one's own assets, without having to trust another entity, is at the heart of the crypto – and, by extension, DeFi – ecosystem.

First, it is important to realize that a crypto wallet does not actually store your tokens. Unlike a physical wallet, it does not contain funds. A blockchain is a ledger of transactions that everyone can see, but you can only move funds from one address in the ledger to another if you have the private key for their current address. Therefore, a wallet is simply a way of storing this private key, which is a unique string of numbers and letters.

At its most basic, a private key may be written down on paper ('paper wallet') or engraved into metal for longevity, but most people tend to use either hardware wallets such as Ledger or Nano or, for less-secure purposes, a browser-based wallet such as MetaMask, which supports multiple networks including Ethereum, BNB, Avalanche and Fantom and Layer 2s such as Polygon and Arbitrum.

The most important thing to remember is that you, and you alone, are responsible for backing up your wallet. If you accidentally lose access to your bank account, your PayPal account or even your Binance and Coinbase account, you can normally restore it reasonably easily. If you can't do it yourself, there will be someone in the support team who can. But if you lose the 12-word secret phrase that allows you to access your MetaMask wallet or ledger, then all your funds are gone for good. Or, to be more precise, they are locked in a cryptographic limbo where you will never be able to unlock them. There are other hazards than forgetting your back-up phrase too. While smart contracts are designed to be publicly viewable and thus obviate the need to trust third parties, the number of people who can read the code in a smart contract and spot any bugs in it is vanishingly small. Many people have lost eye-watering sums of money in the form of tokens and NFTs simply by connecting their wallet to a malicious smart contract that contained instructions to remove all their assets to the thief's address.

These concerns are understandably off-putting for many people new to DeFi, which is why the majority of crypto users tend to stick to custodial wallets offered by the likes of Coinbase. Some of the most popular are given in Table 3.2. For decentralization enthusiasts, however, the idea that the individual is in control of their own money is one of the most exciting aspects of DeFi, as is the idea that you can effectively log in to any DeFi application

TABLE 3.2 Examples of popular software wallets

Wallet	Blockchain/s
MetaMask	Ethereum, BNB Chain, Polygon, Avalanche, Fantom, EOS, Celo
Coinbase Wallet	Arbitrum, Avalanche C-Chain, Bitcoin, BNB Chain, Ethereum, Gnosis Chain, Fantom Opera, Optimism, Polygon, xDai, Solana
Trust Wallet	More than 60 networks, including Bitcoin, Ethereum, BNB Chain, Polygon and many others
Phantom	Solana only
crypto.com	More than 15 blockchains, including Cronos, Crypto.org Chain and Ethereum

NOTE not a recommendation

anywhere using your wallet, without having to create different passwords or wait for someone in a company to set up your profile.

In-wallet swaps, wrapped tokens and bridges

Some wallets also offer the ability to swap tokens directly within your own wallet instead of visiting either a centralized or decentralized exchange. To do this within MetaMask, for example, it is as simple as clicking the Swap button, and ensuring that you have edited any advanced options such as those that allow you to set your custom slippage tolerance. This is a useful feature that allows anyone to diversify their portfolio directly within their wallet without having to use an external dApp.

Wrapped Bitcoin

When navigating various Ethereum DEXs and protocols, you may see trading pairs that offer Bitcoin – or, more accurately, 'wrapped' Bitcoin, or dApps where you can lend or borrow Bitcoin. How can traders and investors possibly interact with Bitcoin on the Ethereum network? It would be like loading a Nintendo game on a PlayStation console or trying to install an iPhone app on an Android phone. The technologies are simply not designed to work interoperably.

The answer lies in a mechanism known as 'wrapping', where an ERC20 token is minted in response to the equivalent sum of a digital asset being deposited in a vault secured by (in this case) custodian service BitGo. The most popular wrapped token is wBTC, which represents more than $10 billion in assets. Once you have completed whatever transactions you want, the process works in reverse: you send your wBTC back to the entity that minted it. They burn it and you are able to redeem your original Bitcoin from the vault. It perhaps goes without saying that this is an entirely centralized bottleneck in the system and that any Bitcoin deposited in exchange for wBTC is stored at the user's own risk.

You can also use your wallet in conjunction with a special type of dApp called a 'bridge' in order to port your tokens from a Layer 1 blockchain to a Layer 2. This takes the form of a protocol such as Hop, where you visit a specific website, connect your wallet and are able to transfer funds such as ETH, USDC, Matic, Dai and USDT between Ethereum's mainnet and the Polygon, Optimism, Arbitrum and xDai networks.

Why might people want to switch to a Layer 2 network? The primary answer is fees, which can make trading smaller quantities of digital assets uneconomic on Ethereum's main network. Traders need to bear in mind that they will need to pay these fees each time they bridge back to Ethereum, but increasingly, solutions are springing up that enable assets to remain on Layer 2s. A prime example is Quickswap, the best-known DEX on Polygon, and over all, one of the primary Layer 2 DEXs (remember that Polygon – previously Matic – is a Layer 2 on the Ethereum network).

It is worth visiting Quickswap to see the range of tokens and pools available. *Note that this mention is in no way a recommendation of its services.* As just specified, bridging back to Ethereum is neither free nor particularly fast – it may take several hours to complete.

What else can you do with DeFi?

A cursory visit to Uniswap or any of the other DEXs mentioned in this chapter shows that swapping tokens in liquidity pools or adding liquidity to these pools are not the only ways to get a return. Many DEXs also offer lending and borrowing services as well as trading-related opportunities. There are also DEXs that specialize in derivatives, perpetuals and other complex financial instruments.

The next chapter looks at the growth of DeFi products other than simple trading pairs and evaluates the future of this expanding sector.

References

Haig, S (2022) 'Uniswap faces class action lawsuit from trader who lost money on altcoins', *The Defiant*: https://thedefiant.io/uniswap-class-action/ (archived at https://perma.cc/TT3C-GN4N)

Regan, MP (2021) 'Uniswap restricts fake-stock tokens as regulatory scrutiny grows', *Bloomberg*: www.bloomberg.com/news/articles/2021-07-26/uniswap-restricts-fake-stock-tokens-as-regulatory-scrutiny-grows (archived at https://perma.cc/XB96-JK5K)

SEC (2018) 'SEC charges EtherDelta founder with operating an unregistered exchange': www.sec.gov/news/press-release/2018-258 (archived at https://perma.cc/FWH2-K5G5)

SEC (2022) 'SEC charges former Coinbase manager, two others in crypto asset insider trading action': www.sec.gov/news/press-release/2022-127 (archived at https://perma.cc/Q9PU-BN8B)

Torres, CF (2021) 'Front-runner Jones and the Raiders of the Dark Forest: an empirical study of front-running on the Ethereum blockchain', *Unsenix*: www.usenix.org/system/files/sec21-torres.pdf (archived at https://perma.cc/Y96Z-UKTJ)

04

Beyond DEXs: other DeFi protocols

CHAPTER OBJECTIVES

- Learn about staking
- Understand collateralized loans
- Understand composability and how DeFi protocols are interoperable
- Learn about gamified savings projects
- Find out about more complex loans
- Understand how derivatives, perpetuals and options are created in DeFi
- See how institutions are starting to use DeFi

The previous chapter looked at how decentralized exchanges can in some sense replicate many of the functions of their centralized equivalents by replacing traditional order books and matching engines with liquidity pools.

We have seen how this is not simply a semantic difference, or a mechanism for evading regulation, but one that has an important built-in security imperative in that it encourages investors to take responsibility for their own funds and hold them in a self-custodial wallet rather than in an exchange wallet.

Of course, swapping assets is only one activity performed in the financial markets. In order to create a DeFi infrastructure that can more closely mirror our traditional financial systems, we also need to have access to ways of lending, borrowing and earning yield on our assets, as well as methods for representing off-chain assets on blockchains and creating more complex financial instruments. We may also want to buy insurance for our assets and have access to off-chain data about real-world assets such as stocks and commodities.

If the current system is already providing all these functionalities, why would we want to develop a parallel system that replicates them in a more energy-intensive, slower, less scalable and less private way? One reason is that the centralized database systems that make up the existing financial system introduce high fees levied by intermediaries and delays in settlement, in addition to the technical challenge of maintaining many different types of legacy architectures that are not compatible with each other. An open financial system removes these intermediaries and introduces a principle of common standards, based on interoperable smart contracts that can easily be read and understood by multiple parties.

This chapter looks beyond DEXs to dig into progressively more complex areas of decentralized finance and discuss how they differ from their centralized counterparts.

Staking

In its simplest terms, staking a token simply means that the person who owns the token sends it to a smart contract, where it is held in exchange for a reward. The exact terms and conditions depend on the way the smart contract has been coded. Some contracts might specify that the reward is only paid or the token withdrawable after a certain time. From the investor's point of view, the closest analogy in traditional financial services is either a deposit savings account or a bond, depending on the entity where the token is staked, and whether there is a fixed term for redeeming the asset.

One way to stake tokens is to become a validator on a blockchain that is secured by proof of stake consensus (described in the following section). Providing liquidity to liquidity pools on decentralized networks is also a type of staking, looked at in the previous chapter. Here, we discuss other types of staking, such as committing tokens to be lent out to other users, and also staking in specific reward programmes.

Whatever type of staking is under discussion, the yield or reward is the most important element. Without this incentive, token holders would not be prepared to forgo the chance to make money from trading their tokens, or to take the risk that the smart contract might be flawed or malicious.

In an environment where interest rates on bank deposits or the yield on bonds is historically low, the chance to make double-figure returns on riskier protocols or even 4 or 5 per cent staking of Ethereum is rapidly drawing more and more hopeful investors into the DeFi space. Let's first look at how staking works to secure a network.

Staking on proof-of-stake networks

Bitcoin – the first blockchain-based digital currency – and those tokens that immediately followed it were based on a consensus mechanism called proof of work. In a proof-of-work system, the broadcast transactions are picked up by the different nodes that have joined the network, which compete to solve a mathematical puzzle and produce the definitive block of transactions that forms the next link in the chain. The computing power needed to solve this puzzle increases and decreases as programmed in the algorithm, but the block rate – the time in between blocks being produced – stays more or less constant.

The main objective of the network is to find consensus between the nodes, so that there is one single source of truth. The 'winning' node that produces the block is rewarded with a certain number of tokens, which offsets the operator's power costs and provides an incentive for remaining in the network. We refer to these nodes as 'miners', but their purpose is simply to validate the transactions on the network.

Its proponents see proof of work as the most secure way of validating a network, but its detractors argue that its power consumption is excessive – particularly during a tumultuous geopolitical period when these resources are scarce. (These claims are examined in greater detail in the next chapter.) In 2012, the developers of PeerCoin proposed a system where node operators offer their tokens as collateral in exchange for joining a pool of validators. Nodes are chosen at random from this validator pool to 'mine' a block, and are rewarded for this function. This is the most simplified description of proof of stake.

Criticisms of proof of stake include the degree of centralization that is inevitably introduced as more and more rewards accrue to existing token holders, resulting in an oligopoly. Consequently, variations on the theme – such as delegated proof of stake systems – have sprung up in an attempt to address these concerns.

Proof of stake operates on the basis that, if a validating node acts in a dishonest way – for example, validating fraudulent transactions – the operator is punished with the loss of their stake. The underlying idea is that having 'skin in the game' keeps people honest.

Blockchains that offer staking

There are many different blockchains that offer staking yield, but the best known of these is Ethereum – or, more accurately, the upgraded version known as Ethereum 2.0. Ethereum was launched as a proof-of-work block-chain, but has been evolving towards a new version based on staking for the last few years.

On 1 December 2020, the Ethereum 2 staking contract was deployed. By August the following year, it had become the largest holder of Ether, and by March 2022 it hit the milestone of containing 10 million Ether. By simply locking up (in other words, staking) 32 Ether, nodes are able to become validators on the so-called Beacon Chain, which ran alongside the original Ethereum blockchain until it moved fully to proof of stake in September 2022 (in the 'Merge'). 32 ETH is a significant amount of capital, limiting the number of Ether holders who are able to benefit from staking. However, centralized exchanges such as Kraken and Coinbase, as well as protocols such as Lido, offer individuals the chance to participate in a collective stak-ing enterprise, allowing those with smaller holdings the chance to benefit from staking yields.

Ethereum is not the only chain in town: many competing Layer 1 networks have come along that offer yield in return for validation. As with Ethereum, in many cases, the minimum amount needed puts this yield out of the reach of ordinary users other than via exchanges.

CONTROVERSY SURROUNDING ETHEREUM'S MERGE

While the Merge was undeniably a success from a technical point of view – conducting a major upgrade like this on a live network is an extremely challenging task – dissenting voices were heard in the days and weeks that followed as the price of Ether fell.

Not only were miners annoyed that a major source of income had disappeared with no compensation, but criticism emerged of the degree of centralization in the new network. Most stakers had nowhere near the 32 Ether required to run their own node, so majority control was effectively handed to exchanges and protocols. The geographic concentration of nodes in the USA also drew the attention of the SEC.

With no palpable improvements in either price or performance, some critics grumbled that appeasing the green lobby by reducing energy consumption had come at too high a price.

Staking for network growth and rewards

There are many alternatives, however, to staking tokens in order to become a validator on a proof of stake chain. Chapter 3 showed how staking coins in liquidity pools on decentralized exchanges – whether you are providing both sides of the trade or only one – can earn yield. This chapter takes a look at how the protocol tokens earned as a reward for liquidity provision can also be used to earn even more yield.

Let's explore a concrete example of this. Imagine you are an early adopter and supporter of a DeFi project that issued cryptocurrency tokens called A Tokens. The DAO or other entity running the project has a key objective of increasing liquidity for A Tokens, so they create a liquidity pool on Uniswap that allows traders to swap A Tokens for Ether. You deposit your A Tokens, with an equivalent value of Ether, and, as explained in Chapter 3, you receive a share of transaction fees for any swaps that take place in the pool. In addition, when you provide liquidity to the pool, you receive a liquidity-position (LP) NFT, which remains in your wallet until you remove liquidity from the pool (or decide to sell it).

If the issuers of A Tokens decide that one of their primary objectives is to encourage liquidity providers to lock up their tokens in the pool, they may well run a scheme (time limited or otherwise) that allows holders to lock up their LP NFTs in another smart contract and earn yet more A Tokens in exchange for this. This is a simple example of yield farming, where investors are able to gain different types of yield from locking up one type of token.

Liquidity-position tokens may be staked in a variety of different ways, not simply as a reward for holding a particular token. However, it is important to bear in mind that, if you stake your LP tokens in a protocol where the smart contract may be questionable and you lose your tokens, you also lose your share of the liquidity pool and you will not be able to remove liquidity and reclaim your original tokens.

This scenario is an example of staking LP NFTs, but there are many different ways to stake tokens directly, without having to deposit them in a liquidity pool first. For example, dedicated staking protocols such as Lido offer the opportunity to stake a variety of different Layer 1 and Layer 2 tokens, including Ether, Solana, Polygon and Kusama. Lido stakers lock up their original tokens in a smart contract and are rewarded with the corresponding Lido token: stETH for Ether, stKusama for Kusama, and so on (with 'st' meaning 'staked'). These staked tokens can in turn be deposited in protocols such as Curve or Yearn to earn further rewards.

Unlike a traditional savings account that pays interest monthly or sometimes even annually, most DeFi protocols accrue daily or even hourly yield, which is compounded. This can add up to a significant difference in yield over time, even where the headline percentage yield appears low.

Loans

Lending crypto-assets to an individual or a company is another way of earning yield. There are different ways to do this via either centralized or decentralized organizations. We will focus on decentralized lending protocols, but it is first worth mentioning centralized companies who have offered this opportunity, such as the cautionary tale of BlockFi.

BlockFi and other crypto lending companies

BlockFi is a wealth management company headquartered in New Jersey, which was incorporated in 2017. It offers US dollar loans in exchange for crypto collateral. The loans are over-collateralized, which means that a borrower has to deposit far more in crypto value than the amount of the loan. Depositors who want to lend money can deposit their crypto assets and earn a small amount of interest. The interest earned is less than the potential yield on DeFi protocols, but is usually more than offered by a bank savings account. Unfortunately, BlockFi filed for bankruptcy in November 2022 as the effects of FTX's failure cascaded across the industry.

One question often asked is why someone with, for example, $100,000 in Bitcoin or Ethereum would want to take out a loan – not just paying interest for the privilege, but also forgoing the opportunity to make money on their assets elsewhere and not simply exchange their crypto for fiat currency.

The answer lies in the volatility of crypto prices against US dollars and other state-backed currencies. If you hold cryptocurrency and are convinced that the price will rise over the medium term, you may decide that you would do better to hold your assets in their current form rather than cashing out and having to buy back in at a higher price. Taxation laws are another incentive to use crypto assets as collateral rather than sell. In many jurisdictions, taxes become payable on crypto sales but a collateralized loan is not a taxable event. When taking taxes and potential losses on price into account, it often makes sense to borrow fiat currency against crypto assets.

Celsius is another example of a centralized crypto lending project. Like BlockFi, its story is a cautionary tale that highlights many of the problems of companies operating within the DeFi space in that they are exposed to all the risks without in turn offering their customers the transparency that comes from decentralized solutions.

The Celsius freeze on withdrawals

One of the events that shook the world of DeFi in 2022 was the news that Celsius Network had frozen withdrawals, and later went on to be declared bankrupt. The problem with Celsius, as with so many other projects in the sector, is that it was somewhere in the middle, promising the transparency of decentralized finance with the convenience of a centralized company. This meant that individuals and institutions could use a single, uncomplicated interface to deposit their tokens, and all the complex decisions around which lending protocol or liquidity pool to use were abstracted away.

This might seem like a good idea in principle, but in many respects, it can be the worst of both worlds to present users with a slick user interface that looks like a traditional bank when none of the normal checks and compensation arrangements apply. Organizations such as Celsius bring an unwelcome degree of centralization, without the benefits. It later emerged that it owed its 500,000 creditors a total of $5 billion.

Decentralized lending protocols

Companies such as BlockFi and Celsius were popular precisely because they allowed investors who are used to interacting with traditional web inter-

TABLE 4.1 Lending protocols by chain and TVL (total value locked)

Protocol name	Network	TVL ($)
Aave	Ethereum, Arbitrum, Fantom, Polygon, Optimism, Harmony	5.54bn
JustLend	Tron	3.16bn
Compound	Ethereum	2.26bn
Venus	BNB Chain	630.12m
SushiSwap	Ethereum, Arbitrum, BNB Chain, Fantom	313.05m
Solend	Solana	267.94m

SOURCE Defi Llama, September 2022

faces to earn a return on their crypto assets, or for the crypto-affluent to borrow dollars against their Bitcoin or Ethereum.

These services are still centralized, however, requiring crypto holders to trust their assets to a third party rather than keeping them in a self-custody wallet. There are, of course, advantages to this approach: users can retrieve their password if they forget it, for example, and it provides a smooth onboarding experience for new entrants into the crypto space. However, this is not DeFi – and when things go wrong, as they did for both Celsius and BlockFi, the fallout can cause reputational damage to the entire DeFi ecosystem.

For a decentralized alternative to the likes of BlockFi, we have to look to lending services such as Aave and Compound. (See Table 4.1 for these and others.)

Aave

Aave is a decentralized non-custodial liquidity market protocol. Aave v3 introduced lending on various Layer 2 chains including Optimism and Arbitrum (Polygon was already available in v2), as well as additional Layer 1 networks including Fantom.

The experience and user flow are different for lenders and borrowers, so let's first look at how Aave works from a lender's point of view.

- As with Uniswap and various other DeFi protocols, Aave has been through more than one iteration, so it is important to note whether you are accessing v2 or v3 in the dropdown that appears when you launch the application.

- Connect your wallet in the usual way in order to see any assets you have supplied or borrowed. Elsewhere in the app, you can select the Markets page for an overview of the different tokens you are currently able to deposit and see the different yields that are on offer.

- When choosing a deposit amount and a network, it is crucial to take account of transaction fees. For example, making small transactions on Ethereum is unlikely to be worth it as the fees will vastly outweigh any yield returned. Yield is based on a share of the interest paid by borrowers calculated against the average borrow rate. (Aave provides a useful spreadsheet to illustrate this calculation.) In addition, lenders earn a share of the flash loan fees corresponding to 0.09 per cent of the flash loan volume. (There is more on flash loans later.)

- For serious yield-seekers, Aave offers other opportunities, too. Depositors receive aTokens in exchange for their deposits, which, in a similar way to the liquidity-position tokens illustrated in the last chapter, can be staked and used elsewhere in the DeFi system in order to earn extra yield.

- Additionally, holders of Aave's native token Aave (formerly Lend) can stake it in their Safety Module, which is, very loosely, a kind of insurance scheme designed to keep reserves in hand in case of fund loss. As expected, when stakers are taking on the risk of losing up to 30 per cent of their assets in a potential mitigation event, the 'Safety Incentive' rewards are set higher than normal staking yields.

Composability

Now is a good time to talk about a word that often comes up when talking about DeFi: *composability*. This term simply means the way decentralized protocols and applications can be used in conjunction with each other in different configurations: a 'plug and play' model where as many things as possible are interoperable. You may also hear this being described as 'DeFi Lego', referring to the way Lego pieces clip together to construct entirely new creations that the manufacturer may not have thought of.

Let's think about how this contrasts with the traditional model, where financial service companies are in competition with each other and generally their services are not interoperable. For example, wealthy individuals or companies may be able to use assets they have bought somewhere as collateral for a loan on another platform. But these kinds of transactions require legal agreements, escrow and other kinds of friction, which slows the process down.

Within decentralized finance, assets are free to flow to wherever they can generate most yield, reducing friction and opening up financial opportunities to people in different countries and of varying financial status. This composability and interoperability is usually a good thing, although it can mean that, if instability is introduced in one protocol, it can have negative knock-on effects on others. We look at these risks in more detail in the next chapter.

Compound

An example of composability in action is Compound, which, like Aave, is one of the largest DeFi lending protocols. Among the assets you can supply to Compound is Aave. So, you can supply Aave tokens to Compound and receive interest on them. A parallel to this in real life would be a situation where you receive air miles as rewards for spending on a credit card – and you are then able to deposit your air miles at an unrelated financial institution and earn interest on your balance. This is exactly the type of use-case that could be interesting at the intersection of fintech and DeFi.

Of course, this level of connectivity and dependence between products can also mean that contagion spreads quickly and introduces systemic risk. Given how quickly events can spiral out of control (such as Luna falling from nearly $80 to much less than a cent within seven days in May 2022), this same composability that is hailed as a feature can actually turn out to be a bug. And, while Compound is regarded as one of DeFi's success stories, even this successful protocol has fallen victim to bugs. In October 2021, it emerged that a smart contract had an error that let borrowers claim more Comp tokens than they were entitled to.

The bug happened as a consequence of a software update, and was not noticed until after $80 million worth of tokens had been distributed to the wrong people. The team quickly identified and fixed the problem, but that was not the end of the story. Because Compound is a decentralized protocol, community members had to vote for the fix to be deployed to the main network, and there was a week between the proposal being created and voted on. The vote passed, but not before another $68 million disappeared from the project's vaults. We discuss this and similar pitfalls in community governance in Chapter 6.

In a strange coda to the tale, which sums up the sometimes cult-like weirdness of the DeFi/social media intersection, Compound's founder Robert Leshner appealed directly on Twitter to the better nature of those who had received tokens in error, begging them to return the Comp to the community. As unlikely as it might seem, his appeal was successful and half the funds were returned.

COMPOUND TREASURY

The Compound website offers details of a Compound product that is different from any of its others, and which offers something completely different from other DeFi lending protocols: Compound Treasury.

This is a custodial service that offers institutions the chance to deposit their US dollars in exchange for USDC, which are held in custody for them and deposited on Compound to return a fixed 4 per cent yield, accrued daily. (Not that depositors would necessarily be aware of what is going on under the hood.)

The service also has the distinction of being the first institutional DeFi offering to be scored by a major credit rating agency, gaining a stable B-rating from S&P Global in May 2022.

Gamified savings projects

In the traditional financial world, particularly in Anglophone countries, saving has, to some extent, gone out of fashion. When Bitcoin came along, many of its early supporters shared the philosophical view that saving for the future and holding a form of money that could not be debased by governments was preferable to the consumerist dream of living on credit cards, personal loans and 'buy now pay later' deals, which are sold so heavily to millennials and Generation Z.

Other than the possibility – not guaranteed, of course – that the purchasing power of Bitcoin will outpace that of US dollars and other government-issued currencies, it does not provide a return. DeFi savings protocols offer yield as an additional incentive to put aside capital for future purchases or financial freedom.

There is, of course, considerable crossover between staking, savings and lending protocols. All are theoretically a way of locking away your investments so you don't spend them and of earning interest. However, this section looks at savings-specific protocols rather than the generalized staking schemes described earlier. So, let's look at two projects that focus on either the community element of savings groups, or gamification (or both), by building on top of other DeFi protocols.

PoolTogether

PoolTogether is a crypto-powered prize savings protocol – a type of no-loss lottery operating on the same principle as Premium Bonds. Savers deposit funds using their choice of network (Ethereum, Polygon or Avalanche) and these are pooled together with everyone else's funds and in turn deposited to other DeFi protocols where they earn yield.

Every day, a winner is selected randomly using a ChainLink oracle, and this winner receives the collective yield that has accrued on the pooled funds over the period. While savers are incentivized to leave their savings untouched to maximize their chances of being the prizewinner, they can withdraw their funds at any time: the protocol is fully liquid.

HaloFi

Gamification is also one of the elements of HaloFi, a DeFi savings service whose team believes that saving should be 'easy, rewarding and fun'. HaloFi founder Rachel Black explains:

> We provide the incentivization piece that builds on top of the other DeFi Legos that are out there. We build on Aave and Moola and we will have more yield strategies coming in the future as well. We solve the age-old problem that people have the intention to put away money or assets and build up their portfolio, but they don't always do that because other things happen in life.

HaloFi savers deposit Dai (US dollar-pegged stablecoins) into a savings pool that has multiple rounds, each with a fixed duration. To win, they need to make a deposit every round, before the deadline expires. Unlike PoolTogether, everyone who hits the pre-defined savings goals is a winner. Rachel Black explains:

> We split the interest in yield just among those who have been hitting all of their targets – so-called good savers. But we have designed it to be no loss, so if you did miss one of your deposits, you'll still get back your principal amount. On top of that, we're also adding on some more layers of gamification, for example an XP points system, NFTs and so on.

Essentially, we're building on top of the DeFi infrastructure that's out there and just making it more accessible and providing the incentives for people to make those weekly or monthly deposits.

Borrowing

So far, we have looked at how staking works and how investors can deposit assets in lending protocols to earn yield, either choosing the protocol themselves, using an aggregator such as Yearn or a savings interface like PoolTogether or HaloFi.

There is another side to lending protocols, however: the people who borrow the deposits and pay the interest that becomes the lenders' yield. Just as liquidity pools on decentralized exchanges contain two different tokens – one for each side of the exchange – when someone supplies funds to a lending protocol, there is a counterparty. In the case of protocols such as Aave and Compound, there is one side who deposits and another person who borrows.

In Chapter 1, when describing MakerDAO, we addressed the question of why someone who is already asset-rich needs to borrow money. In retail finance, borrowers are often those with few assets or savings, who may need money to fund a large purchase. In the case of a collateralized loan within DeFi, this may also be tax-efficient, because in the simplest case of depositing Ether and borrowing US dollars, many jurisdictions do not impose a tax on cryptocurrencies unless they are actually sold. So, it may make sense for someone to make a purchase while locking their Ether as collateral for the loan rather than selling the Ether for a central bank currency.

Other advantages might also include the speed of the loan: unlike a bank loan based on your credit record and subject to identity checks, a collateralized, decentralized loan is paid out instantly, with no waiting around for a human or an algorithm to make a decision about who you are and how credit-worthy you are.

Democratizing finance

Proponents of DeFi borrowing also point out that it also democratizes the act of taking out a loan, no matter what country you are in or what your personal circumstances are – as long as you already hold sufficient assets, that is. Someone in a low-income country whose economy is suffering and where interest rates might be high can access loans at the same interest rate as someone in a low-interest territory. This is an important aspect of the new decentralized finance offering from payments giant Block (formerly Square), tbDEX. Angie Jones, VP of developer relations for tbDEX, explains:

> We believe this open, decentralized financial system will enable all people to exchange value and transact with each other globally, securely, and at significantly lower cost and more inclusively than what traditional financial systems allow. Beyond reinventing money itself, we recognize smart contracts also have the ability to fundamentally reshape how the financial infrastructure of the future can work, and we'll utilize them in our protocol to complement our approach.

Borrowing US dollars in order to make purchases of physical items or buy assets outside DeFi is a small proportion of DeFi loans. Often, individuals or institutions may wish to borrow an asset which, if invested elsewhere, will give them a higher return than the one they possess. Unlike the example we have just looked at, the asset raised in the loan does not leave the DeFi system, but circulates within it, and loans simply become a tool for creating more and more complicated financial instruments. Critics of DeFi borrowing argue, on the other hand, that the volatility of cryptocurrencies make these products dangerous for investors at the lower end of the income scale.

More complex loans

In many cases, a loan is chained into a whole series of transactions across other protocols – and sometimes this sequence of events is encapsulated into a series of steps within a single contract so that all linked instructions are executed within one single transaction. This is known as a flash loan. Unlike the more common scenario in traditional financial services, where a loan may be applied for and received in a period of days or weeks, the loan is taken out, used elsewhere and repaid, along with any interest, all in a matter of seconds.

Flash loans came into common use in January 2020 on Aave and, by June 2021, more than $4 billion in flash loans had been issued and repaid. Unlike more traditional loans, flash loans do not need borrowers to put up collateral because blockchain networks like Ethereum are able to roll back transactions that are not completed correctly. So, if someone creates a single transaction that borrows funds, does something with those funds and then pays them back with all the associated fees and interest, but the last step fails because of a miscalculation or other error, the other steps are rolled back.

While the risk to the borrower is minimized because their collateral is not at risk of being liquidated, there are still some costs associated with failed transactions because gas fees still need to be paid, and the more complex the transaction, generally the higher the gas fees are.

How do flash loans work?

Flash loans are often used to take advantage of arbitrage opportunities. To give a concrete example of how they work, imagine there are two decentralized exchanges (DEXs), which both offer swaps of Token X against Dai:

- DEX A has a price of 100 Dai for every Token X
- DEX B offers Token X at 110 Dai.

A borrower could write a smart contract that:

1 borrows 5000 Dai from a lending protocol
2 buys 50 Token X from DEX A
3 sells the 50 Token X on DEX B, receiving 5500 Dai
4 returns 5000 Dai to the lender and keeps the profit of 500 Dai.

All these steps are carried out in one single transaction. Of course, this is a trivial example as the gas fees – and any fees payable to the lending protocol – would eat into the 500 Dai profit. But it is easy to see how, when larger sums are borrowed, huge profits can be made with minimal risk to the borrower.

In reality, especially on Ethereum, it can be difficult for average users to take full advantage of flash loans, both because of the technical knowledge needed to write the contract, and also because of front-running, where bots continually scan transactions in the mempool to spot profitable arbitrage opportunities and pay a higher fee to get their transaction mined first and thus take advantage of the opportunities. The next chapter looks in more detail at the issues of front-running and miner extractable value (MEV), which could be just about worth an entire book to themselves.

If flash loans are relatively low risk for borrowers, they can be high risk for protocols, and are a frequent source of attacks. Many protocols, including Compound, Balancer and Cream, have been the target of flash-loan attacks that have drained tens of millions of dollars from DeFi platforms. These attacks have frequently targeted the weak point of pricing oracles: when inaccurate prices have been supplied, bots can spot this and take advantage of these vulnerabilities.

While flash loans are an example of something it is possible to do within DeFi that it is not possible to do in centralized financial markets, does this automatically mean that we should be trying to do them? Many critics of public blockchain networks have pointed to their transaction costs and latency as barriers to replicating sophisticated financial instruments. The risks inherent in having your transaction sitting, visible to the world, in a place where it can be easily front-run is just one example of these barriers.

Derivatives

In traditional financial markets, derivatives make up a vast proportion of financial products and services, having a market capitalization of as high as $1 quadrillion. A derivative is, of course, a type of financial contract that derives its price from an underlying asset, which may be a currency but may just as easily be a commodity or a stock.

Synthetix is one of the best known DeFi derivatives platforms. Founded in 2017, it allows investors to trade in synthetic assets (Synths) backed by Synthetix Network Tokens locked into a smart contract as collateral. As well as a range of synthetic cryptos, such as sBTC and sETH, synthetic fiat currencies such as sGBP and sYEN are available, as is sDEFI, a DeFi index derivative. At one point, it was also possible to buy a small range of synthetic tech stocks on the protocol, but these were withdrawn in the third quarter of 2021, with a view to relaunching on Layer 2 networks at a later point.

Perpetuals

Perpetuals are a special type of derivative that operate like futures but without the complexities of settlement dates, meaning that you can hold your position for ever – or until you are liquidated. Perpetuals are popular on centralized exchanges such as BitMEX, FTX and Kraken, but the best-known decentralized market for perpetuals is dYdX.

This allows up to 10 times leverage and anyone is able to perform liquidations and earn the liquidation fee, so these would be risky products for inexperienced investors. To trade perpetuals on a centralized exchange such as BitMEX, a trader has to undergo KYC verification, but to participate in perpetuals on dYdX, they simply connect their non-custodial wallet and deposit USDC as collateral.

Perpetuals allow traders to bet on the price of the underlying asset without holding it. A long position indicates that the trader believes the price will rise, and a short position indicates the opposite. The funding rate is the financial reward for being on the correct side of the bet: if the price of the underlying asset rises (for example, Bitcoin against the US dollar), then traders holding long positions will receive profit and those holding shorts will lose money. DYdX calculates the funding rate by the second and settles payments every hour, and every trader has a profit-and-loss account) and can withdraw their funds at any time.

Proponents of decentralized perpetuals argue that the greater transparency and the automated nature of smart contracts is a step forward when compared with their centralized counterparts. Hourly settlement with no extra cost in terms of manual intervention or checks is certainly one example where smart contracts provide these benefits.

Options

We have seen from the examples so far that many concepts from centralized finance are easily applied to crypto – and options trading is no exception. Options are a type of contract that gives investors the right to buy or sell an asset at a particular expiry date.

In centralized finance, describing options as American-style or European-style simply means that, if you hold the former, you have the right to exercise the option at any time before the expiry date, while the latter allow you to do so only on or after the expiry date.

European-style options are by far the most prevalent in DeFi, and the automation element inherent in smart contracts means that the buy or sell action can be programmatically executed at a particular time. Investors are able to long the underlying asset by taking out a 'call' option (the right to *buy* at a particular price on the expiry date) or to short it by taking out a 'put' option (the right to *sell* at a particular price on the expiry date).

Opyn is probably the best known DeFi platform for options. We will see in the following sections how investors can protect themselves to some extent against smart contract bugs or hacks by taking out insurance via a decentralized insurance protocol, but, in fact, using an Opyn option to hedge their other positions is another protective measure that traders can take to protect their funds.

DeFi options vaults (DOVs)

Options trading can be complex and risky, so perhaps it is not surprising that we have recently seen the emergence of DeFi options vaults (DOVs), a structured product that allows investors to deposit funds in a smart contract that aggregates them with funds deposited by others and invests these into a range of different options, according to the strategy and level of risk desired by the trader.

Using a DOV means that, instead of having to calculate dates and prices themselves, the smart contract is doing the hard work for the trader, and for this there is a fee payable. Ribbon Finance is the best-known provider of DOVs. In the CeFi world, these products are available only to qualified investors, but the steady rise in their popularity shows that there is an increasing demand for these sophisticated products across the whole spectrum. Whether this is a good thing or not is discussed in Chapters 5 and 8, where we see how regulators are dealing with these thorny challenges.

Insurance

Given that DeFi in general is risky because it deals with cutting-edge technologies for which the security and incentive structures have not yet been proven, and where government-legislated compensation is not applicable, it is worth considering the options available if investors want to mitigate some of these risks. Only a tiny percentage of DeFi positions are currently covered by insurance protocols.

Nexus Mutual is one of the best-known insurance protocols, and offers cover against smart contract bugs and hacks on a limited range of DeFi services for around 2 to 4 per cent per year. Nexus offers decentralized insurance, and the total cover available depends on how much has been staked against each product. It works on the principle that stakers can 'bet' on the security of a particular product by buying Nexus' native token

(NXM) and staking it against a product that they believe to be relatively secure. If an insured product fails and those investors who have bought Nexus cover are reimbursed, this reimbursement comes from the staker's capital.

Creating your own financial instruments

Critics of DeFi – who also make many very valid points about the dangers of financially naive investors piling money into experimental and untested smart contracts, let alone the presence of outright fraud within the ecosystem – often overlook some of the truly interesting innovations that are happening.

One of these is the possibility that specialists in a particular field, who have deep knowledge of a particular sector, can create their own futures market to manage risk or hedge against volatile prices. Providing the infrastructure to make it easy for individuals or institutions to do this is likely to become a key part of the DeFi universe in the future.

Vega Protocol, for example, is a decentralized derivatives network that allows traders to propose new markets as well as creating liquidity. Its vision of truly democratizing access to the type of financial products that have previously been limited to a small number of investors is one where decentralized protocols can provide incentives for better data provision on a wide range of assets, resulting in more efficient markets, particularly for those that are currently under-served. For example, manufacturers would be able to create their own market to hedge their risk of price depreciation while products were being shipped, even if there is no pre-existing precedent for this.

In a world where anyone can create markets on any underlying asset, a range of new business models become possible, unleashing a wealth of specialist knowledge and ideas that may not otherwise have come to light via the traditional corporate route.

Institution-focused initiatives

Earlier, we touched on Compound Treasury, the institution-focused offering from DeFi protocol Compound. Unsurprisingly, other products and services are now gradually appearing on the market that have specific appeal to institutions, offering permissioned trading with enterprise-grade identity checks. Aave Arc is Aave's institutional product, offering a much smaller subset of tokens than is available on the main Aave protocol, but where participants are limited to white-listed suppliers and borrowers.

Another institutional development to watch is J.P. Morgan's Onyx Digital Assets blockchain, where trades are settled in the bank's in-house token, JPM Coin. By September 2022, Onyx had $350,000 in trading volume and is involved in various pilots across the world. It is already possible to trade tokenized versions of BlackRock's money market fund shares on Onyx, and there is a pilot underway in Singapore to test institutional DeFi using permissioned liquidity pools containing tokenized bonds.

Evaluating risk

As with any product or service that involves money, would-be investors should think carefully and be aware of all the downside risks before taking part in DeFi transactions. The dangers of being liquidated, especially when markets are volatile, are high – and using leverage in any situation can risk everything.

Losses can also, of course, be compounded by a background of generally falling prices in the crypto assets sector – and even stablecoins, designed to mitigate this problem, are not immune to crashing in value if the underlying value of their collateral falls or if the algorithm that guarantees their stability has bugs or logic errors. It is worth being especially cautious around products whose returns appear too good to be true.

For traders – and in some cases, developers – who have only ever known rising markets, it can be easy to make assumptions that are based on economic good times, without accounting for the extreme stress that will be placed on an algorithmically driven protocol in a period of rapidly falling prices. These dangers are unfortunately inflated and exacerbated by the effects of social media.

Social media influencers are able to create hype around tokens and protocols that return wildly inflated yields, and financially naive investors have piled millions into them, with dire consequences. As with investments that are promoted in traditional financial markets, the principle should always be that, if something looks too good to be true, it usually is. With this in mind, the next chapter looks at challenges and risks – for both investors and institutions integrating with DeFi protocols – and how to balance these against the opportunities that are on offer.

Further reading

Allison, Ian, 'JPMorgan wants to bring trillions of dollars of tokenized assets to DeFi', CoinDesk, 11 June 2022:
www.coindesk.com/business/2022/06/11/jpmorgan-wants-to-bring-trillions-of-dollars-of-tokenized-assets-to-defi/ (archived at https://perma.cc/HBW5-CV93)

Francus, Lily, 'Capital inefficiency & DeFi options', *Midnight on the Market Momentum*, 3 April 2022:
https://nopeitslily.substack.com/p/capital-inefficiency-and-defi-options?s=r (archived at https://perma.cc/8Q7J-T8A7)

Haig, Samuel, 'Why Compound might ditch its yield farmers', *The Defiant*, 19 April 2022: https://thedefiant.io/compound-incentive-overhaul/ (archived at https://perma.cc/JZM6-QWHF)

Hamacher, Adriana, 'What are flash loans? The DeFi lending phenomenon explained', *Decrypt*, 18 June 2021:
https://decrypt.co/resources/what-are-flash-loans-the-defi-lending-phenomenon-explained (archived at https://perma.cc/RXR6-57JB)

QCP Capital, 'An explanation of DeFi Options Vaults (DOVs)', *Medium*, 12 December 2021: https://qcpcapital.medium.com/an-explanation-of-defi-options-vaults-dovs-22d7f0d0c09f (archived at https://perma.cc/7XM8-YQFW)

Roberts, Liam, 'The current state of under-collateralised lending in DeFi', *DeFi Mullet*, 9 May 2022:
https://defimullet.substack.com/p/the-current-state-of-under-collateralised?s=r (archived at https://perma.cc/L4CS-UFLT)

05

Risks and challenges

> CHAPTER OBJECTIVES
>
> - Learn about scalability and transaction fees
> - Evaluate governance risks
> - Understand why insufficient decentralization is problematic
> - Learn about miner extractable value
> - Understand how to work with open-source code
> - See the technical risks of integrating with legacy systems
> - Know why DeFi is sometimes regarded as a systemic risk

The previous two chapters examined the nuts and bolts of how some of the products and services within DeFi work, and looked at some of the activities that would-be investors might engage in. We have also seen how certain protocols can offer higher yields than many returns available outside the DeFi ecosystem.

However, in a sector where capital is not protected by government guarantee schemes, and where customers may not understand what they are investing in, how do we manage risk and communicate to potential investors, who are not necessarily knowledgeable about open-source software or decentralized governance, about who is ultimately responsible for securing the safety and integrity of public networks or who might be deliberately trying to defraud and scam them?

The technical architecture of blockchain networks is a work in progress, with scalability problems that are still being solved and game-theoretic challenges around front-running transactions on transparent public networks, as well as the fact that transparent public blockchains offer visibility that may not even be welcomed.

There may also be risks – both financial and reputational – to banks, fintechs and other institutions seeking to integrate with the wider DeFi ecosystem, depending on where they are located. There are also many practical challenges, both technical and regulatory, that stand in the way of such partnerships.

The dependence of DeFi protocols on open-source code that can be easily copied by anyone and which is in the process of being battle-tested in the wild is a culture shock to many institutions, with their emphasis on process and safety over speed and agility. How can these competing requirements be reconciled?

The high-profile collapses of FTX, Three Arrows, Terra and others was a reminder that great risk often accompanies great rewards – especially those that appear too good to be true. What lessons can we learn from this particular incident, and how can institutions protect themselves and their customers if they decide to integrate with these new protocols?

And – perhaps most importantly – what does the small but increasing number of touchpoints between DeFi and TradFi mean in terms of systemic risk to the whole international financial ecosystem?

Blockchain-specific challenges

In the ICO (Initial Coin Offering) boom of 2016–2017, there was scarcely a sphere of human economic activity that was not targeted by blockchain start-ups. The idea that instructions of many different kinds could be encoded in smart contracts and executed entirely autonomously in a transparent manner was one that seized the imagination of innovation teams and investors in a range of industries.

However, most of these start-ups failed. Architecting such systems to perform efficiently is difficult – and the trade-off in terms of efficiency and speed is often not worth it. The number of use-cases where a blockchain might add value is actually very small. The entirely public nature of permissionless blockchain networks has also proved to be a sticking point, particularly for the financial industry, whose participants desire privacy for both their own and their customers' transactions. While many of the projects that raised money in 2017 are no longer functioning, those that survived prove that, where blockchains are genuinely useful – for securing transactions between parties who do not know and trust each other – they are very useful indeed, and the trade-offs are worth it. Let's look at some areas where blockchains still present significant challenges to their mainstream adoption.

Scalability and expense

Computation and data storage consume power. In the age of cloud computing, where it is possible to run powerful servers remotely and where the price of storing huge amounts of data has fallen sharply over recent decades, it is easy to forget this. A distributed system like a blockchain network requires the record of all transactions to be stored in multiple places (for transparency) and be cryptographically validated (for security). On a smart-contract-based system such as Ethereum, what this means in practice is that the same computations are executed over and over again, in such a way that all nodes in the network reach agreement. (Over the last decade, multiple books and articles have been written and videos created to explain how blockchains work, so there is little point in repeating this at length.)

This system is extremely secure because the resulting consensus means that it is difficult for bad actors to game the system. However, it can also be expensive in computational power and monetary terms.

Ethereum's transaction fees

Ethereum was designed in a way that its scarce resources (the 15 or so transactions that it is capable of executing per second) would not be abused by malicious entities spamming the network with nonsensical transactions, and the mechanism for this is to impose a fee on transactions that rises and falls depending on how busy the network is.

While considerable progress is being made in upgrading Ethereum and in the development of Layer 2 networks that can alleviate some of this load, Ethereum's high fees remain a sticking point. It is also not the case that Ethereum 2.0 will have lower fees by default, as some people have made the mistake of believing.

As many would-be savers and NFT collectors have found to their cost, transacting on Ethereum can feel like a privilege reserved for the already wealthy, and the unpredictability of these costs can be a strong deterrent to corporate interest, particularly when the volume of transactions on Ethereum hits a bottleneck due to some hyped event or deadline.

As an indicator of how extreme these pressures can be, the much-hyped Otherside NFT sale carried out by Bored Ape creators Yuga Labs was notable for its extreme gas costs, with some users having to pay more than $4000 per transaction. Other unhappy users reported spending thousands on fees for failed purchases, which were later refunded by Yuga Labs (Irwin, 2022).

Naturally, all transactions that are carried out on computers carry some costs, but the advent of hyper-cheap computation and storage using cloud providers such as Amazon Web Services, Google Cloud and Microsoft Azure has meant that processing and storage costs are not something that developers have to think too deeply about in most cases. To replace or augment an extremely-low-cost system with one that incurs a significant charge for even the most basic transaction means that there would need to be very real advantages that could not be gained in some other way, to justify the extra costs. And, whenever extreme events such as the Otherside NFT sale are taken into account, it is a brave company that would take the risk of a customer dissatisfaction event on this scale.

Governance risks

A corporate structure is easy for anyone to understand. Hierarchies are normally top-down and the suite of executives is tasked with optimizing return for, and representing the needs of, the investors and any other stakeholders. The decision-makers are humans, appointed by other humans, who sign contracts and letters of intent, and who promise to compensate clients if service-level agreements (SLAs) or other commitments are breached.

Integrating with a public blockchain is entirely different from integrating with proprietary software offered by a corporation, with all the guarantees and service expectations that this implies.

We look more closely at DAOs (decentralized autonomous organizations) in the next chapter, but, for now, what DAO-based decision-making means in practice is that, if your company or organization is unhappy with a particular aspect of the software or performance of a DeFi protocol, there is no CEO or account manager to call up and complain to. Technical changes that are made to the protocol may have to be agreed by the community: a faceless agglomerate of individuals from all over the world who may have all kinds of competing agendas that do not necessarily coincide with your own. For example, MakerDAO founder Rune Christensen has talked openly about why the community should plan for an emergency shutdown of the multi-billion-dollar protocol should the US government impose sanctions that stakeholders in the protocol felt were too onerous and compromised too many of their principles (Haig, 2022).

Insufficient decentralization

Embracing this entirely new paradigm can offer great rewards for those organizations willing to take the leap, however unfamiliar the principles seem. An important and somewhat counterintuitive principle is that real risk and uncertainty arise when a network is insufficiently decentralized and no one is sure where responsibility begins and ends. As we have touched on in earlier chapters with the bankruptcies of Celsius and Three Arrows Capital, by far the worst consequences of the 2022 DeFi crash fell on the shoulders of those who had invested in centralized companies assumed to be more decentralized than they actually were. An investment manager I spoke to emphasizes that it does not matter if a project is somewhat centralized in the beginning, as long as its originators have an authentic plan to work towards a future where power and decision-making are more distributed:

> It can introduce a systemic risk if a centralized chain is not operating in good faith or they're not working towards progressive decentralization. From what we've seen over the years, it's fine to start as a centralized protocol, as long as you commit to progressive decentralization, as long as you commit to growing the user base and growing the distribution of the validators at the very similar pace so you don't get more end-users than you can actually handle. It should be fine in the short term, but we should all commit to progressive decentralization. Otherwise, we introduce a lot of systemic risk.

In other words, this kind of 'decentralization theatre' creates a situation where there is the worst of both worlds: power concentrated in the hands of one or several people whose motives may not be transparent, coupled with a lack of structure and oversight that would otherwise be provided by a company.

Financial cryptographer Ian Grigg, famous for his invention of triple-entry accounting, which pre-dated the development of Bitcoin, points out that many DeFi projects are not quite as decentralized as they may seem, with all the implicit risk:

> Probably a large number of the contracts that are out there turn out to be actually centralized or there's one in the hands of a few big players. There's one person who runs the contract and can change the conditions or run this API or save the day or whatever.

Even where keys and passwords are not at the mercy of one or two individuals, there is the potential danger that one individual or interest group can dominate decision-making.

We look at governance – and particularly DAOs – in the next chapter, but it is also worth bearing in mind that, when a protocol is governed by a DAO, decision-making may be hijacked by those with nefarious intentions, if insufficient safeguards are not put in place. In February 2022, Build Finance DAO lost $470,000 when one user amassed enough tokens to seize control of the treasury and was able to drain it. This was not the result of a hack or a technical exploit: it was simply the result of the DAO's governance model being insufficiently rigorous in that the voting structure easily allowed one individual to grab critical financial decision-making powers (Copeland, 2022). Traditional corporations wishing to integrate with protocols that are governed by DAOs should be mindful of votes that may affect the smooth running of the protocol in unexpected ways.

Maximal extractable value and front-running

Governance issues such as those just mentioned are not usually a consequence of bugs affecting a project's code: the project may have been coded exactly as conceived. However, tokenomics, governance and incentive design are all very new fields and it is often difficult when designing a system to predict exactly how end users will behave in any given situation.

Unlike an incorporated company, which is able to set out the terms and conditions under which its customers interact, anyone who interacts with a public blockchain network does so according to a set of predefined rules that are encoded into the smart contracts deployed. If anyone – whether an end user or a DAO member – can find a way around these rules via a loophole that someone has not thought of, then, while some people might argue that this goes against the spirit of the project, it is not strictly a hack.

One of the behaviours that falls into this grey area is front-running – along with the related idea of miner extractable value (MEV). Within the world of traditional finance, front-running is banned by regulators, and transgressors are penalized heavily, sometimes even with jail sentences. In traditional finance, the rules are clear. Brokers working on behalf of clients are not permitted to use their insider knowledge of upcoming trades to make their own deals. If a broker has been commissioned to buy a large block of shares for a client, they are not allowed to submit their own order first and then watch as their client's purchase pushes the price up. Every firm has checks and balances in place to ensure their employees remain within the law.

Public blockchains present an entirely different challenge. Investors carry out their own trades instead of involving an intermediary, but, because every transaction is public, their order to buy a certain quantity of a token or other financial product can be seen by anyone in the world – and potentially intercepted and overtaken by someone else's transaction.

How MEV works

Mining software on public blockchains is designed to order and prioritize transactions in the most profitable manner for the miner. It is all part of the incentive mechanisms that keep these networks running.

When Bitcoin was created, its primary purpose was to transfer value from one peer to another. If someone needed a transaction to be confirmed particularly quickly, they could opt to pay a higher transaction fee to incentivize miners to include it in a block as a higher priority, but all that they received in return was a faster transaction.

With Ethereum, however, came smart contracts and the opportunity to create complex financial transactions that interacted with different – or often, multiple – DeFi protocols in chained transactions. Examples of this include arbitrage and liquidations. In the case of DEX arbitrage, a trader may spot a difference in the price of a token pair on different DEXs. A smart contract allows that trader to buy on one exchange and sell on another in a single atomic transaction, taking advantage of the higher-priced token on the second exchange.

Liquidations are another way to profit. Protocols such as Aave allow anyone to call in a collateralized loan on behalf of the lender if the collateral falls below a certain point. The liquidator receives a fee for this, so multiple bots roam Ethereum and other DeFi-enabled blockchains, looking for liquidation opportunities.

Flash loans are yet another example. As described in the previous chapter, these borrow assets, trade them to make a profit and then return the assets, all in one complex smart contract. If the price of the trade at which they make a profit changes before the transaction can be completed, the entire transaction is unwound and the trader makes no profit at all, and has to pay transaction fees for the failed attempt.

In all these cases, third parties can easily – and legally – find out what arbitrage opportunities or other profitable transactions are waiting to be processed. They use bots known as searchers to constantly scan the mempool for upcoming transactions and, if they find a profitable opportunity, are prepared to pay validators a high fee to ensure their transaction wins the race to execute the contract first.

The use of searchers is a profitable enterprise, but validators still end up with most of the MEV as they ultimately have the power to include or exclude transactions from blocks. It is also worth noting that in many cases, validators themselves can front-run these transactions.

In addition to front-running, MEV can also be used to back-run transactions. Back-running is a technique where someone (usually in these cases a bot) spots an opportunity to profit from a higher price immediately following a trade. For example, an upcoming transaction that is large enough to move the price of a token in a liquidity pool may benefit someone who is selling the token whose price has increased. In these cases, paying the validator to order your transaction so that it immediately follows the transaction that has forced the price higher can be worthwhile.

A sandwich attack combines front-running and back-running. The attacker might, for example, first front-run a transaction to profit from an arbitrage opportunity that someone else has spotted and pay a lower price for a token. The original transaction happens next and pushes the price higher. The attacker then makes their second transaction immediately afterwards, profiting from the higher price. The victim's transaction is sandwiched between the attacker's two transactions, hence the name.

Many analysts draw a distinction between 'toxic' MEV, which is effectively extracting value at someone else's expense, and 'healthy' MEV, which can be seen as a way of producing more efficient markets.

Where is MEV an issue?

MEV exists on all smart-contract-enabled networks where node operators are responsible for ordering transactions, whether these are proof of stake or proof of work (the principle remains the same, even if some of the details are different). Some people argue that MEV is a necessary ingredient for efficient decentralized finance markets as it aids price discovery and smooths out inconsistencies.

However helpful MEV is for the market as a whole though, anything that pushes up fees and promotes front-running is a negative for individual traders. Some initiatives that have aimed to reduce transaction fees have even increased MEV. For example, EIP1559, which was released as part of Ethereum's London hard fork in 2021, removed the variable gas fee paid to miners. It was replaced with an algorithmically set fee, which was then burned. This was supposed to make fees more predictable – but it meant miners had to rely even more heavily on making revenue from MEV.

Ethereum's move to proof of stake was not designed to impact MEV one way or another. After the Merge, miners were replaced by validators, and these also have the power to order transactions to take advantage of MEV, or to delegate this function to other actors in the network. Any attempt to change the protocol code itself to disallow this would simply mean MEV payments would happen off line. Meanwhile, independent projects such as Flashbots offer the chance to send transactions to miners for priority ordering without submitting them to the public mempool. This means that they cannot be front-run.

The grey area of where system attributes that look like bugs – for example, the fact that miners are able to affect transaction ordering and either enable front-running for others or front-run themselves – are actually part of the incentive design that governs the core behaviour of the blockchain but are difficult for people to get used to.

Projects that combine elements of privacy and obfuscation in pending transactions, such as Flashbots, are attempting to solve the problem, but it is clear that any system that allows its users to pay for priority transaction ordering cannot easily eliminate front-running.

In traditional finance, such transaction prioritization has traditionally been gamed by large institutions paying to set up their own networks to gain a speed advantage when conducting high-frequency trading (as per the book and film *Flash Boys*, from which Flashbots gets its name). A casual observer looking at a large Ethereum trader operating front-running bots and paying heavily for the privilege might well ask what the difference is.

Open-source code and its liabilities

Open-source code is the foundation of DeFi protocols. In itself, it is not necessarily a significant risk, even for the most traditional of financial institutions, as trends in technology over the last decade have meant that open-source libraries and frameworks are much more commonly used than they once were, particularly since the advent of open banking and of fintech in general. The days of banks using only proprietary software run on licensed platforms are disappearing rapidly.

Open-source code has many advantages in a composable system that is public and based on transparency. In an ecosystem where the code of a smart contract is open to public view and where anyone can copy it and experiment with it, anyone can, theoretically, spot bugs before they become problematic and indeed, in a small minority of cases, detect deliberate loopholes that developers might use to steal or divert funds.

It may seem counter-intuitive to open up the inner workings of a financial system to scrutiny by bad actors as well as good, but the general consensus seems to be that such transparency is the best way to encourage developers to work together for the common good. There is an expression, 'Sunlight is the best bleach.' This means that bugs or general fragility are more likely to become problematic when obscured and hidden in dark corners than when exposed and dealt with in public view. Think about how it feels to be told after the event that there was a catastrophic bug in your banking app that could have drained your account, but that you should not worry about it because the bug was detected and fixed. With no knowledge of how the bug occurred, was noticed or was fixed, it may leave you with an uneasy feeling.

However, it is also important to say that unnoticed flaws in code have nevertheless been the cause of considerable financial loss and heartbreak, regardless of transparency and openness. It would be a mistake to think that otherwise successful projects are immune. The $150 million hack of Compound in October 2021 was a case in point – although the resilience of the project as a whole was proven by the team's response to the hack, and the fact that the project is still successful today.

Audits do not offer guarantees

An average saver and investor, while theoretically able to look at the source code of a smart contract, is unlikely to do so – and even more unlikely to understand the inner workings of the complex, interconnected contracts that make up a DeFi protocol. The composable nature of DeFi building blocks make the possible bugs that are exposed at the integration points between these blocks even more difficult to detect. Even among developers experienced in working with smart contract programming languages such as Solidity, there is a relatively small proportion who would be capable of spotting obscure or edge-case bugs.

Specialist audit firms such as Omniscia, Peckshield, Certik and Solidified offer services that validate a project's smart contracts meeting a certain security standard. Audit by one of these recognized providers is a baseline guarantee that due diligence has been carried out, but does not in itself mean that the system cannot be gamed in some other way. Protocols that use game theory for their incentive mechanism – as all public blockchain networks do – are always vulnerable to someone who interacts with the protocol discovering a novel way to gain an advantage at the expense of other users.

Izabella Kaminska, founder editor of *The Blind Spot* media site, has interesting points to make about this distinction between 'hacking' and arbitrage-seeking by traders in situations where incentive design has been poorly thought through. Referring to the Terra de-pegging, she wrote (Kaminska, 2022):

> What's really cute is that the crypto community is referring to the unstitching of the peg as a hacker style 'attack' on the stablecoin. But by all accounts the 'exploit' was simply the unpicking of a poorly constructed value system through a legitimate arbitrage-exploiting exercise… I love that the worlds of crypto and finance have now collided in such a way that we can finally expose everyone engaged in arbitrage hunting, from Paulson to Soros, as nothing more than a hacker.
>
> (Of course there is an element of truth to this. Good traders look for bad value assumptions or vulnerabilities in current arbitrage mechanics. They then exploit them and make squillions. This is seen as an exercise in making the market more efficient in the long run. As a result, I think this fusing of terminologies tells us more about how we view computer hacking than it does trading. If most hackers — at least those who don't depend on social engineering or disinfo — are just arbitrage hunters, it's fair to say they have gotten a bit of a bad rap for exposing vulnerabilities and making the market more efficient. Though, I guess, that's the point of offering hacker bounties in penetration testing environments.)

Hacks, heists and other disasters

Unlike depositing your money in a bank savings account or an ISA, investing in DeFi protocols is a high-risk venture. When something goes wrong – as frequently happens – there is no government-backed insurance scheme ready to compensate you. For comparison, while bank failures in Britain are a relatively rare occurrence, the Financial Services Compensation Scheme is designed to pay back the first £85,000 of any individual's savings in the case of a bank collapse. Of course, it is entirely possible to buy shares whose value falls to zero, to suffer the erosion of savings caused by inflation or to save into a pension scheme that fails or to fall victim to a scam whose perpetrators are acting outside the law, but the underlying message is that money deposited in a regulated savings scheme is safe and will be returned to you in the unlikely case of company failure.

If you have this expectation and you see influencers and friends buying tokens with their cash and depositing them in DeFi savings protocols, then it is likely that you may not think too deeply about what happens if things go wrong. Making yourself aware of these risks is crucial, however, for anyone wanting to interact with DeFi technology, and also for businesses deciding to offer these services to their own customers. In the brief history of DeFi, many tens of millions of dollars have been lost to theft or unproven, experimental computer code.

It is probably true to say that a system becomes more resilient as its participants learn from bad experiences, but that is little comfort to people who have lost their life savings – or, worse, have ended up heavily indebted after borrowing to invest in the latest 'sure thing'. In 2021, DeFi investors lost more than $10 billion to theft and fraud, according to crypto analysts Elliptic.

Two of the three biggest DeFi hacks in history (one on the Wormhole bridge and the other on the Axie Infinity play-to-earn game, targeting the bridge to its Ronin side chain) demonstrated that bridges – the intersection point between different networks – are still a very difficult area to get right. $326 million was lost in the first exploit, while an eye-watering $620 million disappeared in the Axie Infinity hack (Kharif, 2022). See Table 5.1 for more.

TABLE 5.1 DeFi hacks in order of severity

Name of technology hacked	Type of technology	Sum lost ($)	Date of hack
Ronin	Bridge	615.5m	March 2022
Poly Network	Bridge(s)	602m	August 2021
Wormhole	Bridge	326m	February 2022
Beanstalk	Stablecoin protocol	181m	April 2022
Compound	Lending protocol	150m	October 2021
Vulcan Forged	Gaming studio	140m	December 2021

There is rarely a story in DeFi – or within crypto in general – that is totally straightforward, and the Poly Network hack, in which $611 million was drained, is a case in point. In a rare case of a hack with a happy ending, the Poly team reached out to the hacker and negotiated a solution where the hacker explained that they were merely trying to teach the team a security lesson, before returning the stolen funds.

Perhaps nothing underlines the huge gulf between DeFi and traditional finance as much as the open letter the Poly Network team released on Twitter in an attempt to contact the perpetrator, which began with the infamous salutation: Dear Hacker…' (Pearson, 2021).

CASE STUDY
The collapse of the terra ecosystem

The de-pegging of the TerraUSD (UST) stablecoin is an event discussed several times in this book. It is hard to overemphasize the negative impact it had on the perception of DeFi – and of algorithmic stablecoins in particular. While it was happening, and in the short period directly afterwards, there were many rumours and accusations flying around on social media that the large UST liquidations that triggered the beginning of the de-pegging event were part of an orchestrated attack by two large financial companies. This did not turn out to be the case. Even if this had been true, one could reasonably argue that the possibility of such purchases should have been foreseen, and that the algorithm underlying UST should have been battle-tested and resilient enough to withstand them.

When committing funds, time, integration efforts or reputation to a project like this, it is always crucial to bear in mind that most of this technology is being used in a particular context for the first time, and, rather like a rocket launch that has not been attempted before, the consequences may not all be foreseen.

Knowledge and education challenges

Established businesses and fintechs alike need to tread a fine line when deciding to provide access to DeFi protocols via their apps and platforms. The growing market of younger millennials and Gen Zs, who are open-minded about crypto and who have either dabbled in DeFi themselves or who have heard friends and influencers talking about it, will ultimately drive demand for these integrations.

If companies miss out on the chance to offer these integrations as part of a unified financial portal, they are likely to be beaten by crypto companies moving further into the fintech space. However, any company working in TradFi is likely to face considerable barriers to adoption: not simply technical hurdles, but issues arising from concerns around reputation, or from lack of knowledge among their product teams.

Ioana Surpateanu feels that there are pockets of understanding but that these people are in a minority:

> I don't think there is sufficient understanding of DeFi within TradFi, at scale. There are various teams within very relevant traditional financial services entities that do understand crypto, but in a more generic fashion. And some teams are equipped with DeFi experts, but it's small teams of people compared to the overall magnitude of that specific institution.

Hanan Nor sees the human side to this hesitancy:

> People worry about their jobs. They can be very keen at innovating to a certain extent, but that extent is one in which their jobs will still be protected.
>
> So, if someone is a head of digital, for example, and they're developing a new app, that does something like a faster approval process in a bank account, then that is good in their books. But if someone else comes in and says, oh, we can encourage people to buy cryptocurrency and it's an app in an area in which they have no knowledge of and which they have to take responsibility for, that is a risk to their career.

Risks around technology and integration

Challenges in integrating DeFi services into traditional apps and platforms is not simply a matter of psychology, however, or encouraging financial service employees to take a deeper, more crypto-native interest in the sector. There are very real technical challenges associated with integrating blockchain-based products into Web 2.0 products and services.

Most developers are used to dealing with systems in which there are service-level agreements (SLAs) about up time, and where transactions are instantaneous because they are simply recorded in a single, centralized database. It can also be difficult to make decisions about which blockchain to use, or whether to use a Layer 2 solution, in a world where technology moves at lightning speed.

The typical lifespan of a technology project within a bank or traditional financial services institution can be many months or even years, and may need to go through multiple layers of approval by different management teams. Many are not capable of mounting a rapid response in a situation where a more suitable network may emerge, or where technical issues may make using a particular blockchain uneconomic.

Dealing with the latency of blockchain transactions and developing solutions for situations where transaction fees can fluctuate are relatively new challenges. Deciding whether to provide custodial wallet services or instead educate users on the need to deal with securing their own decentralized wallets is another pain point. Once a company goes down the custodial route, this suddenly means a return to the same kind of centralized architecture and protective security systems that banks have traditionally provided.

There may also be issues recruiting software engineers in large enough numbers. Many blockchain-specialist developers are used to living the life of digital nomads, and salaries that are considerably inflated by token incentives, and are not as easily lured into a corporate lifestyle where their physical presence may still be demanded on site.

Product challenges

Creating user-friendly interfaces is another major pain point when developing products that integrate with any kind of decentralized finance service. The 'move fast and break things' approach of current DeFi projects relies on a willing audience prepared to learn new skills and operate at the bleeding edge of technology that may not always work correctly – yet these people are a tiny minority compared with the general population who are busy with their work and families and who just want financial products that work for them with the minimum of fuss.

Sometimes it seems that the target users of crypto products – and DeFi protocols in particular – are prepared to endure significant inconvenience and put in place different technical workarounds in order to ensure that their experience is as decentralized as possible. For the vast majority of mainstream users, however, convenience is king, and decentralization may be an unfamiliar concept, and one for which no one is particularly willing to make sacrifices.

One anonymous source highlights the need for a user-friendly experience that is currently lacking with existing DeFi products:

> A lot of people don't understand the current financial system. They don't really understand how the bank works or where their money is being stored. Most people just don't care about these things. They don't want the hassle of managing their own money end to end because it can slowly become a full-time job, especially if you have a bigger portfolio. So, one of the hurdles to that adoption is essentially producing products that are easy enough to use and also feed into more generalized use-cases.

Ala Haddad, a Web3 strategy specialist, agrees that one of the biggest hurdles to adoption, both among retail investors and within the financial industry, is lack of knowledge – and a certain reluctance to make the effort to learn about something that is totally new:

> It's such a shift in paradigm that no one is really one willing to put in the time to learn, at least from my experience, or think it's too complicated to learn about it. People really don't care about the technology. They don't care about the revolution. They don't care about how it works. They just see it as a way of making money by investing in it rather than making money by actually doing or building things. I always recommend people to go down the rabbithole and learn about how things work: get a wallet and buy an NFT or whatever instead of just jumping onto Binance and buying different coins.

For TradFi companies to take full advantage of the opportunities available from integrating DeFi services into their products, it is therefore likely that they will need to hire specialized resources or rely on existing team members to voluntarily sink a significant amount of personal development time into researching and experimenting with decentralized products in order to bring their knowledge up to the standard of crypto-native users.

Conversely, new hires entering traditional companies from crypto may find themselves lacking knowledge in the administrative, regulatory or process aspects of their new environment and will have to adjust their expectations.

Systemic risk

The Bank of International Settlements (BIS) released a paper in December 2021 that highlighted concerns around high leverage and liquidity mismatches, as well as the interconnected nature of the DeFi system (Aramonte, Huang and Schrimpf, 2021). It makes some interesting general points about the current degree of centralization and the illusion of decentralization, which it argues applies to most protocols at the moment.

The paper notes that, while the relatively small size of the sector and the small number of on/off ramps and other intersection points between CeFi and DeFi mean that contagion to traditional markets is for now limited, stablecoins are a particular area of concern. Specific concerns around stablecoins focus on the risk of a stablecoin having to sell its reserve assets, thus triggering funding shocks for corporates and banks that could ripple out to the wider financial system.

The future of DeFi as an integral part of the financial system

As we will see in Chapter 8, regulation is a key piece of the jigsaw that makes up the integrated fintech and DeFi landscape. Regulatory arbitrage for DeFi founders is not necessarily about choosing jurisdictions with the most lenient or lax regulations but about choosing places to do business where governments are prepared to allocate time and effort into researching solutions that will be permanent and resilient. Founders need certainty more than anything else, and there are few things more dispiriting than pouring resources into hiring staff and establishing a base in a country on the understanding that crypto regulations have been well thought through – only to discover a few months down the line that someone is about to propose a hasty and badly-thought-through new piece of legislation, often as a knee-jerk reaction to something or other.

In my view, and in the view of many people I have interviewed, the integration of certain elements of DeFi into traditional financial services is more likely than not least because the genie is now out of the bottle, and younger, crypto-native users are pushing for these products.

The big question is who will provide these new integrated products: existing firms within the fintech or banking space – or crypto start-ups themselves, with their rapid-response and agile development teams, who are leveraging open banking in order to provide new types of applications where users can switch between fiat currencies, tokens, shares and DeFi positions with fluency and easy on/off ramps.

What is also clear from talking to insiders and reading research papers is that DeFi needs to be integrated into user-facing apps in a manner that reflects its decentralized nature and spells out the risks. A banking app that offers government-guaranteed savings accounts on one side and on the other a high-APY on a stablecoin staked on a DeFi savings protocol with no commensurate guarantees, for example, would be sowing the seeds of confusion.

Mitigations might include providing self-custodial wallets where passphrases are split into parts and held by third parties who could help with recovery, and also the implementation of best practices, coding standards and custodial conventions to limit the damage that can be caused by hackers and thieves. Price volatility is something that is difficult to guard against, although if stablecoins work as they have been designed to do – in other words, not how TerraUSD worked – then this in itself is a useful mitigating factor.

In the meantime, while retail users are accessing these protocols directly, it is worth looking at how technical risk is currently managed.

Insurance, bug bounties and audits

As we have seen, the number of security researchers and developers capable of carrying out audits on very complex systems is tiny – and that is why most reputable blockchain audit companies currently have a long waiting list for audits to be carried out. Also, while a successful audit, with developers having fixed all non-trivial bugs discovered in the process, shows good intent and that a certain amount of due diligence has been followed, it is in no way a guarantee that the protocol is bullet-proof.

An audit can reveal that developers are competent and have followed reasonable best practices, but it cannot necessarily reveal what will happen in particular market conditions, or where a trader is using other protocols to stack different loans and transactions in a configuration that would amount to an attack.

In addition to using open-source code in development, it is common for crypto projects to open-source testing, too, in the form of bug bounties. Bug bounties are a great way to provide incentives for white-hat hackers (benevolent security specialists) to find loopholes in projects' contracts in return for substantial rewards. (Table 5.2 shows a list of bug bounty platforms, both Web3-specific and more general.)

Some of these rewards can be millions of dollars. While this may seem excessive to outsiders, it is a sign of a project that values security and is prepared to pay for specialist knowledge. The popular Ethereum Layer 2 network Polygon paid out $2 million in rewards for the discovery of a bug

TABLE 5.2 Bug bounty platforms

Name	Web3 specialist?
HackerOne	No
BugCrowd	No
ImmuneFi	Yes
HackenProof	Yes
SafeHats	No
Hats.finance	Yes

that would have cost them $85 million. The Wormhole bridge project paid $10 million for the detection of a bug that would have fatally locked up potentially hundreds of millions of funds – earning kudos from the community for fixing the bug the same day.

For observers who are not used to seeing projects asking for crowd-sourced help like this, the approach may seem unsettling and chaotic. In fact, bugs that are discovered in this way and fixed transparently, rather than being hidden away behind layers of secrecy, are the key to developing a public, trustless system that works for everyone.

Conclusion

We have been looking at these issues through a prism of traditional corporate structures and conventions because this is the system with which most people are familiar. We have seen that, while an absence of clarity around DeFi regulation is a risk for institutions, in that it may lead to inadvertent non-compliance, it is only one of many risks, including: the hazards implicit in working with new technology that has not been fully battle-tested, unpredictable transaction fees if using public blockchains, and the challenges of interfacing with software that is community-governed rather than supplied by a traditional partner.

A lack of education among investors is undoubtedly one of the greatest challenges in DeFi, along with the technological hurdles that are inherent in scaling blockchains. However, it is not simply the technical differences between blockchains and other types of data structure that bring challenges to mainstream understanding of DeFi: a major obstacle is the gap in understanding how decisions are made in a decentralized context, and the mechanics of how billions of dollars of value can end up deposited in networks that are governed by the votes of disparate groups of individuals.

The next chapter takes a closer look at the incentive models coded into DeFi projects and what these mean for decision-making processes. Many such projects are run by DAOs – decentralized autonomous organizations – so we also examine the tokenomics that underlie DAOs.

References

Aramonte, S, Huang, W, and Schrimpf, A (2021) 'DeFi risks and the decentralisation illusion', BIS: https://www.bis.org/publ/qtrpdf/r_qt2112b.htm (archived at https://perma.cc/D5JD-3JSC)

Copeland, T (2022) 'Build Finance DAO suffers "hostile governance takeover," loses \$470,000', *The Block*: www.theblock.co/post/134180/build-finance-dao-suffers-hostile-governance-takeover-loses-470000 (archived at https://perma.cc/5853-WXW9)

Haig, S (2022) 'MakerDAO may execute "emergency shutdown" if sanctions hit DAI', *The Defiant*: https://thedefiant.io/tornado-impact-makerdao-dai (archived at https://perma.cc/PC26-NEGU)

Irwin, K (2022) 'Yuga Labs sees \$561 million in Otherside Ethereum NFT sales within 24 hours', *Decrypt*: https://decrypt.co/99156/yuga-labs-sees-561-million-in-otherside-ethereum-nft-sales-within-24-hours (archived at https://perma.cc/F5FP-TFNA)

Kaminska, I (2022) 'In the Blind Spot (Terra, diesel, cartels)', *The Blind Spot*: https://the-blindspot.com/in-the-blind-spot-terra-diesel-cartels/ (archived at https://perma.cc/XJ9H-C69D)

Kharif, O (2022) 'Axie-Infinity developer to reimburse hack victims, restart Ronin', Bloomberg: www.bloomberg.com/news/articles/2022-06-23/axie-infinity-developer-to-reimburse-hack-victims-restart-ronin#:~:text=Hackers%20stole%20173%2C600%20Ether%20and,since%20the%20attack%20took%20place (archived at https://perma.cc/F5Z6-FHK3)

Pearson, J (2021) '"Dear Hacker": crypto platform begs for money back after losing \$600m', *Vice*: www.vice.com/en/article/v7ejxx/dear-hacker-crypto-platform-begs-for-money-back-after-losing-dollar600m (archived at https://perma.cc/ZL5A-P6H8)

Further reading

Benson, Jeff, 'DeFi users lost $10.5 billion to theft and fraud in 2021, mostly on Ethereum: report', *Decrypt*, 20 November 2021: https://decrypt.co/86503/defi-users-lost-billion-theft-fraud-2021-mostly-ethereum-report (archived at https://perma.cc/889W-6EA7)

Cuming, Reid, 'Compound Treasury Receives S&P credit rating', *Medium*, 9 May 2022: https://medium.com/compound-finance/compound-treasury-sp-credit-rating-897aff3a6f8c (archived at https://perma.cc/Y5E3-P6HF)

Genç, Ekin and Graves, Stephen, '13 biggest DeFi hacks and heists', *Decrypt*, 19 April 2022: https://decrypt.co/93874/biggest-defi-hacks-heists (archived at https://perma.cc/4UGD-PU9P)

06

DAOs: decentralized autonomous organizations

CHAPTER OBJECTIVES

- Learn about the history of DAOs
- Understand how DAOs differ from traditional organizational models
- Recap the 2016 DAO hack
- Learn about five different types of DAO
- Understand how governance issues complicate DeFi DAOs
- Understand DAO vulnerabilities
- Learn about working for a DAO

We touched on governance risks in the previous chapter. Let's now dig into these in more detail. Many DeFi networks and applications are not owned and administered by traditional companies but by a loose federation of individuals and organizations whose roles, rules and decision-making processes are encoded in smart contracts. These are generally known as DAOs – decentralized autonomous organizations.

How this governance works – and who is ultimately responsible for the software – is a topic that constantly recurs in DeFi. Even if the rules of a protocol are encoded in computer code that runs on servers all over the world, that protocol is still centralized if one person – or one organization – is responsible for setting these rules and is able to update the software to enforce new rules.

Traditional organizations and companies operate according to decisions that are made by people working in a hierarchical structure. Less important decisions are devolved, but the important decisions are usually taken by the person or people at the top. One of the primary goals of these decisions is, often, to represent the interests of the shareholders, and these interests may or may not align with those of customers or employees.

While, certainly in the case of publicly traded companies, activist investors can influence decision-making, most of the choices that determine a company's direction are taken by different levels of management, depending on the importance and complexity of the decision. We are so used to the idea of top-down hierarchies, where the person at the top of the pyramid makes the big decisions and is reputationally – if not financially – liable for them, that it is sometimes hard to imagine an alternative model. CEOs in these traditional corporations become associated in public opinion with the fortunes of the companies themselves, with the result that a change of management can send a share price shooting up and down. Think of the power that Elon Musk wields at the helm of Tesla, for example.

What is a DAO and how does it differ from traditional company models?

The concept of a DAO radically challenges the way decision-making happens in traditional corporations, whether these are small, private, limited-liability companies or billion-dollar multinationals whose shares are traded on one of the big stock exchanges.

DAOs can be considered as a kind of cooperative, whose initial rules are encoded in software and whose subsequent decision-making is carried out by votes made by community members (usually the holders of the cryptographic tokens that denote membership of the DAO). We look at different voting strategies later in the chapter. These are important because simple 'one token – one vote' rules can easily lead to a concentration of power in the hands of one party whose interests may not be aligned with those of the DAO as a whole.

DAOs usually administer work or tasks that cannot be carried out by software alone – for example, community management or planning new development work – and so their encoded rules need to allow for the delegation of certain jobs to individuals or other organizations. In a world where corporations are the default, the notion that projects can be run by communities whose rules are specified and voting facilitated by nothing more than code running on computers can be a hard one to grasp.

Of course, it is not quite as simple as that may seem. DAOs are an emerging idea, and, as with any emerging technology or social innovation, sometimes ambition can outstrip reality and things can go disastrously wrong.

This chapter looks specifically at DAOs: how they work, what they are used for and how they fit into existing legal and regulatory structures, particularly in the context of DeFi. We also look at some success stories, and other case studies where DAOs have caused more problems than they have solved.

Despite the challenges they have faced, it seems unlikely that DAOs are going to vanish, so it is worth understanding the underlying principles of decentralized governance and tokenomics that enable them to function.

The history of DAOs

DAOs are not a new idea. The idea of intelligent organizations running entirely according to software-based rules is one that has cropped up repeatedly in science fiction, from the *Culture* series by Iain M Banks to Neal Asher's *Polity* books. Of course, artificial intelligence is not yet at the stage where it is capable of running even a single factory on its own with no human intervention, let alone running a corporation or an entire society. Hence we can think of DAOs as a staging post along a continuum from a traditional company to an organization run entirely by software.

In other words, the process may be largely automated and the rules set in advance and encoded in software-based rules, but today's DAOs work on decisions that are made by humans. As we shall see in this chapter, this has its own advantages – and disadvantages.

Other than in the pages of novels, the origin of DAOs was prefigured by internet pioneer John Perry Barlow in his seminal 1996 'Declaration of the Independence of Cyberspace', in which he stated, 'Cyberspace consists of transactions, relationships, and thought itself.' This abstract sentence encapsulates the idea that somehow the peer-to-peer nature of the internet would enable a new type of structure, completely different from the hierarchical organization that has been prevalent throughout human society.

This early idealism of course proved to be optimistic, as large corporations began to take control of the internet, which had originally been envisaged as a liberating, peer-to-peer and equalizing technology. However, with the invention of a peer-to-peer payment system in the form of Bitcoin, came a new hope that decentralized technologies would bring a return to these early possibilities.

A 2014 blog post by Vitalik Buterin, the creator of Ethereum, shows that he was thinking deeply about the opportunities that smart contracts would open up for creating these new organizational structures. He writes of a DAO as an 'entity that lives on the internet and exists autonomously, but also heavily relies on hiring individuals to perform certain tasks that the automaton itself cannot do'.

Collaboration in pursuit of a common goal

Just as DeFi enables financial transactions between individuals who do not need to know each other's identity, so DAOs allow strangers to collaborate in pursuit of a common goal without having to know and trust each other.

In his 2014 post, Buterin draws an interesting distinction between DAOs and DACs (decentralized autonomous companies):

> There is a concept of shares in a DAC which are purchasable and tradeable in some fashion, and those shares potentially entitle their holders to continual receipts based on the DAC's success. A DAO is non-profit; though you can make money in a DAO, the way to do that is by participating in its ecosystem and not by providing investment into the DAO itself. Obviously, this distinction is a murky one; all DAOs contain internal capital that can be owned, and the value of that internal capital can easily go up as the DAO becomes more powerful/popular, so a large portion of DAOs are inevitably going to be DAC-like to some extent.

As Buterin states, the idea of internal capital is fundamental to most DAOs in the early 2020s. Many are designed purely as investment vehicles that enable individuals to pool their assets and have attracted huge inward flows of capital. The Ethereum Foundation (2022) lists three purposes of a DAO:

- Member-owned communities without centralized leadership
- A safe way to collaborate with internet strangers
- A safe place to commit funds to a specific cause.

The third point is the most frequent use-case for DAOs within DeFi, enabling individuals to accumulate funds in a smart contract and allowing members to vote on proposals for investments, grants or other purposes. These DAOs are, in a sense, the institutional investors of DeFi, whose size and investment capability gives them great power. Take BitDAO, for example, with $2.5 billion under management and investors who include Peter Thiel and Alan Howard. In this definition, the phrase 'to a specific cause' is doing some heavy lifting, as the specific cause for most DAOs is to increase the wealth of its particpants rather than some loftier purpose.

The 2016 DAO hack and its impact

It is only since 2020 that DAOs have again become a hot topic, after the first well-publicized attempt ended in abject failure.

The original DAO, whose smart contract was deployed and hacked in 2016, had, for some years, such a negative connotation that few people were willing to risk being associated with something similar. The infamous hack not only lost investors huge sums of money, but also almost brought down the entire Ethereum ecosystem. It is entirely possible that, without these dramatic events, the development of DAOs would have progressed much faster, although it is also fair to say that valuable lessons were learned along the way.

In her excellent book *The Cryptopians* (2022), Laura Shin presents a gripping, hour-by-hour account of the DAO hack, pieced together from the first-person stories of those at the centre of the drama. In order to understand both the opportunities and risks of DAOs as they exist today, it is worth revisiting the events of 2016. (See Figure 6.1 for some of the key dates.)

The world's first decentralized autonomous organization was launched, with great excitement in the Ethereum community, on 30 April 2016. It was

FIGURE 6.1 Timeline of the DAO hack

designed as a kind of decentralized venture capital fund, where participants could buy DAO ERC20 tokens (issued at the rate of 100 DAO per Ether) in exchange for the right to vote on whether a portion of these collective funds should be allocated to support specific projects.

Of course, many people who eagerly deposited their Ether in the smart contract in exchange for DAO tokens did so in the hope that the value of DAO tokens would rise and make them a fortune, rather than because they necessarily believed in the grand philosophical principles underlying the idea. No one knew, however, that, when the DAO contract was deployed, there was a fatal programming error lurking within its lines of code.

Within six weeks, 14 per cent of the entire Ether supply, worth $150 million at the time, had been sent to the DAO, but, on 17 June 2016, disaster struck. An unknown attacker managed to exploit a coding error and was able to withdraw $70 million worth of Ether. For many observers, the bug seemed obvious in retrospect – although as all software professionals know, it is easy to be wise in hindsight. One fundamental mistake in the smart contract code meant that users were able to withdraw the same funds over and over again – as though you could withdraw the same $100 from your bank balance many times without your bank account ever being debited.

Perhaps in some respects life would have been easier for the Ethereum community if the funds had been stolen and a line could have been drawn under the whole sorry affair. Lessons would have been learned, and, while the Ethereum ecosystem would have suffered a body blow and a temporary hit to the price, everyone could have moved on. However, written into the DAO code was a safety mechanism that specified that any withdrawn funds should be frozen for 28 days. This meant that the hacker could not spirit them away to a wallet or an exchange, and instead they remained in limbo while a heated debate ensued about what action should be taken.

In *The Cryptopians*, Laura Shin presents a fascinating inside story of the conversations that were happening behind closed doors, but the open nature of crypto development, particularly in 2016, meant that much of the conversation happened in public developer forums or even on Reddit.

Evaluating the fallout from the hack

Reading these posts several years later is a salient reminder of the ethical issues that ensue when technical discussions become tangled in the financial interests of those taking the decisions. Many of those who had bought tokens were long-term Ethereum enthusiasts, including developers who had direct responsibility for contributing to Ethereum's code and technical underpinnings. The public nature of the debate also meant that even where those responsible did not themselves risk losing many thousands of dollars, the flow of desperate and often aggressive messages from DAO investors aimed at the decision-makers also took its toll.

With the deployment of one faulty smart contract, a problem that had initially been one for the DAO developers to solve spilled over into the wider Ethereum community. After a less invasive solution proved impossible, it became clear that the only way to clean up the mess was to make a change to Ethereum's code that would reverse the hack. It was a straightforward choice between doing nothing or implementing a hard fork where the offending transactions would be rewritten to divert the stolen Ether to a refund wallet.

For a protocol that was supposed to be decentralized, and whose value was derived from the immutability of transactions written into the blockchain, this was hugely contentious. The entire Ethereum community – everyone who held Ether – was invited to vote on the proposal, and a furious debate raged on social media.

The group who favoured taking no action felt that, as Ethereum's primary purpose was to provide an immutable, trusted record and that the quote 'Code is law' had been frequently employed as a shorthand for the reliability of smart contracts, then the existing state of the blockchain should be respected and events should be allowed to take their course. The faction who wanted to restore investors' funds and confiscate them from the hacker argued that the ecosystem was evolving, that code was not yet law, however much that remained an aspiration, and that more reputational damage would be done to Ethereum if attempts were not made to remedy the situation and recoup investors' money.

After an anxious period, the vote to restore funds won the day and the blockchain was forked. However, when the new version of Ethereum's software was released, a proportion of individuals who remained ethically opposed to the fork continued mining and transacting on the older version of the software. In practical terms, this meant that there were now two Ethereum currencies, sharing a common history up until the moment they diverged. 'New' Ethereum continued to use the exchange ticker code ETH, while Ethereum Classic, as the original version of the code was quickly dubbed, gained the code ETC. The fork caused much argument and bad feeling at the time, but ETC has continued to thrive, albeit on a smaller scale, and more than two years on, software updates are regularly released that keep Ethereum Classic interoperable with Ethereum.

Users who held Ethereum at the time of the fork now had the same amount of ETH and ETC. This might sound like it was a great way of making money out of thin air, but in fact the whole DAO hard-fork debacle had hit the Ethereum price so badly that Ethereum holders were out of pocket overall.

The aftermath of the hack – and new beginnings

The shadow of the DAO hack hung over the crypto community for some time afterwards, so inextricably linked was the acronym with the hack. However, as decentralized finance began to proliferate, so did the need for new ways of organizing and incentivizing people to work together for a common goal.

It is probably true that many DAOs as they exist today are little more than a smokescreen for a small group of committed individuals working on a project in the same way they would if contracted by a typical company. There might be occasional decisions devolved to community governance, which generally means an outer ring of enthusiasts and token-holders communicating via a medium such as Discord, but with important decisions still made by founders or a small handful of core developers. Such a situation is often disparagingly cited as 'decentralization theatre'.

There is, however, a valid argument for what is known as 'progressive decentralization', where initial decisions are taken by a smaller group and the project is gradually farmed out to a wider community. We will consider this later, but first let's look at some examples of DAOs that have sprung up in the last couple of years, and their different uses.

DAOs for different purposes

A DAO simply provides a technology-assisted way of coordinating human decision-making. While the financialized element (owning tokens that represent voting rights) has so far meant that the majority of DAOs tend to be focused on investment funds or financial enterprises (hence the inclusion of this chapter in a book about DeFi), a DAO structure can be used as effectively to administer a social club or community enterprise as a lending protocol or decentralized exchange. Figure 6.2 gives examples of some better-known DAOs and what they were created to do.

FIGURE 6.2 DAO examples

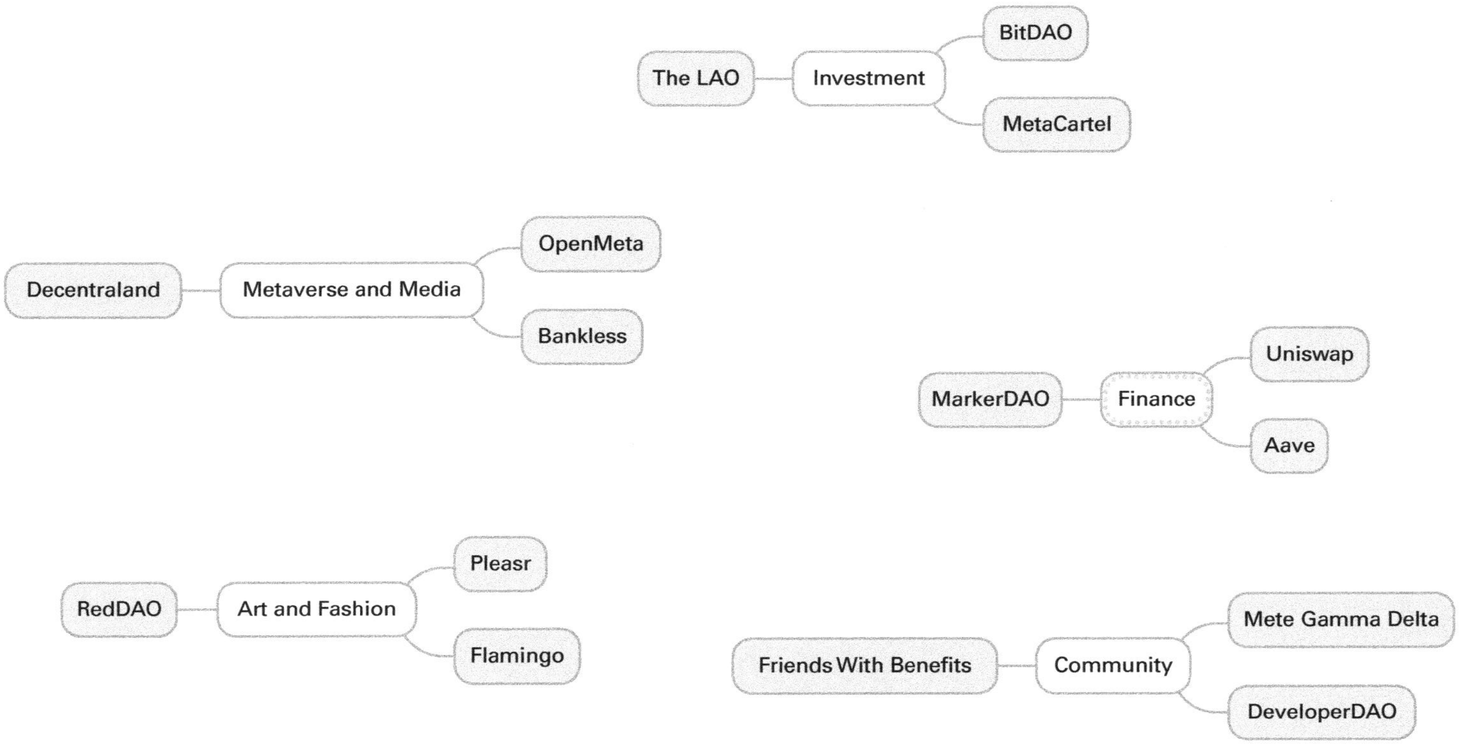

Investment: BitDAO

With a treasury of more than $1 billion, BitDAO is somewhere between an accelerator and an investment fund. Its purpose is to provide capital across industries, blockchains and products. With a list of high-profile founders and backers including Peter Thiel, holders of the DAO's Bit token can have their say on how treasury funds are allocated, thus potentially benefiting from any increase in the value of the projects invested in, as well as the value of the Bit token itself.

NFT investment: Pleasr

The next chapter looks in detail at non-fungible tokens (NFTs) and the points at which these interface with decentralized finance, but it is worth mentioning here that the growth in NFTs – and particularly the involvement of large corporations and celebrities – was one of the big stories of 2021–2022.

Along with this upsurge in interest came an exponential increase in the market capitalization of NFTs, particularly artwork, and this in turn opened the door for specialist funds that allowed individuals who could not afford to buy well-known art themselves, to pool their assets into a smart contract that collectively owned NFTs. With members that include Wikipedia founder Jimmy Wales, Pleasr was designed primarily to collect artworks of cultural significance. A detail that illustrates the interconnected nature of crypto networks is that BitDAO is an investor in Pleasr.

Fashion NFTs: RedDAO

Fashion NFTs are a subset of this fast-growing world. With a projection that as much as 15 per cent of clothing fashion will be primarily digital by 2030, there is a possibility that fashion NFTs minted now may accrue value in future, as they become vintage finds in their own right.

The purpose of the DAO is to support the emerging world of digital wearables and fashion by investing in items and maintaining an archive of these purchases. RedDAO is heavily focused on active membership, with a weekly community call, and includes fashion writers and industry figures among its initial 45 members.

Metaverse: Decentraland

One of the prime locations where you might find yourself wearing digital fashion is in one of the many blockchain-enabled virtual worlds that include Decentraland, the Sandbox and CryptoVoxels.

While Decentraland was conceptualized by Esteban Ordano and Ariel Meilich, decisions relating to its development and ownership are now taken by the Decentraland DAO, which votes on such matters as deciding which businesses and locations should be added to the map, and which wearables should be added to the wearables registry.

Single-purpose DAOs: Constitution DAO

Smart contracts provide lightweight and easy-to-use tools for managing a pool of funds contributed by strangers on the internet, which means that they are particularly useful for one-off purchases, whether these are successful or not.

Constitution DAO shot into the headlines in 2021 when it raised $42 million for the sole purpose of buying the original copy of the US Constitution. Ultimately it failed in its glorious mission, and those who contributed were able to claim a full refund. Critics of the project pointed out that one of the likely reasons for the project's failure was that other bidders knew in advance what the DAO's maximum bid would be, because of the fundamental transparency of public blockchains. However, this does not negate the fact that the DAO proved the case for crowdfunding and collective enterprise in this way.

Community enterprise

Community enterprise is more of a speculative use-case than a concrete example, but, in future, it is entirely likely that DAOs – or similar organizations – will be a suitable mechanism for orchestrating and administering non-profit community enterprises such as shops and pubs. (I expand on this idea in an essay published by the Nesta foundation, in which I write about ideas such as volunteers being able to build up stakes in community enterprises and why legislating for these new structures could be socially useful: Lewis, 2020.)

The idea that rules written into code can provide an out-of-the-box framework for people of like mind to club together in situations where money is involved is a compelling one – and one that has seen great traction in Web3.

Women-focused groups such as Meta Gamma Delta (funding Web3 projects built by women) and HerDAO have created strong networks and friendships, while DeveloperDAO and the GitCoin DAO focus on educating Web3 developers and funding useful projects.

Tech entrepreneur Balaji Srinivasan takes this idea one step further with his book *The Network State*, in which he describes how groups of people might ultimately come together digitally to create whole new countries, with a view to buying land and establishing themselves as nation states.

DeFi DAOs: Uniswap and Compound

Finally, and most importantly, we come to the primary use of DAOs today: within DeFi. Most of the leading decentralized protocols, such as Uniswap and Compound, are run by a DAO. For those from a traditional finance background, it can be challenging to accept the idea that billions of dollars of value can be stored in software whose code is not only visible to the outside world, but which is administered by a group of people, often anonymous, who sometimes have no further qualification than simply owning whichever tokens are issued by the protocol.

As we see in the section on voting mechanisms later, DAOs only work if careful attention is focused from the beginning on encoding the right incentives into the smart contracts that make up the protocol. Game-theory models are often used to predict how users will behave in certain scenarios. The normal process for decision-making in a DAO such as Uniswap is that any qualifying DAO member is able to make a proposal, which is then voted on by other members. It makes fascinating reading to look at the list of recent proposals and the votes attracted on Snapshot. (In the tooling section later, we explain exactly what Snapshot is and why DAOs use it.)

A Uniswap proposal in April 2022 highlights some of the complex decisions taken in the open by token-holders voting on technical and strategic issues.

An earlier vote had approved in principle – in a 'temperature check' – the deployment of Uniswap v3 on Gnosis Chain. Comments on this vote requested more detail on three topics:

- the team who would be carrying out the technical work
- the bridge used to facilitate cross-chain governance for Uniswap v3 on GC
- timelines and logistics for transferring funds relating to the liquidity incentives.

Legal liability and legal standing

As befits an idea that no one owns, has copyrighted or controls, there is no standard definition of a DAO, although I personally like the Gnosis idea that describes it as a *digital cooperative*. There is not even a specific requirement that a DAO needs its own token, although, in principle, most do, in order to facilitate group decision-making and ensure that those voting have skin in the game. The Gnosis idea of a minimum viable DAO being little more than a multi-signature account and a communication channel is an interesting one (Kei, 2021).

While laws around the legal responsibilities of companies and limited-liability entities vary from country to country, it is inaccurate to believe that, because a DAO does not fit the legal definition of a company, it sits entirely outside the rules of a particular jurisdiction. After all, a DAO is far more than just software: it represents the collective ideas and choices of real human beings, who are subject to the rules and regulations of the nation state where they reside.

Although there are influential individuals, such as technologist and futurist Joseph Raczynski, who believe that DAOs will eventually have a place in the real world, rather than being confined to the metaverse or digital world (Raczynski, 2021), this is not currently the case. In order to meet the requirements of the law in particular jurisdictions, DAOs must sometimes make compromises in terms of centralization by setting up limited companies to take on responsibility for certain DAO activities.

This is, in fact, the approach taken with the original and eponymous DAO. While the code itself was transparent and decentralized, provisions were put in place to allow the entity to interface with the real world, including the legal aspects of contracting individuals or companies (known as Contractors) to carry out funded work on its behalf. In order to make these contracts legally enforceable, a limited company (DAO.link) was set up in Switzerland.

In September 2022, the Commodity Futures Trading Commission (CFTC) in the USA sent shockwaves reverberating around the DeFi industry with their federal civil enforcement action against members of the Ooki DAO for running an unlicensed exchange. This included anyone who had ever used their tokens to vote in a DAO governance decision, or who had been involved with the DAO in any way. Whether or not this case and any subsequent action will dampen the enthusiasm of US citizens for getting involved in DAOs in future remains to be seen (CFTC, 2022).

Working for a DAO

Many futurists see DAOs as the future of work, appealing to those of the Generation Z cohort who tend to want more than the inflexible, top-down structure of a traditional organization.

One of the few DAOs that is also incorporated as an LLC (in Vermont) is dOrg. A *Time* interview with four of its employees makes for interesting and eye-opening reading (Chow, 2022). dOrg's legal standing as an LLC means that the legal and accounting duties of salary payments and so on are carried out in the normal way, but for other DAOs it is not so easy.

Payment via a service company, as outlined earlier, is one option, but other DAOs work on a more informal basis where ambassadors (generally responsible for community management and content creation), developers and other contributors are voted into position for a fixed period and rewarded with the native token of the DAO. In this case, it is the contributor's own responsibility to declare the value of the token on their tax return and deal with all associated administrative duties.

Ioana Surpateanu is a fan of DAOs – but only if they are conceptualized and created properly, in such a way that attracts talented people. She cautions that this needs to be done right from the outset:

> You need to have some financial rewards for it, for sharing your knowledge and for supporting a project – especially in this market where we see these fluctuations. The precursor to that should be creating a valuable product that then attracts people for whom you can then build the correct incentive mechanisms to get them involved in the governance process.

She is, however, realistic about the current state of play:

> Unfortunately, aside from some Tier 1 DAOs, the rest are just mimicking what a DAO should be and this is something that sort of the market needs to address and I hope it gets addressed, because I also am fascinated by DAOs and what the power of the community can generate.

Working for a DAO – or several DAOs at the same time – is an increasingly popular way of making money and gaining exposure to the Web3 world. Rachel Black, founder of HaloFi, describes some of the pros and cons:

> There's a whole conversation around how you compensate people in DAOs, and a lot of DAOs are experiencing a situation where there's a few people in the DAO who are doing a disproportionate amount of the work. How do we measure that? There are definitely difficulties here, especially when it is more complex and nuanced work.

She sees a number of potential answers:

> There are different solutions to this – potentially either smaller DAOs or not everything being on chain. On the positive side, if you are working for a DAO, you are given the freedom and autonomy to deliver, which most people would want as an employee. There is a balance between having all decisions made on-chain against people having the flexibility to work in the way they want to.

Negatives of decentralization

One important thing to remember about decentralized technologies, and DAOs in particular, is that this is experimental technology – and where experimental technology and human nature intersect, unforeseen consequences frequently come into play.

Ethical dilemmas

The huge sums of money that are concentrated in many DAOs' treasuries offer a honeypot to anyone who is both smart and unprincipled, and many governance dilemmas revolve around situations where bad actors are not strictly breaking the law, but rather exploiting poorly conceived rule sets.

The same applies when even well-intentioned people decide to do something that may not be in the interests of other DAO members, such as when Fei Labs decided to withdraw from Tribe DAO after an exploit.

Inability to act quickly

When proprietary software is compromised, while fixing it might be a headache for the development team involved, the processes are straightforward. In the case of a DAO, a decision to fix a bug is often subject to the same voting process as adding a new feature. Take the Compound protocol as an example. After $80 million in Comp was sent to the wrong people, the team rushed to patch a fix. But before any fix could be implemented, the protocol required a governance proposal to pass. By the time the community had accepted the fix – seven days after its proposal – the vaults had lost a further $68.8 million. This type of scenario is one of several raised in the DeFi paper by the Bank of International Settlements in 2021, which argued that some degree of centralization is sometimes necessary to provide fast operational decisions (Aramonte, Huang and Schrimpf, 2021).

Taking these issues into account, we can see that decentralization in many cases needs to be a journey rather than fixed at the start, and thus we talk about the concept of 'progressive decentralization', which essentially means that a small group of people take critical decisions at the inception of a project, which is then broadened out to let the wider community take control.

This tendency towards stasis and the barriers in the way of quick decision-making were highlighted in an important post on the MakerDAO forum, by its founder Rune Christensen, where he recommends a detailed road map based on smaller DAOs, named MetaDAOs, and points out the inherent tension between the governance processes and political dynamics involving MakerDAO and the reality of processing real-world financial deals (Christensen, 2022).

What is progressive decentralization?

As a protocol or project moves towards full decentralization, where the community takes on responsibility for decision making, the following elements need to be considered:

- product and technology
- economic sustainability
- ecosystem funding
- treasury management
- community participation
- token distribution

All are crucial for the success of a decentralized project, and, without a handful of dedicated individuals putting in the initial work, a successful product can be hard to coordinate and achieve success in each of these five metrics.

Ioana Surpateanu cautions that it is impossible to create a successful DAO without getting the incentive mechanisms right, and that is why so may fail to attract the required numbers of talented community members to sustain the organization:

> Without the right incentives, either material or in terms of the quality of
> the project that you want to support, then you cannot really get organic
> participation. And I say that with a heavy heart because I know the industry
> very well and have witnessed some DAOs and their operational models can be

extremely centralized and filtered. This applies to many DAOs, aside from the blue chip DAOs, the original ones like Maker and Aave, which were built by people who do genuinely believe in community input.

After all, what does it mean to have a DAO? Some just create a Discord group and they have discussions there or a forum and they put some Snapchat voting systems, they activate those. But the reality is that as an admin, you can filter who participates, you can filter voting proposals. So, I think we have a long way to go. There's this frenzy of creating a DAO for almost everything which kind of defeats the purpose.

She is an advocate for building a product and a community first and progressively decentralizing:

The way that I think DAOs should happen Is that you first need to build a very strong community first. So, you have to have the right product and then the network effects happen and the community is organically being built and then you can move towards a decentralized governance structure.

This means the whole idea is done ethically. The idea is, in time, that you hand over everything to the community, from treasury to product decision making to strategy, decision making, etc. To do this, you need to build the correct incentive mechanisms. They don't always have to be material, but I think in most cases there needs to be a material angle.

Many others emphasize this pragmatic approach, where the idealism of total decentralization is balanced against the need to build a strong product which can later be handed over to the community. Rachel Black points out the advantages of progressive decentralization:

Early on, there may be some benefits to having a smaller team and maybe even more centralized decision making. I think the bigger you become and the more voices there are, it's good at that point if you are maintaining something that's already been built rather than needing to take quick, hard decisions.

Voting mechanisms

Voting within DAOs is generally based on token ownership: the more tokens you own, the more votes you get, thus ensuring that votes are taken by those with skin in the game, rather than random participants or bots. In this way, game theory ensures that the interests of voters remain aligned with those of the DAO as a whole. This does not tell the whole story, however. With huge honeypots at stake, it is important that voting cannot simply be captured by those with the most money, who may take short-term decisions that are not for the long-term benefit of the DAO, or where the DAO is seen to be over-reaching its responsibilities.

A case of the latter occurred with the Solana-based lending protocol Solend, whose DAO came in for severe criticism after a controversial proposal was passed. The proposal recommended that the protocol should simply take over one particular user's account and forcibly liquidate it because the position was so large that a chaotic liquidation could threaten the financial integrity of the protocol itself. The proposal passed, but such was the backlash that a second proposal was later approved that would reverse the outcome of the first and prevent any further proposals along the same lines being approved.

An example of DAO governance going horribly wrong is the Build Finance DAO hostile takeover, where a single entity was able to vote them-selves into power and drain the entire treasury. This is an extreme example, but it shows how important it is to set important voting parameters, such as reaching a quorum.

Stipulating that a certain proportion of token holders must vote may seem like common sense, but, if the quorum is set too high, it may mean that no proposals are ever voted on and the community loses interest in partici-pating. Other solutions include quadratic voting, where one token equals one vote, two votes cost four tokens and three tokens nine, and so on; differ-ent forms of sponsorship, where proposals must be sponsored by a quorum by being voted on; and liquid democracy, where votes are delegated to specialists who are more likely to have the technical knowledge to make informed decisions.

Additionally, there are factors such as the human tendency towards the majority view in a situation where voting preferences are public, as they are on a blockchain or on a tool such as Snapshot.

Lido and Dragonfly: DAO democracy in action

An interesting example of DAO governance working as intended happened in 2022 when a proposal was created in the Lido DAO (Lido is the largest liquid staking protocol in DeFi) to sell more than 1 per cent of Lido's token supply to a venture capital outfit called Dragonfly, on particularly advanta-geous terms for Dragonfly. Dragonfly already held 1.5 per cent of Lido's circulating token supply, so was able to legitimately influence the vote in this direction. However, the proposal, which would have overall been negative in impact for other DAO members, was voted down and a new proposal submitted with more reasonable terms, which later passed.

In summary, DAO governance and voting mechanisms are a highly interesting area of development as decentralization enthusiasts learn by trial and error how to organize themselves.

Mainstream finance interaction with DAOs

DAOs seem like such an unfamiliar idea to many, that it is hard to believe there are already some mainstream financial institutions interacting with them, but this is indeed the case.

While much institutional DeFi has centred on permissioned access to DeFi infrastructure and white-listing participants (for example, J.P. Morgan's Onyx), there have been cases where institutions choose to interact directly with a DAO, such as Huntingdon Valley Bank's decision to open a $100 million stablecoin loan vault with MakerDAO.

Tools and software for DAOs

In order to automate processes as much as possible, and also ensure transparency, DAOs must reduce reliance on human input. Hence, a whole new software-as-a-service sub-sector has sprung up to meet this need, providing management applications that allow DAO members to interface with the organization and contribute to its decision-making. Key areas include:

- treasury management, where multi-signature solutions such as Gnosis Safe are used to ensure that funds allocation cannot be carried out by a single person
- voting interfaces, either on-chain or off-chain (the latter to reduce costs) – Snapshot has become the default solution here for many DAOs
- badges and rewards, where a POAP token or a custom NFT dropped to a DAO member's wallet can provide token-gated access to different subscription services
- automated task-tracking software to validate that a particular task has been completed and can be rewarded, without the bias implicit in human judgement.

Conclusion

This chapter has touched on new governance models and the prospect of a totally different type of organization that could – partially at least – replace many of the roles of established corporations. We have also examined the considerable challenges posed by these newly fledged entities controlling literally billions of dollars of assets.

Chapter 8 explores some of the challenges faced by regulators in devising appropriate rules within their jurisdictions for dealing with software that, to all intents and purposes, runs autonomously on global networks, with no one formally in charge of it. Before then, however, Chapter 7 takes a closer look at a type of investment that we touched on in this chapter: NFTs, both as digital assets in their own right and as a type of proof that gives a person, whether identified or pseudonymous, the right to access particular subscription or membership services.

NFTs are such an important story that they deserve a book in their own right, but in this book we will concentrate on their intersection points with the DeFi system. The next chapter demonstrates why anyone seeking to learn about decentralized finance should understand the basics of NFTs.

References

Aramonte, S, Huang, W and Schrimpf, A (2021) 'DeFi risks and the decentralisation illusion', BIS: www.bis.org/publ/qtrpdf/r_qt2112b.htm (archived at https://perma.cc/6BY2-B7FM)

Barlow, JP (1996) 'A declaration of the independence of cyberspace', Electronic Frontier Foundation: www.eff.org/de/cyberspace-independence (archived at https://perma.cc/9YPL-EHRW)

Buterin, V (2014) 'DAOs, DACs, DAs and more: an incomplete terminology guide', Ethereum Foundation: https://blog.ethereum.org/2014/05/06/daos-dacs-das-and-more-an-incomplete-terminology-guide/ (archived at https://perma.cc/UGF2-4CV7)

CFTC (2022) 'CFTC order finds, and complaint alleges, Ooki DAO is liable as an unincorporated association': www.cftc.gov/PressRoom/PressReleases/8590-22 (archived at https://perma.cc/Q4QC-RTTW)

Chow, A (2022) 'No bosses: what it's like working for a DAO', *Time*: https://time.com/6146406/working-at-dao-dorg/ (archived at https://perma.cc/GV9R-TKXB)

Christensen, R (2022) 'The endgame plan parts 1&2', MakerDAO Forum: https://forum.makerdao.com/t/the-endgame-plan-parts-1-2/15456 (archived at https://perma.cc/9VKE-22WK)

Ethereum Foundation (2022) 'Decentralized autonomous organizations (DAOs)':
https://ethereum.org/en/dao/#main-content (archived at https://perma.cc/4U9X-
ERX7)

Kei (2021) 'A Prehistory of DAOs', Gnosis Guild: https://gnosisguild.mirror.xyz/
t4F5rItMw4-mlpLZf5JQhElbDfQ2JRVKAzEpanyxW1Q (archived at https://
perma.cc/3MWQ-7BWV)

Lewis, R (2020) 'How DAOs can revive local communities', Nesta: www.nesta.org.
uk/report/how-daos-can-revive-local-communities/ (archived at https://perma.cc/
R7TL-KSZ6)

Raczynski, J (2021) 'Buying the Constitution: the rise of DAOs in legal', Thomson
Reuters: www.thomsonreuters.com/en-us/posts/legal/daos-business-structure/
(archived at https://perma.cc/W5TF-BR3V)

Further reading

Longarzo, J (2022) 'Fuse exploit post mortem': https://medium.com/@
JackLongarzo/fuse-exploit-post-mortem-76ce18d8974 (archived at https://
perma.cc/5DCF-RLAZ)

07

NFTs within the DeFi system

CHAPTER OBJECTIVES

- Recap of NFTs and their purpose
- Understand the intersection points between NFTs and DeFi
- Tell the difference between liquidity-position NFTs and other types of token
- Understand token gating
- List ways to raise yield on NFTs
- Learn about GameFi and play-to-earn games
- Understand how DeFi plugs into the metaverse

This is not a book about NFTs (non-fungible tokens) and neither is it a book about the metaverse: there is enough information about these to write a whole series of primers. Rather, in this chapter, it is an attempt to contextualize where NFTs intersect with DeFi.

The recent acquisition by various celebrities of multi-million-dollar digital images meant that NFTs were rarely out of the headlines in 2021 and 2022, but they are far more than a passing fad, as this chapter will illustrate.

Why should anyone working in finance care about NFTs?

There might seem a large distance between topics such as options swaps and collectable digital images rooted in memes and popular culture, but, as discussed in previous chapters, the meme-driven nature of DeFi is a natural fit with the world of NFTs, and the intersection point between DeFi and NFTs is an important topic.

This book has repeatedly drawn parallels between DeFi and the traditional financial system, but, when it comes to NFTs, it becomes more difficult to see a common use-case. If we step back and look at NFTs – especially art NFTs – as a special type of digital asset, in the same way that a painting or a limited-edition print by a desirable artist is a valuable asset in the real world, perhaps the comparison becomes clearer.

Just as art has always been an investment that people have used as collateral in order to raise finance for other purposes, so NFTs are increasingly being used within DeFi. Falling prices throughout 2022 may have meant the celebrity headlines are fewer and further between, but the interoperability of NFTs with decentralized finance means that they can be bought, sold or leveraged just like any other digital asset.

A Chainalysis study in late 2021 revealed that just 1 per cent of NFT transfers in the first three-quarters of 2021 were institutional. The majority were crypto-native institutions, but the $150 million purchase by Visa of a CryptoPunks NFT showed that interest from mainstream financial institutions was present, at least in a nascent form (Shumba, 2021).

The announcement by Mark Zuckerberg's Meta that NFTs would be supported on Instagram – unleashing an audience of more than a billion potential NFT owners – was also significant. The ability of NFTs to plug directly into finance networks and thus act like any other digital asset or store of value is important to understand.

With NFTs from cult collections such as Bored Ape Yacht Club and CryptoPunks changing hands for many millions of dollars, and Beeple's *The First 10,000 Days* selling at Christie's for $69 million, we can see that NFT art offers the same type of collectability as, say, a limited-edition Damien Hirst.

Note that this book does not make a value judgement about the prices paid for particular NFTs nor attempt to draw a parallel between the artistic merit of NFTs and traditional artworks. This chapter is merely an attempt to make sense of why people have paid so much money for them – and how they might use them.

Collectors may buy physical pieces of art for their bragging value or because they enjoy looking at them for their aesthetic merits, but works of art are also bought as investments on the basis that they will maintain or increase their value. However, artworks, antiques and other collectables have a major disadvantage when compared with other types of valuable assets: they are fundamentally illiquid. Their owners cannot easily use them to collateralize the purchase of other assets, or to generate a yield.

NFTs change this, allowing investors – whether individual, institutional or collectives – to plug their digital assets directly into the wider DeFi ecosystem. This may sound abstract, but we look at specific examples in this chapter. Examples also show how NFTs can be used for many different purposes other than as collectables, and how they can be used as a bridge between finance and gaming, finance and the metaverse and even finance and the physical world.

Previous chapters have discussed the Ethereum ecosystem's composability: the standardized rules that mean that DeFi protocols are able to understand and interpret the actions and attributes encoded in any token or smart contract. This means that, just as a DEX such as Uniswap allows users to create liquidity pools with any pair of tokens that adhere to the ERC20 standard (such as the ETH/Dai pair), developers are also able to create protocols that allow interactions with NFTs. In fact, as we saw in Chapter 3, Uniswap's smart contracts create an NFT that the liquidity provider holds in their wallet to prove that they contributed the liquidity to a particular pool.

This is all potentially confusing for anyone not directly involved in the world of cryptocurrencies and decentralized finance, so let's take a step back and remind ourselves exactly what NFTs are, and what problem they were designed to solve.

What *is* an NFT?

We have touched briefly on the cultural phenomenon of non-fungible tokens and how the celebrity-driven trend for buying collectable cartoons and artworks brought a new wave of buyers into the world of digital assets. Of course, NFTs enable far more use-cases than simply enabling the production of differentiated digital collectables. In order to understand some of these use-cases and how NFTs interact with decentralized finance, we first need to understand the mechanism that underlies them.

The remainder of this chapter focuses on examples using Ethereum-based NFTs. Most major networks have their own non-fungible token standard, such as BNB Chain's BEP721 specification, and the same principles apply.

We discussed the difference between fungible and non-fungible tokens and assets in Chapter 1. To recap, 'fungible' is a term used in economics to denote that one unit of a commodity is essentially interchangeable with another unit of the same commodity, and thus has the same value. For example, a grain of corn is pretty much like any other grain of corn, and a tonne of sand is the same as any other tonne of sand. Money is fungible: a dollar bill has the same value as another dollar bill. The same principle applies to gold, oil and many other commodities.

When we look at other potentially valuable assets, however, such as real estate, artworks or antiques, we see that they are not at all interchangeable and do not have the same pricing uniformity as fungible assets. One house may vary from another in its size, location and the desirability of its decor. A Stradivarius violin may be much more expensive than another made in the same year depending on its condition. A landscape on sale in your local high street, painted by a competent artist, is certainly going to be multiples cheaper than a painting by a household name sold at one of the large auction houses.

The principle behind ERC20 tokens is that they are fungible: every token defined in the smart contract is identical. If you sell an item for 20 Dai, any 20 Dai out of the millions that have been generated can be used in payment. In contrast, if you strike a deal with someone to buy their Bored Ape, this token is strictly non-fungible as each Ape has different assets that make it more or less collectable and more or less expensive.

How are NFTs used in DeFi?

There are three main areas where NFTs can be used to interface with DeFi:

1 as collateral (fractionalized or non-fractionalized)
2 for token gating
3 in specific use-cases, such as liquidity-position NFTs.

NFTs as collateral

In Chapter 4, we discussed collateralized loans, and how investors are able to, for example, deposit Ethereum in a smart contract in order to mint Dai, or deposit tokens in exchange for others in order to take advantage of arbitrage opportunities.

We are now beginning to see the growth of specialized platforms that allow holders of NFTs to use these as collateral. Perhaps the best way to think about this is to recall that people have always been able to raise cash against desirable real-world assets, such as real estate, fine art and antiques.

This allows the borrower to benefit from cash flow, including the ability to engage in yield-generating activities, without having to sell their asset, which may appreciate in value, or simply be of sentimental value.

Where wealthy individuals from previous generations have invested spare cash in hard assets such as real estate, agricultural land or expensive art, digitally native younger generations are more likely to own Web3 assets such as NFTs, or to have accrued rewards from contributing to open-source platforms. In the future, if these people were able to, for example, raise a mortgage or a loan for a car or other purpose by using their NFTs and other digital assets as collateral, this demand would be satisfied.

We may not yet be in a situation where holders of NFTs can raise a mortgage directly against their digital assets, but it is certainly possible now to raise Wrapped ETH (wETH) or Dai against your Bored Ape, CryptoPunks or other collectable.

NftFi (pronounced 'NiftyFi') is the best-known NFT-based lending platform. It relies on a double-audited escrow smart contract to hold the borrower's asset(s) in exchange for liquidity, which can be used to raise yield on other DeFi platforms or to cash out into fiat currency in order to spend on physical goods and services. Unlike standard DeFi lending protocols, it is not possible for bots – or any other third parties – to force liquidations, but if the value of the NFT deposited as collateral falls below the agreed amount, the lender is able to liquidate the loan and walk away with the NFT.

NftFi is therefore a good example of how existing token standards allow NFTs to be used directly within DeFi infrastructure. It is worth mentioning, however, that NFT prices can be even more volatile and more subject to market-sentiment fluctuations than other DeFi assets, so present a high-risk move.

More complex ways to bring liquidity to NFTs

Depositing NFTs as collateral in return for more liquid tokens such as wETH or Dai is a simple process. However, for the more adventurous asset owner, there are more complex mechanisms for benefiting from the value of your NFTs. Another way to bring liquidity to an NFT portfolio is to fractionalize your assets. Platforms such as Unicly and Fractional.art allow users to create fungible ERC20 tokens in exchange for their NFT or collection of NFTs, which can then be easily traded or farmed for yield.

Particularly when markets are volatile, determining the value of an NFT can be difficult, which is why there are so few platforms that allow users to earn yield directly. SudoSwap uses automated market makers to allow hold-ers to interact with liquidity pools in the same way as described in Chapter 4. On its app, liquidity providers can deposit ETH to pools to earn NFTs, deposit NFTs to pools to earn ETH, or deposit both ETH and NFTs to pools to earn trading fees.

Token gating

Token gating is another idea that has been gaining currency over the last couple of years. It is the practice of granting access to a product or service based on a particular token being present in an individual's wallet.

Use-cases for token gating include access to premium content or social networks, loyalty schemes, commerce discounts, extra levels and special features in gaming, and DeFi services such as analytics and profiling. Token gating can also be used for enhanced fee and reward structures: for example, if a contract is deployed that allows ERC20 token holders to earn staking rewards, the percentage reward on a particular platform may be adjusted according to whether the holders also possess reward NFTs issued by that platform.

While a service can be token gated using ERC20 tokens, their fungibility means that all users holding these tokens effectively receive the same bene-fits (although there may be scope to specify threshold balances). In contrast, the attributes and serial numbers encoded in NFTs, which make each one unique, allow the targeting of specific services to specific users.

For DeFi protocols, token gating opens many possibilities, especially when it comes to incentivizing users to take part in DAO activities and so on. Minting NFTs for supporters is an easy way for Web3 protocols to reward participation and interaction, especially when these NFTs can also be used to give access to token-gated incentives. Other people are using NFTs to build communities around sports stars or sports clubs, with the tokens providing access privileges to particular events, or the chance to meet the token holder's heroes. The Dark Horse NFTs minted to help support the career of rising motorsports star Bianca Bustamente is a case in point.

Liquidity-position tokens

Chapter 4 explained how Uniswap issues liquidity-position tokens as NFTs (LP NFTs) when someone provides liquidity to one of their pools. This is a development from version 3 of Uniswap. Previously, in versions 1 and 2, the proof of liquidity provision was minted as ERC20 tokens. Now, substituting these with NFTs has allowed some interesting additional features. One of these is the unique piece of generated art that is created according to your position, with different trading pairs represented by a blend of different colours, and the curve is derived from the liquidity concentration as well as the ratio at which the tokens were initially deposited.

GameFi

One of the most exciting – and in many ways contentious – conjunctions of NFTs and DeFi is in gaming. Computer games have been around long enough that many adults up to about the age of 50 will have childhood or teenage memories of their favourite games or friendship groups centred around gaming, so it is hardly surprising that topics such as the financialization of gaming can evoke strong emotions.

There are two main reasons why a game developer may opt to include Web3 integrations into their game: to broaden the scope of asset ownership, or to add a play-to-earn component to their game (the second is actually more or less a subset of the first).

How in-game assets are owned and traded is a longer-standing debate than anything to do with cryptocurrency or NFTs. Games such as Linden Lab's *Second Life* have long had their own currencies and their own secondary marketplaces, allowing users to profit in real-world currencies from their activities within the game. The game creators had ultimate control of these, however, and assets that were perceived to contravene the rules of the game could be confiscated, with no reparation or compensation due.

Fifteen years ago, there was a flurry of newspaper articles about property sales in *Second Life*, with writers and readers marvelling that it was possible to become a millionaire by selling digital land in an imaginary domain. There were rumours of sweatshops in which legions of young people toiled, playing games in order to earn assets that could then be sold on to wealthier gamers who wanted the bragging rights without putting in the gaming time to earn the assets.

Even today, grey markets exist for assets and currencies in popular games such as *Roblox*. A Web3 analyist I spoke to argued that, if the user experience for NFTs can be improved, then a Web3 approach should result in fairer and more efficient markets:

> At the moment, players can cash out their Robux. It's difficult – it's a grey market – but they can still do it. So, you need to give them something that's easier to use than this. If you communicate to players that they can own all their Roblox assets with the ability to sell them into a completely open market and they could have an actual price discovery and all these things, there would be demand for it.

The same analyst argued that the current learning curve is a challenge, however:

> You just need to make the experience easier. About a year or two years ago, I was looking at how you actually onboard people into crypto and it takes more than 20 steps or more than 40 clicks to actually get to buying the first digital asset. That's what needs to be improved.

It is important to understand the benefits for players that would accrue from Web3 integration into gaming. It sounds like a great idea that players would potentially be able to financialize their assets from plugging them into DeFi infrastructure – using game NFTs as collateral, for example – but it is likely that only a small number of existing players would be motivated or interested in doing this.

Persistent possession

Owning game assets whose possession rights exist independently of a specific gaming platform has many other benefits: for example, the game manufacturer cannot simply change the rules and decide that you are no longer registered to play or that your assets are no longer valid. The real-life analogy of bowling shoes is a useful one. When you enter a bowling alley in the physical world, you hire a pair of shoes for the duration of your visit – unless you are a very enthusiastic player who has their own shoes, of course. The current state of gaming assets is something similar: you retain the use of your assets while you are playing the game, but there is no record of your ownership outside the game.

Mauricio Magaldi, global strategy director for crypto at 11:FS, sees huge potential in this idea.

> With the infrastructure we have today, which is all centralized, you're connecting to a server that belongs to someone and you have your login and you have your account and you play the game and you buy stuff in the game. You don't own any of that. You pay for the privilege to use it. So, when you

shift that to a decentralized crypto infrastructure, what you have now is your private keys and your assets held within the blockchain. Now the platform comes to your data rather than you going to them and having to ask permission to access my data.

This raises the tantalizing prospect that assets represented by NFTs could one day be portable and interoperable between game worlds, in such a way that your avatar could wear the same pair of collectable sneakers in *Fortnite* and Decentraland, for example. Magaldi goes on to say:

> That means that any game could come into my wallet, look at my assets and say, well, this asset that in that other game looks like a sword, here in this game it is a pistol and it has these characteristics. Maybe in another game it is a dinosaur. So, the portability of those assets that can mean wildly different things in different games hasn't yet been tapped because the gaming companies and the traditional gamers are still thinking in silos.

The financialization of gaming

Many gamers may not now be thinking about financialization when they log in to play their favourite game, but many thinkers in the Web3 space see this intersection as inevitable, especially given the current trend towards the gamification of trading and finance in general. It is exciting to consider the possibilities of how this might look in the longer term, but it is crucial to get the economic system right, and she is also adamant that the game and its economic purpose must go hand in hand. 'How do you spin up a financial market on top of a game?' she asks:

> Regardless of what the economic design really is like, how do you create a universal system that will capture these things? There needs to be a team working from a clear understanding of the fundamentals, rather than the current situation, where teams tend to reproduce what's out there already. The game has to be the most important thing. If we look at other sectors, generally the financial system is there to capture the economic activity and to amplify it: the game does not exist simply to create the economic activity.
>
> When it comes to gamers, what we're really missing is a way of explaining what NFTs are. We need to explain it in their language and to build in a way that aligns with their values. The systems are too clunky right now, nothing has been integrated into the really big games and we haven't really seen the use cases play out directly. Going back to *Roblox*, plenty of young gamers will probably use this as an example: why would I deal with crypto when I can deal with Robux?

'Play to earn' games

In many games, owning assets is not the point of the game. In-game assets are something you buy in order to be able to progress more quickly to higher levels or get more out of the game – as many parents whose children have access to their AppStore or PlayStore accounts know to their cost.

However, the ability to own these assets in an untamperable, uncensorable way, and to be able to put them to work to earn yield or generate liquidity by using them within DeFi, raises the intriguing prospect of games where the in-game economy and the ability to earn money becomes as important as the game itself.

As we can see from the following case study, games that have economic potential may also have barriers to entry that can deter all but players who are already rich or who have previous experience within the crypto ecosystem. Getting the tokenomics right, as well as treading the fine balance between creating a financially viable game and one that is fun to play and which goes viral for all the right reasons, is a delicate balancing act. A source within Web3 venture capital told me:

> For the games that actually pay you to earn, you need a comparatively large amount of cash to play and to start earning properly. Or you have the people building play-and-earn systems where it's not necessarily going to be as expensive to start, but it's probably not going to be producing $3000–$5000 a month just from playing. *Axies* is a perfect example. It was a great game. The thing is they grew the user base so quickly that they didn't seem to have enough time to iterate on the token economics properly.
>
> They were doing iterations about every three months on the token or every couple of weeks on the token economy. But even that isn't really enough – at this stage of development, you really need to be looking at what's happening with the tokenomics and maybe it's even a weekly process.
>
> This means that the game design needs to be as modular as possible so you can actually change little parts of these games that won't necessarily affect the big picture on a weekly basis. So far, I don't think we have struck the balance between incentives and gameplay and I'm hoping we will because I think it's important.

Mauricio Magaldi says that game designers should focus on the game itself first and foremost, and that the game experience should not be compromised in the name of financialization:

> Most of the existing games in the play-to-earn and GameFi space are mostly focused on the financialization of the in-game assets rather than the overall

gaming experience. There was an interview from the president of Nintendo where he was asked whether Nintendo was going to explore NFT games. He said, 'Well, yeah, if the games are fun, absolutely.'

This may seem obvious to people outside the DeFi echo chamber, but the experts quoted here are right to call this out: no one is going to waste hours, days and weeks of their time on a play-to-earn game if it is not fun to play or meaningful to them in some way.

Axie Infinity is a blockchain-based game that allows players to battle each other with cute cartoon monsters that can be bought and sold on a secondary marketplace. While players can start playing the game straight away with free Axie avatars, these are not NFTs and have no market value.

The ability to earn SLP (Smooth Love Potion) tokens for successfully winning challenges, and for selling new Axies that players have bred from the Axies they have bought, led to the game going viral. Particularly in the Philippines, many young gamers realized they could make equivalent money to working in a factory from the Axie-based economy.

Because new players needed to own three Axies before they could start playing, at a cost of hundreds or even thousands of dollars, an economy sprang up around the principle of scholarships, where non-playing owners rented their Axies to newcomers who were high on skills but low on cash.

The metaverse: why it's bigger than gaming

In the 2020s, it is barely possible to mention gaming or social media without referencing the metaverse. By the time the Facebook corporation rebranded as Meta in late 2021, we were already well on the way to a future where we spend an increasing proportion of our time interacting in virtual worlds, and where our identity and possessions in the digital realm may be as key to our sense of self as our physical presence.

In order for this to happen, the metaverse needs to have new financial rails that enable a new type of economy where digital goods are at the forefront. Just like the internet felt like a clunky, almost unusable place in the mid-1990s, unrecognizable to today's digital natives, so the nascent virtual worlds of today will seem laughably primitive in 10 or 15 years' time. Hence it is worth considering how the metaverse will interface with DeFi.

The MetaFi thesis

Leading Web3 venture capital firm Outlier Ventures was the first organization to formalize the potential for synergy between DeFi and the metaverse and to coin a name for it: MetaFi. The MetaFi thesis holds that: 'The majority of growth in DeFi will not be driven by CeFi. Instead, we explore how it unlocks value in the Metaverse through what we call "MetaFi": the decentralised financial tools of the Metaverse' (Steis et al, 2021).

Building on many of the principles of Outlier Ventures' earlier paper, 'The Open Metaverse OS', which defines and lists the components necessary to build a Web3 Metaverse, interoperable and open to all, instead of under the control of monolithic Web 2.0 corporations, Steis et al envisage the development of 'a fully-fledged parallel economy bringing hundreds of millions, and eventually billions of users, into the crypto ecosystem over the next decade'.

What is meant by a 'parallel economy'? Quite simply, while the assets you might own in a digital-only world might be entirely fantastical and impossible to replicate in the real world, your metaverse land, collectables and clothing are owned by you in the same way that you own the clothes that are hanging in your wardrobe or the books on your shelves.

The dress that your avatar wears may be made out of fire, ice or even Venus flytraps or snakes; the land you own in the metaverse may be a dreamverse populated by flying dragons and glittering volcanic lava, but both these examples have their own financial value and can be bought and sold in the same way as real-world assets. Gaming platforms such as *Second Life*, *Roblox* or *Animal Crossing* may deal with this possession conundrum by conferring ownership rights themselves and holding the details in their own databases. Advocates of the open metaverse suggest that this approach, while convenient for the individual companies, is sub-optimal because the form of ownership is entirely conditional on the goodwill of the operator and is subject to censorship or – ultimately – the success of the underlying company.

If the players of games or the inhabitants of virtual worlds are able to prove ownership of their assets via ownership of NFTs registered on public networks outside the control of private companies, this is a far more complete form of ownership, which mirrors more closely the type of owner-ship structure we have in the real world. The MetaFi thesis holds that the representation of assets as NFTs, with all the interoperability and common standards that this implies, provides the foundation for an entirely new type of virtual economy, from which value can flow backwards and forwards from the real world via conduits such as the DeFi ecosystem.

Where the metaverse merges into the physical world

For nearly 10 years, computer scientists have been trying to solve the prob-lem of representing real-world assets on blockchains. Provenance solutions are riven with problems, the main one being the impossibility of ensuring that the physical asset is exactly the same entity represented on-chain and has not been swapped for another asset or tampered with in any way.

While this has not been such a significant problem until now, the encroach-ing influence of the metaverse on our lives means that it is a challenge that is gaining currency. As described in the previous section, the use of NFTs to represent our assets in the virtual world – whether these are digital-only wearables or other in-game assets, or are entities with physical twins in the world outside the metaverse – means that the things we own in the virtual world can interface directly with DeFi systems. Hence, instead of depositing your Bored Ape or CryptoPunks NFT as collateral for a loan, imagine being able to deposit the limited-edition sneakers that you keep in a box in your bedroom, or your rare *Star Wars* collectables.

One way to solve the problem of physical asset oracles is to tokenize not the object itself but the promise to exchange it. Boson Protocol is a Web3 start-up whose purpose is to facilitate decentralized commerce, bridging the real world with that of smart contracts and opening the door for brand experiences that seamlessly link the physical and digital realms.

To give a concrete example of how this might work, Justin Banon, co-founder of Boson Protocol says: 'Imagine you go to a designer store, and there's a physical item there that you can't buy. You have to do something in the metaverse, then you activate a bundled NFT that unlocks a digital wear-able, experiences and the physical item' (Kolbrener, 2022).

Essentially, Boson's redeemable NFTs are a type of futures contract for a physical thing, ultimately opening up the tantalizing possibility of being able to plug one's physical assets directly into financial markets via these tokens.

The financialization of everything

An NFT can take any data and record it on a public blockchain in a way that marks it out from any other NFT. Whether this is desirable or meaningful is a separate question, and one that many people have struggled to answer.

The type of ownership that is conferred by an NFT is a particularly hot topic. While Boson Protocol solves the physical asset oracle problem by tokenizing the promise to exchange objects rather than the objects themselves, using NFTs to represent real-world assets has considerable challenges.

Consider a situation where you have a rare collectable item: a guitar that once belonged to a famous rock star or a pair of limited-edition sneakers. You want to wear – or at least demonstrate that you own – this asset in a virtual world such as Decentraland or the Sandbox, so you have an NFT in your wallet that is a digital twin of the tangible original. Let's consider what happens when these two assets become uncoupled in some way. It may be possible to stipulate that the digital token has to be transferred alongside the original when the item is sold, but this does not provide a solution to a case where the original is destroyed, damaged or stolen. This means that the NFT becomes in essence a receipt, rather than an entity that is valuable in its own right. And this can apply equally to digital assets. Take the example of the NFT platform Cent, which makes it possible to mint NFTs of tweets. Jack Dorsey, founder of Twitter, famously minted his own – and Twitter's – first tweet, and it was was sold for \$2.9 million using Cent.

NFTs and ownership: a legal perspective

Owning an NFT of a tweet does not confer any rights over the original tweet or the account from which it was minted. Person A can mint an NFT of a tweet by person B, but this does not prevent person B from deleting the tweet or indeed their own account. Even if person A decides to mint one of their own tweets as an NFT, there is nothing to stop Twitter from removing person A's account, or from taking down their entire platform.

The murky question of rights and ownership of NFTs was thrown into sharp relief after actor Seth Green had his Bored Ape Yacht Club NFTs stolen, and consequently lost the ability to make a TV show based on one of them. He ended up paying a \$260,000 ransom to retrieve it, along with the rights to reproduce and distribute the image (Hogg, 2022).

Theft and copyright violations committed by people minting NFTs of other creators' art has caused a backlash against the technology (discussed in the following section). However, if nothing else, it has generated a debate around the possibilities of attributing value to things that were essentially worthless before – especially as capturing the 'value' of these activities into digital assets allows them to act as financial instruments and plug directly into DeFi protocols. An excellent post in the *Atlantic* sums it up, 'theorizing that NFTs have the power to turn any of the digital data we emit as we go about our daily lives into an asset class for speculative investment' (Bogost, 2022).

Others see the technology as something that can be a tool for generational fairness, noting that younger generations tend to own assets such as in-game purchases, digital music, digital art and other collectables, which have not, until now, allowed them to use them to raise liquidity or earn yield in the same way that older generations have profited from owning real estate, stocks or gold.

In the section earlier on play-to-earn games, we considered the development of technologies that allow gamers to make a living from gaming and profit from plugging their earnings into an entirely new financial system. As Outlier Ventures state in their MetaFi thesis (Steis et al, 2021):

> We believe that the economic activity in the Metaverse will promote
> generational wealth transfer favouring the upcoming generations, not the
> legacy world. It brings inclusion to the digital native, to the digital creative,
> to the digital worker, to the gamer, to the musicians. It will bring inclusion to
> the individuals who have digital value that is not recognised by the traditional
> financial system.

NFTs: the backlash

In early 2022, a much-referenced survey of 2000 gamers found that nearly 70 per cent were opposed to the use of NFTs in games. This is not a loosely held opinion. Gamers who dislike NFTs – and by extension, cryptocurrencies in general – are so hostile to the idea that it frequently spills over into social media attacks and buyer activism. There have been numerous occasions when games creators have announced NFT integrations only to reverse their plans when faced with a wave of fury and boycott calls from loyal customers. So far, EA, Ubisoft, Team17 and others have fallen foul of this.

This resistance has its roots in a history where gamers prefer to pay for their game once, whereas creators often prefer subscription models, or rely on the sale of in-game assets. Gamers see NFTs as a way through which developers and manufacturers can charge more and more for playing rather than relying on a 'one and done' business model. Additionally, the 2022 crash in crypto markets fed into the narrative that the entire sector was essentially a scam, adding fuel to the fire.

It is entirely understandable that gamers are pushing back against financialization. For most people, a game is something in which you immerse yourself, away from the pressures and concerns of daily life. A place of escapism becoming a site for economic activity is undesirable for many people for different reasons and it is important to recognize this. However, in a future where everything will be gamified, including finance, and where game worlds increasingly intersect with the real world in the form of the metaverse, this is a debate that is unlikely to end for some time.

NFTs, the metaverse and GameFi: the future

It is clear that navigating this new world is going to be challenging for many people, and aligning different opinions and understanding other people's viewpoints are going to be key. Those within the Web3 ecosystem cannot simply ignore the valid concerns of those who argue that there are some parts of their lives that they do not want to be touched by financialization, or who are simply turned off by the consumerist excesses of the newly rich NFT elites.

Mauricio Magaldi has a message of hope for games developers, despite the divisions that are currently palpable. He sees huge opportunities for interoperability, despite current challenges:

> What they don't realize yet is that this changes the balance of power. And when game developers realize that everything's permissionless and programmable and composable and they can write new games with other people's assets, this opens up a whole new space that has yet to be tapped into.
>
> There are still a lot of prejudices, which are warranted. People see Bored Apes and they see CryptoPunks and the crazy prices and valuations and it really doesn't make sense because with one Bored Ape you could actually build a software house that develops games. So, people get weirded out with that and I understand it. But I think if we look into primitives and look into how we

interact with data and how companies interact with the data that's now ours, I don't think that we've seen the last of it. I think blockchain games and NFT games have a long way to go, but the opportunity for game developers and for the gaming community – it's completely wild; it's completely untapped.

The financialization of gaming, and of so many other areas of our lives, whether in the physical realm or in the metaverse, challenges the way we think about many first principles. In a world where there was formerly no overlap between, for example, a child's game and the financial system or the creation of a piece of music or art and securities laws, governments and administrators had an easy job. Different departments could deal with different problems, and there was rarely any need for the two to intersect. However, in a world where potentially everything can be a financial instrument, crossing international borders in the blink of an eye, and where potentially taxable events can spring from the most random and inconsequential of actions, it is clear that something fundamental needs to change in the way we look at regulation and cross-jurisdiction rules and guidance.

There is no doubt that NFTs are moving into the mainstream: Meta Platforms (formerly Facebook) announced in August 2022 that it was rolling out NFT collectables on Instagram in 100 countries, and would integrate with Coinbase Wallet and Dapper.

The next chapter considers how regulators are reacting to DeFi in different jurisdictions and at some of the challenges they are facing – as well as some natural advantages of DeFi that may even make their jobs easier.

References

Bogost, I (2022) 'The internet is just investment banking now', the *Atlantic*: www.theatlantic.com/technology/archive/2022/02/future-internet-blockchain-investment-banking/621480/ (archived at https://perma.cc/V3N7-MM33)

Hogg, R (2022) 'Seth Green pays $260,000 ransom for a stolen Bored Ape Ethereum NFT meant to feature in his new TV show', *Business Insider*: www.businessinsider.com/seth-green-pays-260000-return-stolen-bored-ape-ethereum-nft-2022-6?r=US&IR=T (archived at https://perma.cc/744H-7RFN)

Kolbrener, C (2022) 'Boson Protocol and the future of ecommerce', One37pm: www.one37pm.com/style/boson-protocol-justin-banon-interview (archived at https://perma.cc/J684-XYPT)

Shumba, C (2021) 'Retail buyers made up 80% of NFT transactions as sales and volumes have boomed this year: Chainalysis', *Business Insider*: https://markets.

businessinsider.com/news/currencies/nft-investing-retail-buyers-metaverse-crypto-transactions-boom-tiktok-2021-12 (archived at https://perma.cc/KEC2-FWDG)

Steis, M et al (2021) 'MetaFi: DeFi for the Metaverse', Outlier Ventures (see, for example, https://stashberg.com/books/book/58 (archived at https://perma.cc/EAY6-X7G7))

Further reading

Asmakov, Andrew, 'ApeCoin hits one month-high amid Yuga Labs metaverse land sale rumors', *The Block*, 20 April 2022: https://decrypt.co/98257/apecoin-hits-one-month-high-yuga-labs-metaverse-land-sale-rumors (archived at https://perma.cc/KFA6-PKV4)

Knight, Oliver, 'Meta confirms NFT rollout across 100 countries amid Coinbase integration', CoinDesk, 4 August 2022: www.coindesk.com/business/2022/08/04/meta-confirms-nft-rollout-across-100-countries-amid-coinbase-integration/ (archived at https://perma.cc/QD78-WUX6)

Manoylov, MK, 'How a disillusioned former CryptoPunk owner is trying to change the NFT copyright game', *The Block*, 20 April 2022: www.theblockcrypto.com/news+/142696/how-a-disillusioned-former-cryptopunk-owner-is-trying-to-change-the-nft-copyright-game (archived at https://perma.cc/GJJ4-M932)

08

Regulating DeFi

CHAPTER OBJECTIVES

- Understand the difference between anonymity and pseudonymity
- Understand the role of regulators in different territories
- Learn about ethics issues surrounding identity and privacy
- Discover opportunities for regulatory integration

The previous chapter looked at NFTs and how they interface with DeFi systems. This is a great example of how technological innovation introduces new challenges for regulators, who had previously never had to legislate for yield-generating collectable cartoons and financial instruments based on them.

The crypto bear market of 2022 and the collapse or financial travails of high-profile projects and companies such as FTX, Terra, Celsius and Three Arrows Capital, and the consequent losses suffered by retail investors globally, have thrown the regulation debate into sharp relief.

The sanctioning of Tornado Cash and the reverberations following the announcement by the Office of Financial Assets Control (discussed in depth later in this chapter) have also highlighted the interconnectedness of the DeFi ecosystem and raised questions about the legal status of open-source software. It is easy to see why governments want to close up loopholes that they perceive as being too permissive – but knee-jerk reactions that favour short-term punitive action at the expense of a strategic, longer-term view come with their own risks.

A major trap that regulators tend to fall into is the tendency to frame new financial technologies in the terms of the legacy systems they replace; and bolting on new amendments to existing legislation is the worst of all worlds.

Not only does it result in a patchwork of ill-thought-out rules and guidance, but it fails to take into account cases where DeFi tech can help to make financial transactions more transparent and lower cost, and also underestimates the willingness of market participants to work with rule-makers to fashion legislation that works for everyone.

The fallacy of crypto anonymity

There are many misconceptions around DeFi and regulation, among them the view from the outside that cryptocurrency is inherently a scam whose movers and shakers are engaged in a game of cat and mouse with regulatory authorities and stand in opposition to the government. While it is true – and important – that Bitcoin was created as a censorship-proof payment protocol in which governments and other entities could not easily intervene, the view that cryptocurrencies are a major vector for money-laundering and other illegal activity is inaccurate.

The inherent transparency of transactions on public networks and the pseudonymous (not anonymous) nature of those who make these transactions means that there are many circumstances in which blockchain technology can be useful to regulators – and in fact, this transparency acts as a deterrent to many criminals or would-be money launderers.

Crypto analytics specialist Chainalysis reported in 2022 that just 0.15 per cent of cryptocurrency transactions were illicit, compared with an overall figure of 2 to 5 per cent of global GDP in the general economy (Chainalysis, 2022). Even if we take the figure with a pinch of salt – Chainalysis acknowledges that the figure tends to rise retrospectively after more illicit activity is discovered – it appears that financial crime in the crypto sector is not the huge problem that has previously been claimed.

Types of illicit transaction

'Illicit transactions' is an umbrella term encompassing many types of unapproved or harmful activity. It is also worth mentioning that an illicit transaction in one country may be perfectly permissible in another, such as a payment for outlawed political material in a country where the government does not permit the propagation of opposition views. International sanctions are another example: a payment from a US citizen to a merchant in Iran is an illicit transaction from the point of view of the US government, but may be legitimate in various other countries. (We examine later how the role of crypto mixing technologies came into sharp focus in August 2022 when OFAC introduced sanctions on the use of Tornado Cash open-source software.)

The most common understandings of illicit transactions are those that are used to obfuscate the proceeds of criminal activity, or move such proceeds to another jurisdiction; finance terrorism, or evade tax obligations; or those that are carried out without someone's consent (a banking fraud, a hack or any other type of theft).

The role of regulators

While libertarians at one end of the scale would argue that governments should have no business monitoring and interfering with any type of transaction, the general consensus is that potential criminals should not be given carte blanche to launder money and use the proceeds for more nefarious purposes or to enrich themselves. There is also the very reasonable view that, when savers or investors deposit money with a financial institution, they should do so with the expectation of receiving it back when agreed.

The specific implementation details and the small print may vary from country to country, but to prevent the unchecked movement of potentially criminal funding from one jurisdiction to another, there are various international frameworks and agreements that allow governments to oversee financial transfers.

Earlier chapters have examined how high-profile failures such as FTX, Terra, Celsius and Three Arrows Capital brought about the financial ruin of thousands of new crypto investors. With millions of novice investors in hundreds of different countries piling into cryptocurrency and NFTs over the last two or three years, and a percentage of these dabbling in DeFi, it is inevitable that regulatory authorities have been struggling to reach the right balance between encouraging financial innovation and protecting consumers.

To begin with, it is a fallacy that the crypto sector – including DeFi – is a hotbed of criminality. However, while we can see from studies such as the Chainalysis report mentioned earlier that the proportion of illicit transactions in the crypto sector as a whole is small, the rapid growth of this ecosystem, particularly DeFi, meant that the absolute value of financial crimes in crypto exploded in 2021–2022, with $14 billion moving between addresses associated with illicit activity.

Just as different countries take different approaches with crypto-asset compliance and taxation, there are differing approaches to DeFi. The jurisdictions that are most successful in encouraging behaviour that complies with existing know your customer (KYC) and anti-money-laundering (AML) regulation will be those where regulators do not simply adapt existing rules and guidance to accommodate new developments. A more successful and future-proof approach would be to embrace the new possibilities offered by this technology and develop entirely new frameworks to take advantage of a digitally native approach to finance.

Companies and individuals commit huge amounts of energy and resources into proving their compliance – and the current systems are unwieldy and expensive, particularly when it comes to inter-company or international movements. While many companies are looking at incoming crypto-focused regulation as yet another burden, there are some experts working at the cutting edge who see the integration of cryptocurrency technologies such as blockchains and DeFi protocols as an opportunity rather than an obstacle.

Simon Taylor, head of strategy and content for Sardine, the leading behaviour-based fraud, compliance and payments platform, is bullish about the prospect of blockchain-based systems offering improvements in compliance efficiency:

> The biggest problem crypto has is the lack of regulatory clarity. But ironically, it's the most clear and transparent system in the world when it comes to transactions, especially compared with how compliance is managed in the back end of a bank.
>
> Working in compliance in a bank is really hard because you're flying blind: some transaction looks dodgy, but it's happening at another bank. And the only way to figure out what happened in those banks is to call them and say, hey, we've seen this. What have you seen? There's not a golden source of what happened with the transactions. The transparency is really powerful.

The big question, of course, is whether regulators choose to take advantage of the efficiencies and transparency offered by these new technologies, or whether they will continue to bolt on extra clauses and amendments to existing legislation and attempt to fit DeFi protocols into frameworks developed for centralized entities that operate in a completely different way. There are two main aspects to this: first, how crypto assets are classified, and second, who is judged to bear the responsibility for decentralized networks.

Since Bitcoin was created, regulators in different territories have struggled to fit cryptocurrencies and other digital assets into various existing categories: money, property, commodity or security. Different jurisdictions have differing views on this – and how digital assets are classified can dictate not only the regulatory authority that has responsibility for regulating crypto in a particular territory, but also factors such as tax treatment.

However, it is the question of who owns and bears the ultimate legal responsibility for a decentralized network that is currently being debated – and the outcome of these discussions will shape the future of DeFi across the globe. Let's take a look at the current state of play in some major markets.

Regulation in the United States

While the USA does not dictate how the rest of the world regulates crypto assets, such is the size and influence of the US market that rulings by the Securities and Exchange Commission (SEC) or bills proposed by lawmakers tend to send ripples out through the whole ecosystem.

In June 2022, a draft bipartisan Senate bill caused a certain amount of dismay in the crypto – and particularly DeFi – sector after it was leaked. One of the main recommendations was that anyone acting as a money transmitter or an exchange – effectively including DeFi lending protocols and automated market makers – would need to register with US authorities. By definition, a DeFi protocol is simply code that runs on a decentralized network and does not have a centralized organization to carry out the required registration, so the draft as it stood would effectively outlaw the entire sector.

Pro-crypto Republican senator Cynthia Lummis, along with Democrat senator Kirsten Gillibrand wrote various amendments to the bill, to rule that decentralized digital assets are commodities, rather than securities, thus bringing them under the purview of the Commodity Futures Trading Commission.

While much of the debate around regulation has focused on the draconian Tornado Cash sanctions, and the impact of these sanctions on whether or not Ethereum validators will choose to censor transactions based on this, it is important to remember that at least some institutions are progressing on the basis that DeFi integrations will be possible from a regulatory point of view. After all, in the same month that Tornado Cash was sanctioned, Huntingdon Valley Bank pressed ahead with their $100 million collateralized loan with MakerDAO, possibly indicating that it felt any future legislation would be reasonable enough for them to comply with.

ARE TOKENS SECURITIES?

As we see from the draft bill mentioned above, key to the whole debate around DeFi is the underlying question of whether blockchain-based tokens should be classified as securities. This question sounds theoretical, but it has major implications for all participants in the cryptocurrency sector, whether centralized or decentralized.

The world-leading centralized crypto exchange, Coinbase, has expressed unhappiness with the current approach to digital asset regulation in the USA. Chief policy officer Faryar Shirzad wrote an open letter in a blog post lamenting that securities rules simply do not work for digitally native instruments and calling for an updated rulebook that would promote innovation (Shirzad, 2022).

Securities law is, of course, of particular interest to Coinbase because it was the basis of the July 2022 lawsuit in which former Coinbase product manager Ishan Wahi was accused of insider trading by passing on details of forthcoming token listings to family members.

If the majority of crypto tokens are indeed classified as securities, this is where potential enforcement for decentralized exchanges and other DeFi protocols becomes very interesting indeed.

THE STATUS OF DECENTRALIZED EXCHANGES IN THE USA

As early as 2018, the SEC showed that decentralized exchanges would be treated no differently from centralized exchanges (del Castillo, 2018).

Despite not operating an AMM-based model, EtherDelta is usually regarded as the first decentralized exchange, yet the November 2018 SEC charge and settlement with its operator Zachary Coburn showed how 'decentralization' can be a grey area. While the smart contract that formed the operational basis of the exchange was indeed 170 lines of code running autonomously on the Ethereum blockchain, transaction data was also stored in a centralized server, and the SEC case charged that EtherDelta was deemed to be an unregistered national securities exchange.

Decentralized exchanges that followed EtherDelta, which operate on the AMM model and differ from this model in that they do not maintain data stores off the blockchain, are a contentious area. It is a paradox that regulators are so focused on DEX compliance when FTX – an entirely centralized exchange – was instrumental in the 2022 market meltdown.

INSIDER TRADING

While the 2022 investigations into insider trading at Coinbase and OpenSea hit the headlines, it should not be forgotten that both these organizations are CeFi (centralized finance) and, as such, should be subject to the same ethical guidelines as companies in the traditional sector. However, where regulators have found more difficulty pinning down what is – and what is not – insider trading or front-running is within DeFi.

Chapter 5 looked at miner extractable value – the reward that can be made by analysing transactions waiting to be mined on public blockchains and jumping in and paying a higher transaction fee to complete that transaction yourself. In TradFi, the only way to gain access to such privileged information would be to work for the broker who was about to place the deal. However, in DeFi, all transactions are on public display by default, thus removing all stigma from the notion of front-running and effectively negating the idea of insider trading, as there is no insider knowledge to be exploited.

There is more of a grey area when it comes to DeFi community governance and the 'cryptofluencers' who make up such an important part of the token ecosystem and who may stand to receive token bounties, voted on by a loosely bound community of DAO members, for their efforts in hyping up the price.

While many within the crypto industry are hoping that the SEC will take a proactive view that works with the industry to embrace innovation and recognizes the positive aspects of the technology, many worry that the Commission is looking at the sector from an entirely punitive point of view based on enforcement and threats rather than pragmatic collaboration.

In May 2022, the Commission added another 20 enforcement officers, nearly doubling the size of the enforcement division's Crypto Assets and Cyber Unit, with SEC chair Gary Gensler stating that the move would better equip the SEC to police wrongdoing.

TORNADO CASH SANCTIONS ANNOUNCEMENT

It is difficult to overstate the impact of the shockwaves that went around the DeFi sector after the OFAC announcement about the Tornado Cash sanctions.

Tornado Cash is a popular mixing facility on the Ethereum blockchain. Its function is to obfuscate the origin of the funds in transactions, thereby guaranteeing privacy for the person or entity sending the funds. The user sends tokens to a smart contract, where they are intermingled with other users' funds and in return the user receives an encoded key that allows them to spend the funds elsewhere without showing the full trail.

Ethereum co-founder Vitalik Buterin said that he himself had used the service to send funds to Ukrainian relief charities – and the majority of transactions via Tornado originated from similar legitimate aims (Tapscott, 2022). However, OFAC sought to target the 18 per cent of Tornado transactions that were shielding illicit gains, primarily by a North Korean hacker group. The agency published a list of sanctioned addresses with which interactions could mean criminal action would be taken. The code for the Tornado Cash project was removed from GitHub, as were the profiles of its developers – and one developer, Alexey Pertsev, was arrested in the Netherlands.

Crypto web applications – both centralized and decentralized – immediately censored transactions from wallets that had interacted with Tornado or the other sanctioned addresses, highlighting the degree of centralization within various nominally decentralized DEXs and lending protocols.

The Tornado Cash story pulled into sharp focus the principle of whether code is really free speech, as had been generally assumed. Whatever happens, the US government deciding to sanction a smart contract rather than a person or a business drew a new line in the sand and set a precedent for the SEC to do the same thing. It also highlighted the extent to which decentralized protocols rely on centralized user interfaces developed by companies associated with protocols, as well as the extent to which private services such as Infura and Alchemy provide the plumbing via which Ethereum's transactions flow around the network.

While it is entirely possible, although probably not at all advisable – especially for US citizens – to interact directly with the Tornado Cash smart contract and use DEXs and DeFi lending and saving protocols in the same way, thus evading sanctions, the reality is that the vast majority of people will access the contracts through a website or other front end that is centralized and policed.

STATE-SPECIFIC RULES

In addition to rulings from the SEC and other regulatory bodies such as the Commodity Futures Trading Commission, companies and individuals are also governed by local regulations in their state. An example of such legislation is New York's Bitlicense rules, under which a business licence for virtual currency activities is required for cryptocurrency entities trading within the state. At the opposite end of the scale, Colorado passed a Digital Token Act that allows individuals to pay their state taxes with cryptocurrency.

While legislation relating to cryptocurrency varies from state to state, there are not yet any DeFi-specific rulings to compare. However, as decentralized finance makes up a larger and larger part of the crypto ecosystem, this is going to be an interesting area to watch.

Regulation in the United Kingdom

Rules surrounding crypto assets, including DeFi, are still very much under review in the UK. The Bank of England published a report in March 2022 entitled 'Financial Stability in Focus: Cryptoassets and Decentralised Finance'. It covered areas such as systemic risk and the need for consumer protection, but also hailed the positive benefits of technical innovation.

In July 2022, the UK government published a call for evidence around the taxation treatment of DeFi, showing that this is a topic about which they are actively thinking.

Regulation in the European Union

Just as different states in the USA have varying rules surrounding cryptocurrency, so do the various countries that constitute the Eurozone. Many of these differences relate to taxation and how digital assets are treated for tax purposes, and it can be difficult to keep up with the constantly changing landscape. Portugal, for example, has an effective capital gains rate of zero on crypto assets owned by individuals, compared with the current capital gains tax rate for other financial investments of 28 per cent.

While there will still be scope for individual EU member states to create their own tax regimes for crypto, the countries worked together to harmonize definitions and frameworks for the treatment of crypto assets with a bill that was passed on 30 June 2022 known as MiCA – Markets in Crypto Assets (European Commission, 2020).

MiCA in its current draft requires an operator, service provider or an issuer to have a legal entity registered within the European Economic Area – a group of 30 countries, something that is clearly problematic for DeFi projects. In recognition of the fact that the situation is complex, the bill allows for specific regulation of DeFi, and also of NFTs, to be deferred until a later date – although some representatives, particularly those from the Green and Socialist parties, are unhappy about this. An amendment proposed by the Green Party's Ernest Urtasun and Kira Marie Peter-Hansen, alongside Socialists Aurore Lalucq and Csaba Molnár, seeks to make NFT platforms – anyone/thing who acts as an intermediary for importing, minting or trading the assets that represent proof of ownership of artworks or collectables – responsible for fulfilling KYC and AML compliance under EU money-laundering law, according to the document dated June 22.

MiCA defines a crypto-asset issuer as any person who offers crypto assets to third parties.

The MiCA definition of crypto assets includes utility tokens, payment tokens, stablecoins and e-money tokens.

It further limits the provision of crypto asset services to organizations that have a registered office in an EU state and have obtained the relevant authorization.

A source working for a lobby group that is closely working with EU regulators said:

So this is where the member states' interests come into play. And sometimes we have seen this, for example, the debate which agency, which authority should be the one, for example, giving licences to companies, which is going to be the one that is overseeing the whole application process. There's also different interests. For example, ESMA is in Paris, so that also means that for France that would mean additional jobs, et cetera. And then the last one is the Parliament, which in a way was the most vocal because the members of parliament are also tweeting as opposed to, I would say the other institutions.

One of the areas she sees as contentious is the issue of non-custodial wallets: those that are not hosted by a third party, but where the wallet owner controls their own private keys. The same source stated:

This regulates the different crypto service providers that exchange crypto and then they need to follow up with information too, but also from an unhosted wallet from one single person to a process service provider. So, this means that, for example, if somebody would use an unhosted wallet or a wallet to send funds to their own accounts on one of the exchanges, they would need to be, in a way, KYC as they are right now. But they would also need to prove that the wallet is their own wallet and that can be done in practice in different ways.

Some countries, for example, like Switzerland, and some other countries like the Netherlands, which is within the EU, already have some similar rules. And usually what happens is you would need to send a fraction of your crypto to the exchange, and so you would prove that you are in possession of this wallet. There are tons of different practical and legal questions that come into place here, because if you're in possession, are you then really the owner of the wallet? But I would say the main problem that everyone is in a way afraid of is that once somebody has identified this wallet, if you combine this information that a certain service provider has with all the public information that we have online regarding purpose and sections, there could be really a massive violation of privacy.

Professor Dr Philipp Sandner, founder of the Frankfurt Blockchain School, also sees problems with the MiCA definitions of unhosted wallets, as he points out in a post on *Medium* (Sandner, 2022):

> It is worth noting here that authorities use the term 'unhosted wallets', which sounds negative and is prejudicial. Terms such as 'self-hosted wallets' or 'private wallets' are more accurate and should be used instead.
>
> From a privacy perspective, the TFR proposal can be disastrous. Technically speaking, pseudonymous wallet addresses would be associated with their actual owners and their personal information, such as postal addresses. In case such data is stolen or leaked (and government agencies as well as CASPs are vulnerable to hacks), what would be the result? Simply speaking, imagine this threat: a view in Google Maps could be built based on such stolen/leaked data where anyone could inspect clear names, postal addresses, crypto assets (including token-based wealth such as tokenized valuables, properties or collectables) stored and the entire crypto transactional history of a person at the corresponding address.

While the MiCA bill does indeed bring in some clarity around definitions and how crypto assets fit into the general regulatory landscape, the areas where decisions have been deferred – specifically DeFi and NFTs – show the difficulties inherent in incorporating such new technologies into a regulatory structure that was originally set up to deal with a sector that has remained relatively unchanged for decades.

Regulatory arbitrage

There are many aspects to regulation that centralized crypto companies have to consider when deciding where to domicile themselves – and where DeFi protocols are governed by a DAO, the same considerations are important. These may include – but are not limited to – the ability of local banks to provide bank accounts for crypto service providers in a compliant manner and the existence of a road map for ensuring that there will be no nasty surprises when future legislation is devised. As stated at the beginning of this chapter, businesses prize long-term clarity over short-term freedoms that may be rescinded at short notice.

What is true for centralized crypto providers is doubly so for anyone contributing to a genuinely decentralized protocol. Some of the most punitive proposals that have been suggested in different places are to make software developers who have worked on open-source code used in DeFi protocols personally liable for the actions of people using this code. The legal status of DAOs in different countries is therefore something that has been hotly debated within the decentralization community. Ioana Surpateanu summarizes places that she thinks are dealing well with crypto compliance:

> I think there was this overall expectation that the EU would embrace a progressive regulatory stance when the MiCA regulation was initiated. However, even with the regulation now finalized there are still many unresolved issues. As a result, there is a stringent need for additional advocacy efforts stemming from the more decentralized corners of our industry. Successful advocacy will generate a win-win scenario: the correct development parameters for decentralized ventures and the EU as a leader in Web3, DeFi and the Metaverse.
>
> When it comes to a prolific operating ground for DAOs specifically, I would say Switzerland is one of the most progressive jurisdictions. Most projects seeking to be legally registered as decentralized autonomous organizations opt for Switzerland. There is actually a legal format that can be deployed there to be registered and recognized as a DAO in Switzerland – it's called an Association. The downside to Switzerland being one of the very few jurisdictions offering legal clarity for decentralized protocols is an over concentration of projects and subsequently expensive logistics and access to legal infrastructure and services.
>
> Gibraltar, the Cayman Islands, Bermuda are also progressive jurisdictions when it comes to crypto. They're creating and enabling something very different in the market in a slightly aggressive way, and I think that's needed. One year ago, I would have said the EU is far ahead in terms of enabling crypto in comparison to the US. Now, I think they're on equal footing and I'm actually expecting more regulatory traction on the US front.

Regulatory arbitrage, however, has limited possibilities because authorities with overarching international powers are increasingly specifying how cryptocurrency – and, by extension, DeFi – should be regulated. For example, the Bank for International Settlements Committee on Payments and Market

Infrastructures (CPMI) and the International Organization of Securities Commissions (IOSCO) have published guidance on stablecoins which treats them in the same way as any other mechanism for transferring value.

If a stablecoin is used for transfer in this way and might be perceived as introducing systemic risk, it should comply with the Principles for Financial Market Infrastructures (PFMI), just as a different instrument performing that function would have to, according to BIS. It is important to note that this declaration is guidance rather than 'law' and it is up to individual jurisdictions to decide how to apply these rules – but countries that decide on a loose interpretation of this guidance may find it harder to do business with those that have taken a stricter view.

Identity and privacy

The need to comply with regulations concerning money laundering and know your customer guidance is probably the main area people think of when it comes to crypto regulations. However, another angle, other than the need to prevent illicit transactions, is the use and protection of customer data, and the requirement to provide privacy for consumers. This has traditionally been a major challenge for developers of public blockchains as, by virtue of their architecture, transaction data is stored on computers that can be hosted anywhere in the world, and can also be seen by anyone in the world.

As designed, the pseudonymous nature of wallets and the fact that blockchains store wallet addresses rather than real-world names, addresses and other identifying data has meant that those transacting on public blockchains have been able to secure a reasonable level of privacy – though it is worth reiterating that forensics organizations such as Elliptic and Chainalysis are able to derive much actionable intelligence from on-chain data.

However, when regulators apply legislation that requires writers of smart contracts to store extra data about transactions, such as that specified in the Transfer of Funds Regulation (TFR), this is potentially dangerous. In the past, high-profile hacks of crypto exchanges have revealed data such as lists of email addresses that were sold on the dark web. These alone were seen to expose their owners to potential risk from extortion and even violent theft because of the implication that the people associated with these email addresses owned cryptocurrency and potentially had access to large sums secured with a private key.

If providers – whether centralized or decentralized – were compelled to comply with regulations that stipulated that sensitive customer data was stored in such a way that it could be linked with on-chain data, this massive honeypot of information could be hugely risky if it was ever hacked. Even without hacking in the frame, these requirements also naturally cause tension with region-specific legislation such as GDPR, which limits where certain data can be stored. Public blockchains by their very design can store data literally anywhere in the world, so there needs to be future thinking around how data is used in a helpful and positive way that enhances privacy, rather than in a way that puts people's privacy at risk. Someone who has done a lot of thinking about this is privacy technologist Gilbert Hill, who is chief strategy officer at Pool Data:

> Privacy has previously been seen as about stopping things ('I want to stop this company doing this') rather than something that you control, which I think is very interesting both for regulators and for the DeFi industry. For regulators, the opportunity is to move this away from being seen as a cost centre for business and an obligation.
>
> Regulators build on that framework of GDPR and start to plug in modular regulations which focus on key points of tension around trust, but also around points that are currently gumming up data, in particular, things like data from IoT, which is a whole new frontier of data. When you think about all the connected devices from tractors through to printing presses, that data is being siloed and is not being made use of – the latest estimates show that 80 per cent of this data is lying fallow. Similarly, the rights that we have around data portability – getting access to our data and handing it to another service provider to do something for us better or for someone building products in a business context – is very difficult to affect.
>
> We can start to question a raw data layer which is intermediated by proper institutions like data unions and overseen by regulators. And you can start to target people based on their needs and what they are willing to share. And I think that's a huge opportunity. But if we're going to break into the mainstream and attract people beyond the kind of crypto DeFi village, we need to get really serious about baseline privacy. That means complying with the existing regulations like GDPR, being transparent about it, and going on the record about what we do and don't do with data. As technologists in crypto, that is amazing.

Opportunities for regulators

It is important to recognize that everyone can win from a new approach to regulation where the technological benefits of real-time settlement and transparency can be leveraged by those who have oversight of compliance. Those who have been working in the DeFi and crypto space for some time can see great possibilities for regulators to monitor transactions in real time, with very little human intervention and none of the paper trail that is currently required to track transactions through the back offices of banks and institutions.

Mauricio Magaldi calls this approach 'regulatory integration'. His view is that regulators can gain far more knowledge and information about transactions than they currently have – but only if they start thinking in new and creative ways. He describes the current state of affairs and explains how regulatory integration can make things better than the regulatory approach we see now:

> Regulation is just regulating from the sidelines. It's words on a piece of paper that tell you what to do and what not to do, maybe how to do it, but ultimately it's just words on paper. However, when we're talking about this programmable decentralized infrastructure that is public and available 24/7, this is a different paradigm, and old frameworks don't apply to new paradigms.
>
> We need to find new frameworks that work with these new paradigms. How do you get regulations that are written on a piece of paper and apply them to decentralized infrastructure that's programmable, composable, permissionless and completely global? So, when I talk about regulatory integration, the change in stance we'll have to see from the regulators so that the traditional finance participants banks, fintech, insurance companies and brokers can get comfortable in using this infrastructure, knowing that the regulators are there too.
>
> Right now, I don't see regulators doing deep analysis of on-chain data. It's just forensics, just maybe law enforcement, but not banking regulators. For example, the regulators could provide an SDK (software development kit) to financial services providers that says if you use my SDK, you're compliant by default in this jurisdiction. And that has a lot of upsides, which is, if I'm a big bank and I want to delve into this, I know that if I use this SDK, I'm preemptively compliant to everything that I'm going to try. It's not going to let me do anything weird or stupid because I'm using the SDK from my regulator.

And if I'm a tiny start-up company, oh my God, I don't have to pay any of that money to actually get compliance with the jurisdiction because I can use that suite of tools and standards to accelerate my go-to market without having to pay a single dime to a lawyer to review everything.

Magaldi's message is that the new technologies and organizational frameworks that have come into being from innovation in the DeFi sector offer huge efficiencies and administrative improvements for regulators – as long as they take up the challenge and take advantage of them. As he suggests, a proactive move by regulators to deploy software solutions that make it easy for financial services providers to remain compliant would instantly solve many of the reporting issues and lack of clarity, particularly in the crypto and DeFi sectors.

Disclosure NFTs

One example of the type of information that could be automatically available to regulators is disclosure NFTs, as outlined by Georgetown law professor Chris Brummer in his *Medium* blog. Brummer suggests a mechanism where a unique NFT is created to register an investor's interaction with an investment's mandated disclosures, to satisfy regulatory authorities that facts such as risk have been effectively communicated (Brummer, 2022).

Challenges for regulators

One of the main problems facing regulators globally is the fact that it is not enough simply to update existing legislation or even to think about compliance in the same way. When it comes to centralized organizations – exchanges like Binance or Coinbase apps such as Revolut or custodial crypto services offered by banks – it is more straightforward to devise a consistent regulatory approach.

The debate about whether particular tokens fit the definition of securities may be open to interpretation and may be classified differently in particular territories, but the movement and sale of crypto assets in these circumstances can be legislated by extending the current approach. What is more difficult is determining responsibility in a case where a protocol is truly decentralized, or where wallets are self-hosted. For example, as we have seen earlier, the Eurozone's MiCA regulations in their current form require service providers or operators to have a legal entity registered within the 30 countries that make up the EEA. This presents an obvious problem for DeFi protocols – which do not have a legal entity registered anywhere.

This demonstrates the obvious problem with trying to frame an entirely new paradigm in terms of the old way of doing things, and it raises obvious problems in that widely used stablecoins such as Dai would not be legitimate under this guidance. It also raises the uncomfortable possibility that failing to confront this challenge head-on would mean missing out on the very real benefits of a properly decentralized financial system while falling back on centralized solutions that are less robust.

As emphasized in the Introduction to this book, the majority of the high-profile failures in the crypto space in 2021–2022 happened within centralized entities using DeFi protocols, rather than within the DeFi protocols themselves. Celsius failed, but Aave, MakerDAO and Uniswap continued to work exactly as designed. Regulators would be well advised to be mindful of this and to help the retail investors of the future benefit from this resilience, rather than driving them towards riskier centralized cryptocurrency opportunities.

Specific regulatory pain points

There are frequent cases where regulatory authorities and crypto companies do not see eye to eye. Coinbase petitioned the SEC in July 2022, asking for greater clarity around which digital assets should be classified as securities. Their detractors pointed out that that this action came only after an ex-employee was investigated for insider trading. Coinbase came out fighting, restating what many within the industry had already complained about: that crypto assets that could be classed as securities need an updated rule book, while those that are classified as 'not securities' need the certainty that this is indeed the case.

As Gilbert Hill stated earlier, careful consideration needs to be given to the way data is handled by fully or partially decentralized services. To use MetaMask as an example (a browser extension that acts as a non-custodial wallet and allows users to interact with decentralized web applications), even if personal data is not being stored on a centralized server somewhere, it is still being read by the extension. Hill adds:

> Lots of the plumbing around the way that we access the blockchain and we access DeFi is controlled by a handful of companies or foundations. Combine

that with the fact that the more useful a tool is in a default context, as well as in any other technological context for more data, it tends to capture about you. So, you take an example of something like MetaMask, which captures large amounts of data about you in terms of when you use it, where you use it, the carrier, etc, in many ways replicating everything that these Web 2.0 companies are doing, but without any of the oversight because the regulators are still playing catch up.

Hill makes a very important point. While MetaMask has now disabled the default feature that used to leak your Ethereum address to websites that you visit without explicitly alerting you, it still needs to read your IP address, thus potentially correlating your assets to your geographic location, with all the risk this entails should this information fall into the wrong hands.

How regulation will shape the future of DeFi

The next decade will be fascinating: not simply from a regulatory point of view, but also in terms of seeing how the digitally native, internationally inter-connected system of financial rails promised by decentralized finance can transform today's patchwork of local infrastructures and regional frameworks.

Governments can temporarily create bottlenecks that 'protect' their populations from financial systems in other countries, but ultimately, as we have seen with many other technologies, from gene therapy to artificial intelligence, technical innovation can be something of a Pandora's box: once something has been created and released into the wild, it rapidly becomes more and more difficult to put it back in its container.

Some governments see the potential: Australia's central bank chief Philip Lowe, for example, has theorized that getting the regulatory arrangements right will bring advantages such as being able to use properly regulated digital tokens in place of the central bank digital currencies that many other countries are developing. Lowe's viewpoint is interesting because he believes that the private sector is better at innovation and design than the central bank would be (John, 2022). Ultimately the forces shaping the development of DeFi are not governments and regulatory bodies, but technology itself, in conjunction with the culture and societal make-up of individual companies and regions.

The final chapter considers some possible outcomes over the short to medium term, with predictions from some of the thinkers and creators who have contributed their thoughts to the book so far.

References

Brummer, C (2022) 'Introducing Disclosure NFTs': https://chrisbrummer.medium.com/introducing-disclosure-nfts-disclosure-daos-and-disclosure-dids-9579e0e739fe (archived at https://perma.cc/8LK5-2BZ4)

Chainalysis (2022) 'Crypto crime trends for 2022': https://blog.chainalysis.com/reports/2022-crypto-crime-report-introduction/ (archived at https://perma.cc/UF3G-MCZD)

del Castillo, M (2018) 'SEC cyber chief puts a new type of cryptocurrency exchange on notice', Forbes: www.forbes.com/sites/michaeldelcastillo/2018/11/09/new-sec-cyber-chief-puts-cryptocurrency-exchanges-on-notice/?sh=6a7951cd2fb8 (archived at https://perma.cc/5CWW-9RFG)

European Commission (2020) 'Proposal for a regulation of the European Parliament and of the Council on markets in crypto-assets, and amending directive (EU), 2019/1937': https://eur-lex.europa.eu/legal-content/EN/TXT/?uri=CELEX%3A52020PC0593 (archived at https://perma.cc/KHV6-VNAU)

John, A (2022) 'Privately issued but regulated digital currencies have benefits, central-bank chiefs say', Reuters: www.reuters.com/markets/currencies/privately-issued-digital-currencies-likely-better-australia-cbank-chief-2022-07-17/ (archived at https://perma.cc/AS65-N78C)

Sandner, P (2022) 'Germany maintains its pro crypto attitude and opposes the EU proposal on revealing and verifying identities for self-hosted wallets', Medium: https://philippsandner.medium.com/germany-maintains-its-pro-crypto-attitude-and-opposes-the-eu-proposal-on-revealing-and-verifying-ca6ffa3fcc8c (archived at https://perma.cc/4UP4-7RZK)

Shirzad, F (2022) 'The crypto securities market is waiting to be unlocked. But first we need workable rules', Coinbase: https://blog.coinbase.com/the-crypto-securities-market-is-waiting-to-be-unlocked-but-first-we-need-workable-rules-c0ba63eabab3 (archived at https://perma.cc/V7RR-9RTN)

Tapscott, A (2022) 'The recent crackdown on Tornado Cash sets a dangerous precedent', *Fortune*: https://fortune.com/2022/08/19/crackdown-tornado-cash-dangerous-precedent-tech-war-on-code-privacy-crypto-regulation-alex-tapscott/ (archived at https://perma.cc/B9RE-UP5A)

Further reading

Cronje, Andre, 'The rise and fall of crypto culture', *Medium*, 18 April 2022: https://andrecronje.medium.com/the-rise-and-fall-of-crypto-culture-3d0e6fd3e0e9 (archived at https://perma.cc/FLZ2-QKWA)

09

Imagining the future of DeFi

CHAPTER OBJECTIVES

- Understand the implications of generational change for DeFi adoption
- Learn what the future for institutional DeFi might look like
- Understand how central bank digital currencies fit into the picture
- Understand the importance of identity systems

Predicting the future is difficult. Predicting the future of technology and its societal implications is even harder – as the Nobel-winning economist Paul Krugman discovered with his infamous statement that the internet would have no greater impact on society than the fax machine. Just as the internet turned out to be one of those generational transformations with profound and far-reaching consequences, the replacement of traditional financial systems with digitally native, decentralized networks looks to have the potential to upend the way we see the world.

The legacy of globalized systems

To understand the scale of the transformation that is potentially on offer thanks to DeFi, we need to understand that, while we think of the existing financial system as a digital network that spans the world, we are in fact looking at a patchwork of legacy systems that have been painstakingly updated and bolted together. Simon Taylor, head of strategy and content at

Sardine, whose weekly 'Brainfood' newsletter contains some of the best thinking on fintech, distils it thus:

> The existing system isn't global. It was globalized. What you actually saw was a series of national systems that have evolved over decades and were built by the best technology we had at the time. For example, the nature of Swift in the seventies was a massive upgrade from sending cheques around the world and dealing with different central banks and trying to make phone calls to people. We digitized something that wasn't digital before. It was cutting edge when it was built. However, we did it with limited hardware, limited memory, limited bandwidth, and a lot of the standards that we use to this very day still harken back to what we built in the seventies.
>
> We are limited by the context of the time. The creators had limited hardware and software engineering practices by today's standards. We're also limited by the slowest mover in that ecosystem, since each node in the network must upgrade to any new standard itself.
>
> Finance isn't global: it's globalized. It is a patchwork of national systems that have been sort of smushed together. Finance also isn't digital: it's digitized. We took a paper process and we consistently tried to turn that paper process into something that digital technology could make faster and cheaper. We didn't look at what digital can do and started from the point of 'how would we redesign this, given the technology we have today?' From a first principle standpoint, DeFi is the opposite. It isn't national. It's natively global. It's natively 24/7. It doesn't only work when banks are open and there's somebody there to operate the machines. It runs 24/7, and it's natively digital.

As discussed in Chapter 2, the current state of play is infinitely distant from the systems of the future, and transformation on this scale is difficult. Few people in large organizations are empowered to throw away decades of infrastructure and to embrace new ways of thinking that differ so radically from what went before.

Igor Pejic thinks that actively allocating the technical debt of not modernizing to financial institutions' balance sheets would help to concentrate minds. He writes in his blog (Pejic, 2022):

> The degree of legacy is very hard to grasp; for customers, managers, and investors. But often even the IT staff managing the systems is not fully aware of their state. Yet the technical health of an organization is just as important to its future performance as its financial one. Reporting it on the balance sheet might increase transparency and ensure its prominence on the boards' agendas.

Whether or not the issue is forced, as Pejic suggests, in the longer run, it is the institutions that are able to speed up their processes and minimize their costs by introducing new technologies that will succeed – and DeFi can contribute a big part of these efficiencies. Ultimately, the efficiencies and 'always on' nature of these new public networks will likely be too tempting to bypass.

Why am I so confident this will happen and that decades – even centuries – of fixed ideas about the way money traverses the globe will be swept away? At least part of the reason is generational.

Generations Z and Alpha: true digital natives

Even the most technologically literate individuals from earlier generations, including those who have been programming computers for decades, cannot be said to be fully digitally native. That term is reserved for those toddlers whose small hands reach out to swipe through the pages of an analogue book as though it were a tablet, or who perceive no distinction in ownership or relatability between the teddy bear on their screen or the plush version they clasp to their chest.

In the same way that the skeuomorphic design of early computers – graphics representing operating systems with filing cabinets, directories with folders and voice calls with the receiver from now defunct landline telephone sets – makes little sense to younger generations, financial infrastructure that is fundamentally a digitized version of earlier, paper-based processes will ultimately be discarded.

The banking executives of 2022 – and more importantly the regulators – may currently be drawn mainly from Generation X and older millennials, but soon, younger millennials and Generation Z will occupy these positions. In a society where most traditional assets – real estate, private pensions and blue-chip stocks – are held by older generations, it is likely that the new generations coming to power will seek economic value elsewhere. They have grown up with a less rigid idea of money and financial instruments and will be more inclined to create a financial world where settlements are automated and near-instant, and where value flows enable price discovery and liquidity for assets that are currently difficult to value and trade.

Additionally, Generation Z has grown up in an environment where the idea of trading and engaging with financial products is more widespread than for previous generations. Apps such as Robinhood and eToro, and trends such as social trading and copy-trading, have gamified an experience that was once the preserve of wealthy middle-class, usually middle-aged people who telephoned their brokers to place orders on their behalf.

This is not to say, however, that Generation Z is composed of individuals for whom money-making and unbridled capitalism are necessarily priorities. Within younger generations, there is a strong desire to make the world a better place – and many of them see decentralized financial systems as part of a solution that can lead to a fairer world and a rebalancing of incentives – including those that influence the way we treat our environment and the life forms within it.

The ReFi movement

One of the more interesting spin-offs in Web3 is the so-called ReFi movement (an abbreviation of regenerative finance). We can think of ReFi as the equivalent within decentralized finance of ESG (environmental, social and governance) within a traditional context. The main difference between ESG and ReFi is that, while ESG commitments tend to dictate which investments a company or an institution makes, ReFi is focused on creating the tools that directly create a better future.

The aim of ReFi is to reimagine the financial system by putting a price on externalities such as the undesirable side-effects of businesses that pollute or exploit. Its roots lie back in the 1980s, when books such as *Blueprint for a Green Economy* by David Pearce and Anil Markandya (my own former tutors at UCL) and other economists such as Marilyn Waring sought for the first time to fairly price environmentally damaging activities.

The ReFi movement aims to address some of the criticisms that have been levelled at the crypto industry for being energy-heavy, greedy and wasteful, and to focus on the opportunity to use these new technologies for good instead. Projects with explicitly ReFi objectives, such as Celo, commit to principles such as digital inclusion (creating technology that everyone can use, even with the most basic smartphone) and pro-social initiatives that allow individuals to be rewarded for work that is beneficial to their community or to the natural environment (McCormick, 2022).

DeFi will become more institution-focused

While this book has concentrated primarily on the retail side of DeFi, as that is where the majority of the activity has been over the last three or four years, it is likely that, as institutions become more interested in plugging into automated, global, intermediary-free infrastructure, we will see institutional interest rising. For that to work, the plumbing needs to be in place that will allow legacy organizations to integrate more easily, for example with institutional custodial wallets, middleware and dashboards that provide a familiar user experience for enterprise users.

Technical innovation is improving the user experience of crypto wallets aimed at enterprise, and different companies are quietly laying the foundations for a future where businesses will be able to use their assets within the DeFi stack to earn yield without entrusting key management and risky manual processes to individuals. Services such as Fireblocks, which offer settlement, compliance and white-listing, are integral to getting institutions onboard.

Web3 strategy specialist Ala Haddad explains how experience working within the banking sector showed him how such integrations might work:

> One idea was to issue a stablecoin that's backed by assets in the bank, opening up investments for outside investors to buy government funds, commodities or other assets and placing them in a basket. It would be a regulated version of Compound, you fork the protocol, add a KYC layer to it using Fireblocks or similar.

The tools and interfaces need to be ready, too. For example, Ledger, the hardware wallet provider, offers enterprise solutions that promise to allow their corporate customers to execute DeFi operations, such as staking or yield farming, all within the bounds of their own software application.

Add these enterprise offerings from Ledger and MetaMask to the recently announced institutional crypto custody solutions from Nasdaq and BlackRock and to J.P. Morgan's Onyx digital assets platform, and one gains a picture of institutional DeFi integrations that are happening slowly now, but which may suddenly proliferate. A source within Web3 venture capital sees expansive possibilities for this sector over the next decade or sooner:

> A lot of these big investors have very specific mandates, and these very specific mandates are only now in 2022 starting to require some on-ramping possibilities given that they're raising new funds and they're adding digital assets as part of the portfolio and the mandates. Another issue has been the limited range of products for custody. The custodial space has expanded quite significantly, but it's still fairly small when you compare it to the scale of capital that could enter the sector in the next five to seven years.

It is easy to make the assumption that the crypto bear market of 2022 and the high-profile collapses of FTX, Alameda, Celsius, Terra, Three Arrows Capital and others would have served as a deterrent to institutions seeking to integrate with DeFi services or develop their own offerings. Simon Taylor offers a different view:

> As I speak to senior leaders at financial institutions, the appetite to work with Web3 hasn't been dampened as the price has gone down. If anything, it's the opposite: they have gained a lot of knowledge about the sector. They can look at what's really there and what's really not. The same with NFTs. A lot of brands are still accelerating into the space even since the prices have gone down, which I think is a long-term positive.

His message is that change will come, even if it takes time:

> Old institutions tend not to move as quickly, and part of the reason is they can't. They have more risks to deal with, they have more responsibilities, they've got a bigger day job. It's easier to go and start a band when you're 16 than when you're 36 with a mortgage and three kids... But at the same time, those institutions will move. It will just take some time. So, I don't think the appetite is dampened. I do think at the most senior levels the education is seeping through.

The anonymous source also sees strong possibilities for institutional investment in the future:

> We're slowly going into a new space where we're seeing how different projects get more institutional investors on board when it comes to the supply of liquidity. So far in DeFi, we've seen a lot of protocols struggling with liquidity, and the ones that manage to amass enough are slowly working on onboarding next stage of institutional investors because it's a really, really slow process.

Drawing on their experience within venture capital, they added: 'In the past two or three years, we've been looking at teams that are mostly technical founders, and now is the time we're seeing this shift towards more financial engineers and people who are actually coming from the financial space.'

These comments are important because it is those with strong executive and technical experience in the TradFi sector who will have the crossover skills to build the professional-grade DeFi systems of the future.

Integrating identity systems into DeFi

While it is, of course, technically possible to access DeFi protocols anonymously, in the real world there is nearly always an administrative requirement to associate one's wallet with some kind of identity that can be verified by financial institutions or government authorities. In the previous chapter, we looked in depth at some of the challenges thrown up by associating names and addresses with entirely public and transparent records of financial transactions. It is worth restating the personal risk involved in having such data stored in a way that it proves an irresistible honeypot for hackers. Even relatively small-scale hacks of KYC data from centralized crypto exchanges, such as the BitMex hack in 2019 that revealed lists of email addresses, can expose wallet-holders to risks such as theft, home invasion or extortion.

There is also a growing debate around the interoperability of different national identity systems, particularly in countries or areas where not everyone has identity documents. According to a World Bank blog post in 2018, at least a billion people in the world have difficulty proving that they are who they say they are. As financial systems become more natively global, we need to move towards different ideas of identity that are applicable not only to jurisdictions where the legacy financial system is established (Desai, Diofasi and Lu, 2018).

Some of the best thinking on this topic comes from financial cryptographer Ian Grigg, who invented triple-entry accounting in the 1990s, and who has spent many years considering topics such as asset issuance and identity. In his excellent four-part book *Identity Cycle*, he dissects our notions of identity and trust, and suggests that solutions based on community rather than purely technology are inherently more resilient and in tune with the way we evolved as humans. Grigg particularly questions the idea of identity theft (Grigg, 2021):

> When the corporations are hacked, their copy of the me collection, which they call my identity, is shared with crooks. To the corporations, it is convenient to claim that my identity has been stolen, rather than their data. To me, identity theft makes no sense, indeed it is nonsense. Nobody can steal my identity – a fraudster can impersonate me, but they cannot steal the very me that is me. But in some sense that is not legally well defined, labelling the fraud that results from the corporate failure as identity theft shifts the burden from them to me. Identity theft is then yet another case of liability dumping – corporate gain, individualised losses.

Ensuring that the information we provide to governments and corporations is compliant with their rules without handing over tranches of personal data, which not only serves as a honeypot for hackers but which could also be misused by those who purport to be working for us, is a major growth area for DeFi in the future.

Towards a multi-chain future

While most of the best-known DeFi protocols developed on Ethereum, Chapter 5 showed how high fees have acted as a deterrent to smaller investors, because yields tend to get wiped out when gas prices are high. The rapid growth of DeFi on networks such as BNB Chain, Solana, Fantom and Avalanche shows that there is an appetite for low-fee networks – although the Terra ecosystem collapse continues to provide hard lessons for both investors and developers.

There are, of course, questions over the level of decentralization of some of these other chains. Solana in particular has come in for criticism for the level of centralization involved in its technical decision-making, and some critics have put forward the theory that fees will inevitably rise on all these chains as volume and congestion approach levels found on Ethereum. Notwithstanding the ambitious development schedule that is still ongoing on Ethereum, and which will continue for several years yet, it remains to be seen whether Ethereum in its post-Merge incarnation will be challenged as the leading network for DeFi.

A snapshot from August 2022 shows that only BSC, Avalanche and Tron supported any protocols that had a TVL of more than $1 billion – and in each of these cases, only one protocol hit that threshold. However, TVL on other Layer 1 networks has been steadily growing, and it is probable that some kind of multi-chain future will emerge, where DeFi protocols will continue to run on multiple blockchains, connected by increasingly sophisticated bridges.

One factor to bear in mind, however, is that bridges have been a notoriously weak point in crypto infrastructure, with vulnerabilities that are not shared by the networks they connect. The reasons for this include the extra layer of complexity that they bring – connecting two different types of architecture is not a simple endeavour – and also the very practical point that, while Layer 1 blockchains tend to have large teams with big communities and hence more eyes on the code, bridges are usually built by small teams with smaller communities.

Some industry analysts caution against writing Ethereum off too soon – especially when its Layer 2 networks are taken into account. Max Coniglio, investment associate at Outlier Ventures, questions:

> What's their value proposition that is going to beat Ethereum plus Polygon? What is going to be something that beats Ethereum and all the Layer 2 chains that are building on top of it? It's difficult to say that any blockchain at this point apart from maybe PolkaDot really can compete with that.
>
> My advice now would be to look into the things that Ethereum cannot do and then see which other blockchains are doing those things.

DeFi and Bitcoin

When we talk about DeFi's move towards a multi-chain future, one of the opportunities that people frequently fail to mention is Bitcoin. Often, Bitcoin and DeFi are mentioned in the context of Wrapped Bitcoin (WBTC) being the most high-volume wrapped token on Ethereum. However, to assume that the most important role of Bitcoin within DeFi is as a synthetic asset running on Ethereum is to miss the point of the Bitcoin network. The fact that the Bitcoin blockchain does one thing well – peer-to-peer transactions – without burdening itself with the overheads of enabling Ethereum-style smart contracts has proved to be its strength and has not caused its demise as some blinkered Ethereum boosters predicted.

As Jack Dorsey's 'Web 5' work at Block has shown, there are more ways to approach a problem or an opportunity than simply following the same, well-trodden path that others have created. The white paper for Block's new venture tbDEX prioritizes global inclusion and, as mentioned in the Introduction, is interesting because it focuses on Bitcoin rather than Ethereum and its Layer 1 competitors. Instead of facilitating the flow of tokens around a system based on recreating different financial products, tbDEX is focused on the development of a messaging protocol that allows users in all countries to prove their identity easily and thus access Bitcoin-to-fiat on-ramps that they would not otherwise be able to use.

The mission of tbDEX to bank the unbanked

When Jack Dorsey announced he was stepping back from Twitter to focus on his payments enterprise, Block, encapsulating several established companies such as Square and Cash App as well as a new project named TBD, he also made it clear that he saw Bitcoin as an integral part of transforming decentralized finance. Dorsey and his team see the efficient flow of funds around the world as something that can be hugely beneficial for those who have traditionally lacked access to financial services. Angie Jones, VP of developer relations at Block says:

> Bitcoin is adding a crucial new dimension to the global financial system. Its design is inherently global, open, decentralized, and permissionless. People are able to send money around the world in the blink of an eye. This is already making an impact, particularly for the millions of people around the world have been impacted by the pandemic, lost their jobs, and are struggling to get by.
>
> Because the network is transparent and open to all, the most vulnerable users aren't hindered by features of traditional finance such as monthly account fees, credit checks, or overdraft charges.

She emphasizes that inclusion begins with digital identity and providing on-ramps to efficient digital payment systems that bypass extractionary remittance companies.

> A liquidity protocol like tbDEX has the capability to improve lives because it allows individuals to take back control of their finances. Imagine a new paradigm where you could take your phone, open a bank account, create your own digital identity, hold bitcoin or stablecoins, and send money to your family on the other side of the globe, quickly and cheaply, without ever going through an intermediary. With tbDEX, anyone can become a citizen of the new decentralized economy, and we believe this can have a profound impact on the world's relationship with money and ability to participate in the global financial system.

Dorsey has characterized TBD and the ecosystem surrounding it as 'Web5', implying that it is an evolution far beyond existing Web3 technologies.

DeFi on Layer 2 networks

While blockchains such as BSC, Solana and Avalanche are starting to draw market share away from Ethereum, as we have seen, this progress is very slow. Layer 2 networks on Ethereum, on the other hand, provide easy integration with existing protocols and also offer the opportunity for users to transfer their assets back to Ethereum's main chain if they want to. (This is not instant, however: users must wait seven days before confirmation in order to rule out the possibility of fraudulent transactions.) There is also the advantage that decentralized applications and protocols developed for Ethereum can easily be ported over to any of these Layer 2s if required.

Arbitrum, Optimism and Polygon are all established Layer 2 networks, but it is primarily Arbitrum and Optimism that have had most success in attracting TVL. Arbitrum overtook Avalanche as the fourth biggest network in terms of TVL in August 2022, with Optimism not far behind (Table 9.1).

In this new and fast-evolving sector, networks – both Layer 1 and Layer 2 – jockey for position like riders in a horse race. It is clear at the moment that Ethereum's significant first mover advantage is keeping it and its Layer 2 scaling solutions firmly in control of the DeFi market for the moment, but as the long-term effects of the Merge become clear, there could be movement one way or another.

In 2021, the situation was very different, with some analysts tipping Terra and Fantom as possible successors to Ethereum's crown. However, the bear market has changed many things, with Fantom losing 92 per cent of its TVL over the course of a year, and Terra being wiped out completely.

Improving the user experience for DeFi investors

One charge that can be levelled at DeFi that is true of crypto in general is that the user experience still falls far short of the intuitive and slick interactions that users of modern technology expect. Max Coniglio comments:

> The main obstacle that I see is that a lot of Web3 projects are building products that don't make any sense. And that's why people are not onboarding from

TABLE 9.1 Top three Ethereum Layer 2 networks by market cap

Name of network	Market cap
Polygon	1.31b
Arbitrum	979.9m
Optimism	842.48m

Data from DeFi Llama, September 2022

Web2 to Web3. If you add Web3 components to your project and there's no need for them, then you are kind of making a bad product that no one will want to use.

We see just so many of those. So many of the products I see, there's no need for blockchain, there's no need for NFTs. This is a big risk to the sector, because that's what consumers will see and will associate Web3 with these bad projects. That's why people don't like NFTs, because they hear about all these worthless forks of existing PFP projects. That's what they think it is. They don't understand that NFTs are actually the way to prove ownership of something digital. They don't understand that Ethereum gives you the possibility to send money to a piece of code without anyone else owning that money.

Chapter 2 looked at the theory of the DeFi mullet – the principle that an application may look like a normal fintech app on the front but be powered by DeFi at the back – but there are reasons to be cautious about presenting Web3 applications and technologies as a rebranded version of software that works in exactly the same way as familiar financial products.

Many analysts subscribe to the theory that some of the worst failures in the DeFi market were caused by centralized companies using DeFi behind the scenes but presenting it in such a way that users were lulled into a false sense of security and perhaps imagined that the same degree of regulation, due diligence and customer protection existed as for traditional financial products offered by fintechs and banks.

In other words, the cliché that DeFi will have gone mainstream when we don't even realize we are using it is actually wide of the mark. We should accept that most people have very little interest in learning about money or getting to grips with non-intuitive interfaces, but there is still a case for treating Web3 differently. After all, when the internet was becoming mainstream, many critics expressed doubts about the complexity of email and expressed scepticism that 'ordinary' people would be capable of handling the technology.

The explosion in popularity of NFTs has drawn millions of people into the market who are not from the tech or finance backgrounds from which crypto people were often drawn in the past – and many of these have quickly absorbed the idea of wallets and even been tempted to dabble in DeFi.

The big question is how to communicate complex ideas to an audience with no previous exposure to this and, in an increasingly busy world, without the time to sit down and study hard financial and technical information.

Gamification, but with an educational element, is probably the middle way to attract new users but with a responsible focus on education, as Rachel Black of HaloFi explains:

> I think DeFi does have a huge power to bring more transparency. But I also think generally there are challenges with DeFi around accessibility and even understanding it. We've seen this over the last couple of years: NFTs have kicked off and gone mainstream because essentially they're a bit easier to understand than hardcore financial products.
>
> Maybe not everyone needs to know everything about everything, but there needs to be an accessible on-ramp, either at an institutional level or more consumer facing. It will be interesting to see how it pans out. I guess with traditional finance most people don't really know the ins and outs of how bonds or different markets work, but most people have a bank account... a lot of people have investments of some type.

Integration points with central-bank digital currencies

As we look to the future, we should not look at crypto assets in general and DeFi in particular as an isolated piece of the jigsaw puzzle. In *The Cryptocurrency Revolution*, I devoted a chapter to central bank digital currencies (CBDCs) – an ambition which most governments are working on to some degree or other.

The high-level view of CBDCs, as opposed to the digitized dollar, pound or euro that we currently use, is that settlement is able to take place directly with the central bank if desired, thus opening up access to digital payments to all citizens, not just those who are deemed creditworthy or profitable by retail banks. Along with this come advantages such as near-instant settlement and lower costs for both retailers and consumers – as well as a raft of civil liberties concerns, such as the heightened ability for governments to conduct surveillance and potentially restrict access to goods or services that they may not want people to consume.

Some in authority see a place for stablecoins in the digital payments landscape of the future, with at least one – Australian central bank governor Phillip Lowe – suggesting that a stablecoin issuer may do a better job of issuing a widely accepted method of digital payment rather than a central bank. Whether or not these new national currencies are issued by central banks or private or even decentralized issuers, it is likely that the payment apps of the future will have at least some kind of integration with cryptocurrencies and stablecoins, raising the tantalizing prospect that, one day, people might be able to pay a retailer or a friend via an app that seamlessly moves funds from a DeFi platform where they are earning yield until used for payment.

As we have discussed, generational change is likely to be the big driver for such a transformation. There is no question that the world is heading towards a cashless future: the big question is whether governments will choose the authoritarian route of insisting all payments take place using CBDCs or whether they will acknowledge the inherent efficiencies and innovation brought by competition and embrace a future where centralized and decentralized currencies and technologies co-exist.

We are already seeing the foundations of this: PayPal wallets where you can seamlessly buy Bitcoin and Ethereum with your bank account, or the Wise wallet where your balances in different fiat currencies are displayed alongside each other. It's a relatively short hop from here to a theoretical situation where you can deposit any unused currency into a lending protocol to earn yield.

Of course, for any of this to be possible, such products need to be developed within a framework of compliance with existing financial regulations – and this is where the crypto sector is working closely with governments: not to sway them to make irresponsible decisions, but rather to ensure that they are aware of how innovative yet compliant technologies can be developed that embrace the possibilities of DeFi yet provide benefits and assurance for the end user along with the right to privacy.

In terms of the integration of cryptocurrency in general into the mainstream financial system, one needs only to look at the Federal Reserve's August 2022 guidance on which institutions are able to access Federal Reserve Master Accounts to see the direction of travel (Federal Reserve, 2022). Under the new guidance, crypto banks are able to apply for these accounts just as other fintechs are. While this does not necessarily assist genuine DeFi protocols directly, given that, in these cases, there is no centralized entity able to apply for a Master Account, it is certainly a step in the right direction for improving liquidity in on-ramps and off-ramps between fiat currencies and cryptocurrencies.

We mentioned in the Introduction that the ratings sector is already preparing for these possibilities, with S&P Global announcing in May 2022 the formation of a new DeFi strategy group to guide the development of products and services aimed at the sector. When it announced the initiative, S&P stated that it believed decentralized finance has the potential to transform capital markets and develop new capabilities in the execution of financial transactions (McQuaid, 2022).

The financialization of everything

Such assurances become doubly important when DeFi permeates areas that are not traditionally thought of as relating to the financial sector at all: gaming, art, collectables, gambling and incentives, for example.

In more familiar times, a loyalty point in your favourite coffee shop, the air miles you earned on your business trips or your football trading cards were clearly demarcated as something that were not classified as financial assets in any way. However, as games – particularly metaverse virtual worlds – begin to incorporate NFTs, and as loyalty programmes adopt NFTs to represent rewards, it is important to remember (as we saw in Chapter 7) that the composable nature of DeFi means that it is entirely possible to plug these NFTs into savings or lending protocols to raise yield, or even to derive yield from renting out in-game assets. Similarly, a bet on a prediction market on a digital platform run by one of the large betting corporations is simply that: a bet. However, a bet on a DeFi prediction market such as Augur or Polymarket becomes a liquidity position that can be sold or traded. It will take a great deal of work by regulators to provide clear guidelines for such products.

The future of DeFi regulation

The USA in particular seems to be following the road of reactive enforcement rather than collaboration and innovation when it comes to crypto assets – and DeFi in particular. And what happens in the US matters to the rest of the world. The sanctioning of Tornado Cash drove home the message that whatever happens in the US has far-reaching consequences outside its borders, not least because of the reliance of the DeFi system on centralized stablecoins such as USDC.

In addition to US-based legislation that renders certain services or addresses criminal, we are likely to see the growth of region-specific rules that dictate how the treatment of crypto assets differs in various countries – within the bounds of international agreements, of course. Over the next three to five years, we will see different regulations coming into force in countries and states around the world, which could significantly affect the geographic distribution of teams working on DeFi protocols.

As we saw in the previous chapter, the incoming MiCA regulations that stand to change the face of crypto activity across the Eurozone have effectively kicked down the road the issue of specific legislation for DeFi protocols and for the use of NFTs. Until decisions have been made on these areas, and unless favourable signals are sent out, the lack of clarity on their future treatment may well inhibit the willingness of new projects to spring up in the Eurozone. We should also expect to see more clarity from the SEC and equivalent bodies on exactly what is – and what isn't – a security.

As we have stressed, it is wrong to frame the story of crypto regulation as one of cat and mouse. There is considerable potential for innovation and growth in the sector, especially when it comes to technologies that are designed to provide compliance and streamline compliance services. Simon Taylor is broadly optimistic that many of these concerns will be resolved naturally as the sector matures:

> Ultimately, crypto needs something like regulation, or that performs the same role. The industry should be thoughtful about how it manages risks ahead of any national level regulations being implemented. There are opportunities to create standards and best practices that reduce harm to consumers and make markets fairer in a meaningful way.
>
> I think we do have to do more, but at the same time we saw lots of cybersecurity issues in the early days of the internet. We're seeing lots of hacks in defy. But now if you buy Bitcoin on a centralized exchange, it doesn't look like MtGox any more. To me, it's a maturity issue rather than an issue that is intrinsic and unsolvable. I don't think you can eliminate risk altogether, as in other sectors, because I don't think you can eliminate attackers – and scammers are the most inventive people in the world. You're never going to get rid of them. They will find a way, but you can manage and minimize that.

Improbable tales will no longer be told

One prediction is easy to make: the growing pains of the unruly infant that is the current DeFi sector will probably not in the longer term continue to generate outrageous tales and events unlike any that have occurred before in financial history. As Simon Taylor points out, the ecosystem is evolving and maturing, and with it, much of the downright wacky side of DeFi culture will slowly become normalized.

Decentralized identity systems, if administered in the right way, should mitigate some of the issues caused by anonymous or pseudonymous developers working on protocols. We do not necessarily need to compel developers to reveal their real-life identity – we likely would not have Bitcoin if Satoshi Nakamoto had been forced to self-dox – but the ability to discern certain things about certain people in a trustworthy manner would be extremely useful.

In July 2022, a hair-raising story came to light (referenced in Chapter 1), that revealed how developer Ian Macalinao had created 11 identities to work on various interlocking Solana protocols. Names were imaginatively created to suggest developers working in different parts of the world, and, because the protocols all used each other's tokens, this double-counting substantially inflated the reported total value locked on Solana (Nelson and Wang, 2022). This may have suggested to potential investors and traders that the Solana ecosystem was a far more popular and widely used network than it actually was at the time.

While this, and various other tales, might make for an entertaining movie along the lines of *Flash Boys*, the anything-goes era of DeFi is rapidly coming to an end. The larger-than-life characters and the speed of technical innovation that have characterized its growth so far will fade into the background as the sober tasks of integrating DeFi technology into existing systems take over from the anything-goes ethos of the early days. However, in a sector where you can raise a yield on a digital image of a monkey, it seems to be a guarantee that whatever the future holds, it will not be boring.

Lessons from the past inform the future

The final point to remember is that DeFi is an extremely new sector, which has been growing at breakneck pace. Banking has been around for hundreds of years, as has trading of assets such as shares. The world's first bank came into existence in 1472, and the London Stock Exchange was founded in 1801. In contrast, the genesis block of Bitcoin was mined in January 2009, the Ethereum network went live in 2015 and Uniswap launched in 2018.

A scarcely believable torrent of innovation has happened over the last 15 years and it is inevitable that the 'move fast and break things' philosophy has caused casualties along the way – not least because of the failure of regulators in particular to recognize the risks of centralized companies masquerading as decentralized projects, while offering none of the assurances and guarantees required of centralized projects within TradFi.

As Simon Taylor points out: 'The most common form of confusion is to conflate DeFi protocols and liquidity providers and everything that's happening in the DeFi ecosystem with lenders that use DeFi that are companies.'

It is notable that while FTX collapsed, protocols such as Maker and Aave survived and even thrived during the period of extreme turmoil and price fluctuations that marked 2022, with the rules encoded within their smart contracts continuing to do exactly what they were supposed to do.

While the user experience for DeFi applications will undoubtedly improve over the coming years, and while TradFi institutions will undoubtedly integrate further with the DeFi stack, it is imperative that everyone – developers, product designers, banking executives, DeFi founders and regulators – works together to build a new and sustainable system based on the transparency, efficiency and global accessibility of these new technologies, rather than adapting outmoded and inappropriate rules that are ill-suited for the financial systems of the future.

Above all, we need to remember that DeFi should not evolve into something that simply recreates the structures of the past. These technologies offer us the chance to do something other than devise complicated financial instruments that only a handful of people can understand and profit from. The possibilities go far beyond developing fancy toys for a handful of speculators.

Simon Taylor emphasizes the importance of focusing on long-term utility rather than short-term speculation:

> The criticism of Web 2.0 was that it has a lot of users; how will it ever make money? The criticism of Web3 is that it has a lot of money, but how will it ever get users? There's a sweet irony there, but I think the thing to say is both people in Web3 and the critics of Web3 are frustrated by the speculative games that have been the primary use case today. I think a lot of the builders never wanted it to become that, nor is it the long-term core utility of it.

Instead, the potential of technologies such as efficient money streaming, genuinely decentralized and international payment networks that are not under the control of a specific company or country and the possibility to generate minimal-fee yield on even the smallest sums of capital should be something that we can all embrace.

There are dangers inherent in failing to seize these opportunities. Caitlin Long of Forbes Digital Assets warns that banks may be overtaken by tech companies in the field of payments and settlements if they fall behind in the innovation race, either because they have not been bold enough or because they have been constrained by ill-conceived regulations (Long, 2022).

Whether you – like the tbDEX team or those involved in the ReFi movement – see the future of decentralized finance as something that can be leveraged to create a fairer world for some of the world's most financially disadvantaged, or simply wonder how banks' and institutions' processes can be streamlined and made more cost-efficient by integrating with DeFi systems, the story that is currently telling itself across tens of thousands of computers and devices across the world, one transaction at a time, is a compelling one.

References

Desai, VT, Diofasi, A and Lu, J (2018) 'The global identification challenge: Who are the 1 billion people without proof of identity?', World Bank Blogs: https://blogs.worldbank.org/voices/global-identification-challenge-who-are-1-billion-people-without-proof-identity (archived at https://perma.cc/3V73-ETC8)

Federal Reserve (2022) 'Federal Reserve Board announces final guidelines that establish a transparent, risk-based, and consistent set of factors for Reserve Banks to use in reviewing requests to access Federal Reserve accounts and payment services': www.federalreserve.gov/newsevents/pressreleases/other20220815a.htm (archived at https://perma.cc/9MG4-3QHA)

Grigg, I (2021) *Identity Cycle*: www.iang.org/identity_cycle/ (archived at https://perma.cc/XL8J-KWKY)

Long, C (2022) 'Banks are about to face the same tsunami that hit telecom twenty years ago', Forbes: www.forbes.com/sites/caitlinlong/2022/09/23/banks-are-about-to-face-the-same-tsunami-that-hit-telecom-twenty-years-ago/?sh=561929927a7a (archived at https://perma.cc/QHM6-PEW5)

McCormick, P (2022) 'Celo: building a regenerative economy', Not Boring: www.notboring.co/p/celo-building-a-regenerative-economy (archived at https://perma.cc/NQ8K-84H4)

McQuaid, D (2022) 'S&P Global Ratings announces DeFi strategy group', Currency: https://currency.com/s-p-global-ratings-announces-defi-strategy-group (archived at https://perma.cc/2D52-5C7M)

Nelson, D and Wang, T (2022) 'Master of anons: how a crypto developer faked a DeFi ecosystem', CoinDesk: www.coindesk.com/layer2/2022/08/04/master-of-anons-how-a-crypto-developer-faked-a-defi-ecosystem/ (archived at https://perma.cc/74YJ-KP63)

Pejic, I (2022) '5 ways to cut the Gordian knot of technological debt', *Medium*: https://medium.com/@igor_69460/5-ways-to-cut-the-gordian-knot-of-technological-debt-legacy-series-3-3-eda0d41a2d5b (archived at https://perma.cc/R9R5-49FA)

Further reading

Klein, Jessica, 'Michael Wagner: Building a virtual nation-state in the metaverse', CoinDesk, 9 May 2022: www.coindesk.com/business/2022/05/09/michael-wagner-building-a-virtual-nation-state-in-the-metaverse/ (archived at https://perma.cc/9EKY-TG94)

Pearce, E, Markandya, A and Barbier, E, *Blueprint for a Green Economy*, Earthscan, 1989

Waring, Marilyn, *If Women Counted*, HarperCollins, 1989

GLOSSARY

AMM: Automated Market Makers – smart contracts that replace the function of an order book on a decentralized exchange. The exchange rate of a pair of tokens automatically fluctuates according to the proportion of each token in the pool.

Blockchain: An append-only data structure maintained on multiple computers in which transactions are aggregated into blocks and the blocks chained together with cryptographic signatures.

CBDCs: Central Bank Digital Currencies – a purely digital fiat currency issued by the central bank of a nation or territory, which generally allows individuals and companies to make direct app-to-app payments to each other without involving a bank. The most advanced program to date is China's digital yuan, which has been rolled out in a number of areas. A CBDC may or may not use a blockchain.

Composable: Software that conforms to generally agreed standards in such a way that it is interoperable with other software of the same type.

DAO: Decentralized Autonomous Organization – an organizational structure that allows individuals or entities to collaborate according to a series of rules encoded in a smart contract.

Decentralized: A network, protocol or application that is controlled by no one single entity or group of entities.

DEX: A decentralized exchange consisting of smart contracts that enable the swapping of different kinds of crypto tokens.

Flash loan: A loan that exists briefly as part of a sequence of chained actions that make up a single transaction on a DeFi protocol (or multiple protocols). The general principle is that if the loan cannot be repaid within the transaction, the loan does not happen (in other words, it is atomic).

Game theory: A theoretical framework based on mathematics for predicting how people interact with each other in a competitive or hostile situation. It is of particular use when creating applications that involve incentive design.

Impermanent loss: A financial penalty incurred by a liquidity provider who has sent tokens to a liquidity pool in which the value of one token has fallen relative to another. (For a full explanation, see Chapter 3.)

Incentive design: The discipline of designing a system where the rewards and penalties are set at a level that encourages maximum participation and discourages dishonest behaviour.

Lending protocol: A smart contract or collection of smart contracts on a public blockchain that allow individuals to deposit collateral of one type in order to borrow assets of a different type.

Liquidity pool: A smart contract that allows users to deposit pairs of tokens that can be traded by other users.

Liquidity provider: An individual or entity who deposits tokens in a liquidity pool in return for a yield.

MEV: Miner Extractable Value – the extra value that a miner on a proof of work blockchain is able to extract by reordering transactions in order to get paid the highest fee or by front-running the transaction themselves.

Miner: A computer (or the entity operating it) that validates transactions on a blockchain and is rewarded with tokens.

Mixer: A piece of software that allows users to obscure the source and destination of specific cryptocurrency tokens by combining them in a pool of other users' tokens.

Mint: The act of registering an NFT on a blockchain for the first time.

NFT: Non-Fungible Token – one that conforms to the ERC721 or ERC1155 standard on Ethereum (or the equivalent standard on other blockchains) and represents a unique asset that is not directly interchangeable for another asset.

Protocol: An autonomous computer program that replicates at least some of the capabilities of a traditional financial service but in a decentralized way.

Rug or rug pull: To rug users or to execute a rug-pull is a specific type of scam within crypto that involves the founders or developers of an application with a native token hyping up the token's value before it crashes, at which point they disappear with the funds.

Smart contract: Software that encodes a collection of autonomously executing rules on a blockchain.

Staking: The act of locking up a number of crypto tokens in a smart contract in order to earn yield. (For a list of the different types of staking, see Chapter 4.)

Token: A denomination of a cryptocurrency that is created and can be transferred on a blockchain.

Tokenomics: The study of the economic value and impact of a crypto token within its ecosystem, including incentive design and the token's interactions with external markets.

Validator: A computer, or the entity operating the computer, that validates the transactions on a blockchain.

Wallet: Software that allows the user to see the balance of tokens associated with one or more key pairs and to sign transactions.

Whale: An entity (either an individual or a business) that holds such a large proportion of the crypto tokens in a particular market that selling them would cause a major market-moving event.

Yield: The reward that is earned on DeFi protocols for lending or staking tokens or otherwise interacting with the protocol

Zero-knowledge proof: A mechanism that allows one party to prove to another that a particular statement is true without disclosing additional information such as private identification data.

INDEX

Note: Page numbers in *italics* refer to tables or figures

CPSIA information can be obtained
at www.ICGtesting.com
Printed in the USA
BVHW011016260423
663088BV00005B/127